LEADING HIGHER EDUCATION AS AND FOR PUBLIC GOOD

Leading Higher Education As and For Public Good asserts that the purpose of higher education is twofold: *for* public good and *as* public good. Acknowledging that the notion of public good increasingly cannot be taken for granted, the book argues that leading, teaching and learning must be directly connected to its pursuit. It avers and demonstrates how this may be accomplished, articulating specific approaches and dispositions that require cultivation within university communities.

This volume argues that leading higher education occurs within competing and sometimes conflicting webs of commitments, necessitating a capacity to negotiate legitimate compromises. Its empirical chapters expand on this, providing examples of academic developers who use deliberate communication as a method in cultivating leading and teaching praxis. What emerges is the potential of deliberative leadership to be transformative in building sustainable leadership in higher education, while simultaneously renewing commitments to education and contributing to public good.

Leading Higher Education As and For Public Good is essential reading for policymakers, university leaders and administrators, academics, students and all those interested in building a sustainable future for higher education that also contributes to public good.

Tone Dyrdal Solbrekke is Professor of Higher Education and Academic Developer at the University of Oslo, Norway.

Ciaran Sugrue is Professor and Chair of Education at the School of Education, University College Dublin, Ireland.

LEADING HIGHER EDUCATION AS AND FOR PUBLIC GOOD

Rekindling Education as Praxis

Edited by Tone Dyrdal Solbrekke and Ciaran Sugrue

Routledge
Taylor & Francis Group

LONDON AND NEW YORK

First published 2020
by Routledge
2 Park Square, Milton Park, Abingdon, Oxon OX14 4RN

and by Routledge
52 Vanderbilt Avenue, New York, NY 10017

Routledge is an imprint of the Taylor & Francis Group, an informa business

British Library Cataloguing-in-Publication Data
Names: Solbrekke, Tone, editor. | Sugrue, Ciaran, editor.
Title: Leading higher education as and for public good : rekindling
education as praxis / edited by Tone Drydal Solbrekke and Ciaran Sugrue.
Identifiers: LCCN 2019054154 (print) | LCCN 2019054155 (ebook) |
ISBN 9780367205102 (hardback) | ISBN 9780367205126 (paperback) |
ISBN 9780429261947 (ebook)
Subjects: LCSH: Education, Higher--Aims and objectives. |
Education, Higher--Administration. | Educational leadership. | Common good.
Classification: LCC LB2322.2 .L389 2020 (print) | LCC LB2322.2 (ebook) |
DDC 378.1--dc23
LC record available at https://lccn.loc.gov/2019054154
LC ebook record available at https://lccn.loc.gov/2019054155

Library of Congress Cataloging-in-Publication Data
A catalog record has been requested for this book

ISBN: 9780367205102 (hbk)
ISBN: 9780367205126 (pbk)
ISBN: 9780429261947 (ebk)

Typeset in Bembo
by Taylor & Francis Books

CONTENTS

FOREWORD

Lead kindly light: in praise of one step at a time

'Lead kindly light' is an English hymn, the words of which were composed as a poem by John Henry Newman. Well known in the more reflective higher education circles for certain of his essays collected together as *The Idea of the University* (which remains still – more than one and a half centuries after its composition – one of the most influential books on the matter), Newman was also a poet, mystic and theologian, and the first verse of that poem of his runs as follows:

> Lead, Kindly Light, amidst th'encircling gloom,
> Lead Thou me on!
> The night is dark, and I am far from home,
> Lead Thou me on!
> Keep Thou my feet; I do not ask to see
> The distant scene; one step enough for me.

Do we not have resonances here with this book, *Leading Higher Education As and For Public Good: Rekindling education as praxis*? That, at least, in exploring those connections, is the path I wish to tread in the space generously afforded to me by the volume's editors, Tone Dyrdal Solbrekke and Ciaran Sugrue.

What is, or might be, or even should be, academic development in the twenty-first century? It is susceptible to all manner of interpretations, both narrow and wide. Its *more narrow interpretations* would confine it to assisting newish academics in their teaching role, and seeing that assistance as a matter of identifying a portfolio of skills that might be said to be characteristic of good teaching in higher education, not least that of utilising potentials offered by the internet. Hovering in the background, if not in the foreground, would be that portentous signifier 'excellent'. After all, all teaching these days has surely to be nothing less than excellent.

Wider notions of academic development would encompass matters of curriculum, of what it is to be a student (doubtless with the aspiration of ensuring 'student satisfaction'), and of assessment. Still wider notions of academic development would invite participants to reflect on the meaning that 'higher education' has for them, and even what it is to be a 'university' and to imagine possibilities of realising those aspirations in their teaching practices. Perhaps, too, reflective consideration might be given to the student as a 'global citizen' or social justice or to what it is to be an international student far from home. This would be a conception of educational development that constitutes a never-ending journey of critical reflection, of value to university teachers throughout their careers.

Those former narrower interpretations are not just technical but *technicist* in their character, reducing teaching instrumentally to a matter of skills oriented to ends, and limited ends at that. Those latter wider interpretations, on the other hand, are genuinely *educational* in their character, in one of the early meanings of education. They help to lead out participants to understandings and actions that are personally meaningful and have inherent value. They help, too, in promoting continuing reflection and debate as to what it is to be a university in the twenty-first century and to generate internal dynamism in teaching in higher education, with teachers coming to be critically reflective practitioners; even, it might be said, coming to be philosophically reflective practitioners.

Such, I think, is the very broad range of understandings that characterise educational development in higher education today and the way in which it is being taken forward. Each university, and even – in devolved administrations – each faculty in a university, will have its own understanding, whether tacit or explicitly advanced; but I think that most understandings of academic development will be plottable along this narrow–wide array of interpretations that I have just sketched. Both of these poles have been pulled outwards: on the one hand, skill-oriented interpretations have been emphasised, not least as teaching has become more subject to audits and performance management; and, on the other hand, educationally oriented interpretations have also become more sophisticated, not least as the reflective literature on higher education has grown apace and as educational developers have collectively advanced their own understandings of their challenges and possibilities, as well as the challenges and possibilities faced by their own university.

This general pattern of educational development in universities has largely persisted over the past thirty-plus years, with its narrower and wider interpretations, albeit extended at both ends, at once being more technicist and more educational/philosophical. Is that it, then, with a continuing stretching at both ends of the polarity in front of us? Either more technical/instrumental forms of 'educational development', more subject to performance management and learning analytics and, even soon, roboticised *or* more educational, reflective and considerate of students-as-persons with their own unfolding lives? But might another option be available, even orthogonal to this polarity? The ambition of the present volume is just that, to seek a quite different and bold approach, and to do it through the notion of the public good as both the context for *and* the substance of educational development.

Why might it be said that the idea of the public good is *orthogonal* to the instrumental–educational polarity that I have just sketched out? Because the idea of the public good lies in a quite different realm from either the instrumental or the educational polarities. It might be tempting to think that the public sphere is simply an extension of the educational orientation; a point further out on *that* end of the instrumental–educational polarity. But this would be to mistake the ambition advanced here – the connection with the idea of public – and, thereby, what this book stands for.

To speak of the public realm here is to locate higher education in the wider world and to summon up a glimpse of a particular space in it. It is a discursive space, of give and take, of reason and reasoning, of care and sensibility, of unity and difference, of equal participation across members of society and of collective fruitfulness. Such a space is orthogonal to the polarity we have observed. On the one hand, it looks outwards as does the instrumental conception of educational development but it eschews instrumentalism. On the contrary, it sees value in the public realm as a good in itself; indeed, in the public good. On the other hand, it sympathises with the educational arm but in effect also contains a critique of that position as being too inward. A concern with the public realm injects energy into educational development precisely because it senses possibilities for it in helping to further a public sphere that goes well beyond the university.

This book, therefore, is a brave book for it opens a quite new front for educational development that cannot be ensnared within the conventional educational–instrumental territory. It amounts to nothing less than a completely new re-territorialisation of the matter.

See what considerations and implications it brings in its wake. There is, first of all, a bevvy of possibilities precisely in relation to the idea of public. We may wonder, amidst the complexities of a riven age, whether it makes much sense to speak of 'the public'. Famously, Jürgen Habermas spoke of 'the public sphere' (which he wished to see 'transformed') but should we not now speak of public sphere*s* (plural)? Are there not a host of public spheres, and multiple communities, towards which the university, and thereby programmes of study, might be oriented? And is not the title of this book exquisitely chosen, therefore, in its speaking of higher education neither for 'a' public good nor for 'the' public good but simply for 'public good'? This is a formulation that simultaneously orients higher education outward – in that conjunction 'for' – and, in a delicious act of constructive ambiguity, leaves it open as to whether there is a single or multiple public goods. Just in relation to the idea of public, therefore, the book opens spaces and, in this way again, runs outside and beyond the closures of the instrumental–educational framing of educational development.

The title of this book adds another potent twist. It constitutes an argument in favour of higher education not only *for* public good but *as* public good. That is to say that educational development should be construed itself as a contributory part of the public good. The public good doesn't just lie outside higher education but is *in* higher education. Better still, higher education has public good in its veins.

For Tone Dyrdal Solbrekke and Ciaran Sugrue, the idea of public is intimately connected with the concepts both of *deliberative communication* and *legitimate compromise*. We can only sensibly speak of a public realm or a public dimension provided we include a sense that communication has to be deliberate; it has to be careful and intentional and conducted in a spirit of reasonableness. Also necessary here is a spirit of legitimate compromise. The public sphere is one of give-and-take. This give-and-take, though, has to be legitimate. It has to be conducted in a situation of non-domination.

It follows, given this nice set of nuances in this book's title (both the 'as' and the 'for'), the idea of public opens to a *dual set of spaces for the educational developer*. 'Public' here looks both to (i) the immediate pedagogical encounters of educational developers, in engaging with academic staff and in bringing those staff together mutually to explore complex educational matters, *and* (ii) the pedagogical encounters that those academics orchestrate with their students. Both of these educational situations may be constituted, through adroit teaching approaches, as publics. What is sauce for the goose is sauce for the gander. If it is right that meetings of academics – who come together for purposes of educational development – should be open and genuinely discursive, where different views on significant educational matters might be worked through in a spirit of legitimate compromise ('as' a public), so too it must be the case that students in their programmes of study should be encouraged to air their different understandings and work them through together in collaborative reasoning (not only 'as' a public but also with an eye on a higher education 'for' the public).

In neither case – in educational development settings or pedagogical situations in a university's programmes of study – is this to believe that a consensus is possible or even desirable. To the contrary: in prospect here is the possibility, if not the probability, that those involved can be clear about their different, and even conflicting, stances and yet agree to differ in a spirit of 'legitimate compromise'.

In sight here, to draw on another of the key concepts in this book, is a 'responsible praxis'. As is recognised here, 'praxis' is a particularly fraught notion in social and critical theory, and so one has to tread lightly. But this concept, tricky as it is, lies at the heart of the conception of educational development opened by this book. 'Praxis', after all points to action being not merely inflected by but thoroughly *infused* by reason and critical reason at that; and there is an accompanying dialogue of reflection and action. But Dyrdal Solbrekke and Sugrue press us further. Taxing as this never-ending and self-generating combination of critique, reason, reflection and action will be, it should also be 'responsible'.

Is there a larger concept in the English language than responsibility? Responsible to what? To whom? To which set of values? To which organisation or community? To oneself? To the here-and-now or the past or the future? To humanity *or*, as the ecologists would aver, to the whole world, including every creature and non-human entity in it? 'Responsible praxis', then, points to nothing less than an idea of higher education that has inbuilt concerns with and for the whole world. This surely has to become a key – perhaps *the* key – idea for higher education in the twenty-first century, that it should foster among every student a concern, and a care, for the whole world; the whole universe, indeed. (We may recall that the English philosopher and humanitarian Bertrand Russell saw himself as a citizen of the universe.)

In opening up such worldly considerations, of course controversial matters will loom into view. The thinker, whether teacher or student, will find themselves at times – to recall our opening poem – in dark places. What are the responsibilities of science in the modern world? Is knowledge value-neutral? How are those with university degrees to comport themselves in an age of populism? Amidst ecological concerns, how are different interests to be weighed and courses of action determined? The 'webs of commitment' that professionals have in the world open to 'competing logics' (to pick up yet two more of our authors' key concepts).

Such a journey, beset from multiple directions, will not be easy. Recalling the opening poem by Newman, there may even – at times – develop a mood of 'encircling gloom'. One is caught in a situation without a clear path or boundaries. One may feel 'far from home' and yet one has to go forward. However, educational development – of the kind being suggested to us here – will be a form of continuing reflection that may just provide resources that help one go on, if only 'one step' at a time.

And so we come to the final great concept lying at the heart of this book, that of leadership, the appearance of which signifies an additional degree of courage on the part of the authors. The concept of leadership often gives rise to some nervousness in academic circles but, while understandable, such nervousness can be overdone. It is surely not that leadership in itself is problematic (although it is), but rather the kind of leadership that is in question. A bold interpretation is offered here: 'teaching is leading and leading is teaching'; and then we are led into seeing how that view plays out so far as the educational developer is concerned.

One reason, I think, that accounts for a certain squeamishness in academic circles in relation to the idea of leadership is that it poses awkward questions. On the basis of which framework is leadership to be founded? With what or with whose authority? By which authority does X presume to lead Y and Z? These days, questions such as these are deflected with the idea of leadership-as-followership: a leader is only as strong or influential or effective to the extent that she or he has active followers. But this is too easy a get-out. On what basis might one become a follower? Wittgenstein (in philosophy) and Feynman (in physics) were demonstrably leaders. Their authority – and their followers – were gained as a result not only on the basis of their personalities, which were considerable (and, even, in the case of Wittgenstein, disagreeable to many), but much more on account of their being authorities in their respective fields. (Wittgenstein produced two revolutions in his field; Feynman was a Nobel Prize winner.) So leadership in the academy is fraught with difficulty. If management is the art of the possible, leadership is the art of the impossible.

But what, then, is the field of 'academic development'? What is its scope? It is evident, on the view taken in this book, that its territory is very wide and even all-encompassing. For academic development is here understood to be nothing short of embodying the widest possible conception of higher education. It is to be nothing less than that of infusing higher education with its possibilities in the world. It would be a higher education that heeds the world, cares about the world, listens to the world and reaches out to the world. This idea – an idea of higher education – was with us once but now has to be *re-kindled* (or even, dare one say, *kindled*, for we may doubt its pre-existence). Of course, in institutions that are increasingly tightly managed, such a conception of educational leadership has to be handled with subtlety, delicacy and even political nous. It is liable to run into difficulty, above and below. But omelettes cannot be made without a certain amount of egg-breaking. Courage, as in much of higher education, has to be a continuing accompaniment to such a large idea of educational development. Let it go forward in a positive spirit, one step at a time.

And so we are returned to the opening reflections and Newman's poem:

> Lead, Kindly Light, amidst th'encircling gloom,
> Lead Thou me on!
> The night is dark, and I am far from home,
> Lead Thou me on!
> Keep Thou my feet; I do not ask to see
> The distant scene; one step enough for me.

Ronald Barnett
University College London Institute
of Education September 2019

CONTRIBUTORS

Andreas Bergh is Associate Professor of Education at Örebro University, Sweden. His area of research is within the field of curriculum theory with a specific interest in education policy, issues of quality, juridification, and the professional roles of teachers and school leaders. He is currently engaged in studies of higher education, teachers' anti-racist actions and school segregation. Bergh is on the editorial committee for the research journal *Utbildning & Demokrati* (Education & Democracy) and member of the research groups Utbildning och Demokrati (Education and Democracy) and STEP (Studies in Educational Policy and Educational Philosophy). Currently, he has been engaged as external reviewer at the Swedish Higher Education Authority. Recent publications for Routledge include co-authoring articles in *Journal of Curriculum Studies* and *The Curriculum Journal*.

Tomas Englund is a senior professor in the School of Humanities, Education and Social Sciences, Örebro University, Sweden. His research interests centre on curriculum theory and didactics, curriculum history, political socialisation and citizenship education, and the philosophical aspects of education. He has directed the research group Education and Democracy for three decades and has been the general editor of the Swedish journal *Education & Democracy – Journal for Didactics and Education Policy* since 1992. He has written and edited five books in Swedish at Daidalos and published in *Journal of Curriculum Studies* (twice as guest editor), *Studies in Higher Education, Journal of Education Policy, Journal of Human Rights, Scandinavian Journal of Educational Research* and *Education Inquiry*, and contributed to volumes such as *Habermas, Critical Theory and Education* and *The Routledge Falmer Reader in Philosophy of Education*.

Kristin Ewins is Associate Professor and Director of the Centre for Academic Development at Örebro University, Sweden. Since taking up this post in 2013, she has taken a central role in building and leading teaching and learning strategies and practical academic development work within the university. In researching academic development, she has a special interest in the training of PhD supervisors and in leadership for strategic academic development across the sector. She is deeply committed to building a nourishing research environment for studies on higher education at the university and nationally. As part of this work, she leads the steering group for research on higher education at Örebro University, and chairs the organising committee for the second Swedish conference on research on higher education to be held in May 2021.

Trine Fossland is Professor at the Centre for Teaching, Learning and Technology, The Arctic University of Norway (UiT). Her main research interest is academic development, the use of digital technology and teachers' professional development. She is a former member of the national Norwegian University expert group 'Quality in ICT-supported Higher Education' and is one of the former leaders of the Norwegian network for university pedagogics. Her current research is focused on trends and trajectories in the practices of academic developers, and different aspects of quality and institutional quality work in higher education. She has written articles and edited books on ICT in higher education. Recent publications with Routledge include co-editing *Academic Bildung in Net Based Higher Education: Moving Beyond Learning* (2015).

Ester Fremstad (PhD) is an academic developer at the University of Oslo, Norway, and a researcher within the field of higher education. Her research interests includes the societal role of higher education institutions; the societal responsibility of university academics, and the conditions of their work within research, education and public participation; teaching for social responsibility; student formation; as well as the roles and responsibilities of academic developers, and the conditions of their work.

Ragnhild Sandvoll (PhD) is an Associate Professor of Education at the Centre for Teaching, Learning and Technology, The Arctic University of Norway (UiT). She works as an academic developer, and teaches and supervises academics in their development of teaching. She is also the leader of the group of academic developers at the centre. She researches learning and teaching in higher education, and has published work on peer assessment, the importance of teachers' underlying assumptions, and how theories of teaching and learning can contribute to professional development of teachers. Her latest publication is about pedagogical qualification frameworks as incentives for scholarly process in education. She is the project leader of the research project Innovation for Excellence in Teaching Quality in Higher Education at UiT. Sandvoll is the leader of the editorial board at *Uniped, Journal of Higher Education Pedagogics* in Norway.

Tone Dyrdal Solbrekke is Professor of Higher Education at the Department of Education, University of Oslo (UiO), Norway, and Guest Professor at Örebro University, Sweden. She was Head of the Academic Development Unit from 2015 to 2018. Since 2019 her teaching is assigned to LINK – Centre for Learning, Innovation & Academic Development at UiO. Solbrekke has extensive experience as teacher, leader and researcher in both primary and higher education. Her most recent research focuses on the formative aspects of higher education: leadership, teaching, professional responsibility and academic development. She is leading the international project 'Formation and Competence Building of University Academic Developers' (2015–2020) funded by The Norwegian Research Council. Solbrekke was Editor of the *Norwegian Journal of Educational Research* (2003–2011). She has been a board member of the Norwegian Network for Academic Development (2013–2016) and president of the board in 2015–2016. For Routledge previously she has co-edited *Professional Responsibility: New Horizons of Praxis* (2011).

Ciaran Sugrue is Professor and Chair of Education, School of Education, University College Dublin (UCD), Ireland. He has worked in the Irish education system in a variety of capacities including teacher, schools inspector, teacher educator and researcher. Prior to his appointment in UCD, he worked at the Faculty of Education, University of Cambridge, and was a fellow of St Edmund's College. While at the Faculty of Education, he also had a leadership role within the Centre for Commonwealth Education, reflecting a long-term commitment to, and involvement with, educational reform in the global south, sub-Saharan Africa. He was General Editor of Irish Educational Studies (1998–2008) and serves on the editorial boards of several international journals. Previous publications with Routledge include co-editing *Publishing and the Academic World: Passion, Purpose and Possible Futures* (2016) and co-editing *Professional Responsibility: New Horizons of Praxis* (2011).

Molly Sutphen is a Professor of Education at the University of Oslo (UiO), Norway. She is a historian and an academic developer who has worked as a secondary school teacher, teacher educator and researcher on the purposes of higher education for civil society. Prior to her appointment at UiO, she was the Associate Director of the Center for Faculty Excellence at the University of North Carolina at Chapel Hill. For over a decade, she taught at the University of California, San Francisco, where she also conducted research on professional education at the Carnegie Foundation for the Advancement of Teaching, as well as for the Lilly Endowment. She has published in *Studies in Higher Education* and co-edited two volumes with Routledge: *From Vocational to Professional Education: Educating for Social Welfare* (2015) and *Medicine and Colonial Identity* (2003).

Johan Wickström is Academic Developer at the Department of Education at Uppsala University, Sweden. He holds a Doctorate of Theology in the History of Religions, and has been working as AD since 2007. Between 2015 and 2018 he was Deputy Director for the Unit for Academic Teaching and Learning, responsible for the pedagogical content in courses and for strategies of educational development. He has an extensive experience from teaching students and university teachers. Nowadays he mainly teaches Curriculum Theory and Teaching and Learning Theory. He has a background as Senior Lecturer in Didactics of Religion. Prior to his academic work, he was a teacher in history and religion in the compulsory school. He has published research on educational uses of Old Norse myth, and is now interested in critical approaches to dominant theoretical models in higher education. He is also doing research on concepts such as 'religion' and 'social class' in textbooks.

ACKNOWLEDGEMENTS

As editors, we want to express our gratitude to those who contributed to the realisation of this book. The team of authors have been part of a research project funded by The Research Council of Norway (NRC), FINNUT project 246745, from 2015 to 2020. It is this research project, Formation and Competence Building of University Academic Developers (http://www.uv.uio.no/iped/english/resea rch/projects/solbrekke-formation-and-competence-building/), that has provided the impetus, and theoretical, conceptual and empirical material for the book. As always, international projects of this nature could not function were it not for the support of many individuals, primarily located in the University of Oslo, since that is where the project was hosted.

We are grateful for the support afforded by the Department of Education and Faculty of Education to encourage us to apply for research funding, and the department's administrative support by Kari-Anne Ulfsnes throughout the whole process has been invaluable. Ulf Grefsgård created the project's website and has always been hands on to keep resources in the right place, and had them available to the less technically minded among us. Finances too, an integral aspect of project management, benefited from the expertise of Suresh Johnpillai and more recently provided by Trine Labahå, for which we are most grateful.

The research team and the authorship of the chapters that make up this manuscript are one and the same: four Norwegians, four Swedes, one North American and one Irish citizen – one might say, international with a strong Nordic presence. First, we would like to acknowledge the funding of the NRC; it has been a terrific learning opportunity, made possible by the resources, and while inevitably much of the learning is intangible, we are confident that it will continue to have an impact in various systems long beyond the lifetime of the project. Of course, as director and co-director of the project, as well as editors of this book, we express our sincere gratitude to all for staying the course. Your ongoing contributions have been invaluable, and we are grateful also for your patience in responding positively and in a timely manner to our editorial suggestions, particularly during the past several months. Our gratitude also goes to Ronald Barnett, who engaged meticulously with our manuscript to write the foreword. We are grateful too to colleague Jim Gleeson, who at various stages provided insightful feedback on draft chapters of the manuscript.

Words of gratitude are inadequate to convey our admiration for the academic developers who willingly opened up their classrooms to the critical gaze of critical friends and researchers, thus enabling us to provide detailed case studies of leading and teaching while simultaneously deploying deliberative communication as pedagogy and as research method. A sincere thank you. Another sincere thank you goes to all of the university leaders at different levels in their respective universities who agreed to be interviewed to share their reflections on the mission of higher education and the contribution of academic developers to fulfil the purpose of higher education.

Not for the first time, we have reason to be grateful to the Routledge community who, in a very timely manner, offered us a book contract, and have been most helpful at every stage of bringing the manuscript to completion. Thank you.

Finally, when preoccupation with preparation of a manuscript takes hold, those closest to us tend to be ignored or neglected. We readily acknowledge therefore the patience and support of our respective partners who have been more than understanding throughout the writing process.

Tone Dyrdal Solbrekke
University of Oslo
Ciaran Sugrue
University College Dublin
October 2019

PART I

1

LEADING HIGHER EDUCATION AS, AND FOR, PUBLIC GOOD

New beginnings

Tone Dyrdal Solbrekke and Ciaran Sugrue

Introduction

Welcome, reader! We are very pleased that you are about to engage with this book since we consider it very timely. We invite you to join with us in deliberating on how to lead higher education as, and for, public good. For us, the educational mission of higher education is a formative one. Therefore, reflecting and deliberating on the why question, what higher education is for, and what dispositions our leading and teaching approaches cultivate and nurture in both staff and students, are among the most urgent responsibilities in the contemporary landscape of higher education.

We extend this invitation to you wherever you are located in the higher education (HE) sector and possibly beyond in the HE policy and research community. In this opening chapter our intent is to create some common ground, a precursor to further engagement as you make your way through the book's chapters. We do this by introducing the purpose of higher education, and by painting the broad contours of the contemporary higher education landscape. In doing so we also indicate the normative assumptions of our perspectives and the chosen analytical concepts and tools for thinking we draw on throughout the book. We anticipate finding ready resonance with your particular context despite differences in institutional histories, national geography and culture. We want you to journey with us, to emerge in new networks of meaning while entering into a web of commitment that is demonstrably both a contribution to as well as a strengthening of public good. We believe deliberations on the overall purpose of higher education may help us develop a better understanding of the webs of commitments characteristic of leading and teaching in contemporary universities.

Initial mapping of the higher education landscape

A core mission of public universities is to provide societies with highly qualified professionals, leaders and politicians who contribute to public good. Such a mission requires educational leaders capable of leading twenty-first-century higher education as, and for, public good (Walker, 2018). But does such an assertion seem strangely anachronistic in the contemporary higher education landscape, its "super-complexity"? (Barnett, 2011, 2016, 2018). In a fast-paced and turbulent higher education landscape that obliges academics to invest more time in applying for research funding, and in producing more publications to enhance institutional rankings, there is considerable potential to alter institutional missions. Such alterations to the ends of higher education rupture the largely taken-for-granted purpose of higher education, namely to contribute to public good. It has been argued that many public and research intensive universities internationally have become preoccupied with entrepreneurial and innovative orientations (Thorp & Goldstein, 2018). Others argue that such orientations increase the propensity for "commodification of knowledge" which, in turn, influences relationships between academic staff, administrators and students in fundamental ways – the former becoming service agents, the latter clients (Tight, 2013). When combined with internationalisation, these increasing preoccupations create legitimate concern that it is "private good" rather than "public good" that is primarily enhanced in higher education (Deem, 2008). A stronger focus on employability and a certain vocationalisation of university education has also raised concern among many academics about the formative effect on students and their learning (McArthur, 2011). Additionally, in a post-truth world, collective commitments and orientations are increasingly open to challenge, with a tendency towards a vindication of competitive individualism whereby education becomes more commodified and, in the process, a personal and private service to be purchased by those who can afford it (Walker 2018). The rise of "populism" with its strongly anti-elitist and anti-intellectual tendencies makes universities a target (Moffitt, 2017) since they are generally perceived to be on the side of cosmopolitanism, internationalism and other isms deemed anathema by seriously conservative protectionist and reactionary nationalist forces (Appiah, 2006; Benhabib et al., 2008). In the midst of such forces, being clearer about, and committed to, the purposes of higher education has become more onerous and contested.

In such circumstances, leading a public university, embellishing its budget and research profile, promoting internationalisation and building its global footprint to become attractive in an increasingly competitive higher education market may serve to distract from its responsibility to educate as, and for, public good. Whatever your experience of, and perspective on, contemporary higher education, how public universities educate for the public good in the twenty-first century cannot be taken for granted and neither can the multiple meanings such a concept may entail (Walker, 2018). There is increasing concern about the current orientations of higher education even among higher education politicians, policy-makers and university leaders. For example, in the invitation to the celebration of the Bologna

Declaration twentieth anniversary in June 2019, there is concern that public good has been eroded, and that the Bologna process has contributed to dilution of commitment to public good. The invitation to the seminar encouraged participants to deliberate on the following:

- academic and related civic values in changing societies;
- student centred learning;
- providing leadership for sustainable development, the role of higher education;
- the social dimensions of higher education;
- careers and skills for the labour market of the future. (http://bolognaprocess2019. it/abstact-submission/)

The call for such deliberations recognises that while values such as "autonomy, academic freedom, equity and integrity", considered to be among the "core values of academia" and necessary to build "trust and reliability" thus constituting important rallying cries, there is recognition too that "making declarations ... isn't the same as actually embracing them" (ibid.). We are in agreement with the timely nature of the question: how can universities be safe havens of open debate and free expression in times of high political tension? Most likely, you also recognise the necessity to address such an important consideration. You may even wish to insist that such a leading question is the mere tip of the iceberg. While conscious that these are our questions; you are likely to compile your own list of pertinent questions regarding higher education and its current commitment to public good as well as its capacity for such an agenda given the multiple competing interests that it seeks to pursue. Here are a few initial questions to get the cerebral wheels turning:

- What does leading higher education as, and for, public good entail?
- What formative impact does current university education have on students and staff?
- At a time when political leaders seem paralysed or incapable of addressing questions such as climate change, migration and major inequalities in terms of access to health and education, how should public universities in particular lead such challenging agenda?
- How should higher education prepare students for an unpredictable future in ways that enhance their capacities to engage with and to solve these major challenges on a local–global scale?

While not being presumptuous, we hope you will provide even tentative approval for the view that it is impossible to address these pressing questions with any degree of commitment and conviction without addressing the questions of what "public good" entails, and investigate the extent to which the education provided in public universities is actually of public benefit and not merely private gain. We join with others who call for a critical examination of the consequences of the recent years' transnational higher education policies, and what orientations of public universities these have spawned (Barnett 2011, 2018; Deem, 2008; Karseth and Solbrekke, 2016). Although this book is not about governance and financial matters, neither do we wish to downplay their significance for university leaders' priorities with consequences for education. At a time when funding of public universities is being reduced by governments, new systems of governance being imposed, whether in Western liberal democracies, or more conservative secular or religious dictatorships, there are profound consequences for questions of higher education and how public good is construed in these various contexts (Deem, 2008; Walker, 2018). In such circumstances, all academics have a profound responsibility to speak out, advocate for and be public intellectuals for making higher education a public good (Macfarlane, 2012; Said, 1994), especially when their experience is that higher education policies are inimical and counterproductive to the mission of public universities. While asserting this responsibility with sincerity, it deserves to be tempered by an acknowledgement that there are limits to academics' power to influence (trans-)national policies and priorities. Nevertheless, as professionally responsible agents within the field of higher education, we must critically investigate institutional policy and strive to cultivate practices of leading and teaching that promote public good. The task may seem Sisyphean, but commitment to what we believe in and attempt to stand for is more compelling. These are matters that all academics have responsibility for whether or not they inhabit formal leadership positions since all teaching implies leadership (Spillane, 2006).

While not ignoring the wider context, its influences and power relationships, this book thus addresses aspects of some internal practices and in particular the formative aspects of educational leading and teaching. Our ambition is to advocate for, as well as advance theoretically and practically, the leading of teaching and learning processes in higher education as, and for, public good. However, within the structural confines of the book it is not possible to capture all relevant aspects of leading higher education. Selectivity is necessary; choices have to be made. Attention in this book is focused on the contribution of academic developers (ADs) (also referred to as educational or instructional developers (Stensaker et al., 2017; Gaebel et al., 2018), who, in addition to formal leaders, have a particular responsibility to promote the educational mission of the institution.

The significance of ADs' influence on pedagogies in university teaching deserves ongoing deliberation, but not only as general theoretical or abstract discourses among scholars and researchers. It is timely to investigate their practices when leading higher education as, and for, public good, encouraging what Kandlbinder (2007) defines as "deliberative academic development" through critical thinking on the contribution of higher education to society through the relational formative aspects of teaching and learning. As the authors and scribes of this challenging, if not daunting endeavour, we remain confident that we are well placed professionally to document and deliberate on the everyday leading of higher education practices in which we are invested, and sometimes transform through our own ongoing (re-) formation. We need to move beyond espoused normative perspectives, and, in the process, open up some of the black boxes pertinent to leading education.

In order to take up this leading higher education challenge, over time, we have selected what we consider key concepts: tools for thinking as part of our ongoing efforts to understand higher education as, and for, public good, and the identification of possible contributions towards making it a reality rather than a mere aspiration. We are particularly concerned with how educational leadership and teaching practices emerge, and change, in the encounters between institutional traditions, policies, practices, structures and cultures. While we articulate conceptual and theoretical aspects of local and global influences on university education, the book also moves beyond these concerns to address aspects of educational leadership practices and capacity building. Consequently, we connect, and bring into generative dialogue the why question of educational leadership, its relational formative impact on academic development and higher education, and how these are intended to contribute to public good. For this purpose we need some analytical concepts and thinking tools. While there is a variety of concepts and lenses that could have been applied to investigate and analyse leading practices/praxes in higher education, our selection has developed through iterative deliberations among the authors.[1] For the purpose of this book we benefit from previous research on, and experiences with, educational leadership; higher education and its societal mandate; the role of academic developers in contemporary universities; and the webs of commitments that academics in public universities must live and work within.

Structure of book

The book has three sections. Part I (Chapters 1–4) describes the current landscape of higher education while also indicating profound challenges for leading higher education as, and for, public good. Part II, beginning with chapter 5, describes the methodological approach used in the subsequent five case studies (Chapters 6–9) of ADs leading teaching while endeavouring to deploy deliberative communication in different institutional contexts with different groups of academic peers. Part III is home to the concluding chapter where we summarise and critically discuss what has emerged from the foregoing chapters, drawing out the implications for leaders, formal and informal, as well as academics policy-makers and politicians, in order to lead (more successfully) higher education as, and for, public good. In this endeavour, we propose deliberative leadership as a theoretical and practical means of creating sustainable futures consistent with the values, pedagogies and orientations that leading higher education as and for public good entail.

In the pages that follow, we introduce the concepts we have found particularly valuable when deliberating on the questions raised above. Thus, we introduce them here as important conceptual and analytical tools in their own right, while seeking also in Part II of the book to deploy them in discussion and analysis of leading and teaching. In this manner, we consider them to be important signposts on the landscape of higher education. An additional intention in describing these key contours of the higher education topography is to whet your appetite as well as orient you as reader while in the process we also reveal our own normative stance.

Leading higher education: selected concepts

Praxis

As a discerning reader, you may well have observed above that we have used the word "practice" although we consider that the term "praxis" has more to offer depending on how it is construed. Here, we indicate why we are attracted to the term, and the manner in which we intend to use it throughout the book In this regard, we readily recognise that there are disagreements as to its precise meaning, thus it is important that we clarify at the outset the manner in which it is being used in the context of this book. Praxis, as we use it, implies a combination of reflection and action; not one or the other, but both. It seeks to hold in productive tension thought and action through critical reflection. It is important to add that it includes a moral dimension, informed by and imbued with one's values, and beliefs that constitute a world-view. Previously, we have written that praxis combines "critical and ethical reflection with other essential ingredients, such as expertise, humanity and finesse" (Sugrue & Solbrekke, 2011, p. 178). It has much in common with deliberative communication, while we consider that in some respects it captures the affective and human side of deliberation and reasoning that some versions of deliberative communication are inclined to downplay. A core interest in this book is to provide examples on how we may develop an awareness of our own praxes, by reflecting on practices and our arguments for acting as we do in different settings.

Praxis as, and for, public good may emerge in deliberations among staff and students. Sutphen & de Lange (2015, p. 411) argue that the academic community has a responsibility to "engage [students] actively in broad intellectual, moral, political and cultural matters". Having asserted this as a significant formative "out-come" of university education, they question the extent to which "we have an adequate vocabulary for addressing learning about broader moral, political and cultural issues in higher education". Suffice to say that, from a leading education perspective, it is necessary to hold ourselves to account for our stewardship of these moral values (May, 1996) as well as the exercise of a critical reflexivity on the part of the academic community (Taylor, 1989/1992). These considerations are important constituent elements of praxis.

Institutional orientations

Chapter 2 elaborates on the significance and variety of orientations espoused by higher education institutions, frequently projecting more than one, in their efforts to appeal to different stakeholders and constituencies – reflective of Barnett's (2016) "multi-varsity". While the university as a whole is made up of multiple schools, typically discipline based, often organised into faculties or colleges, thus, there are "hard" sciences, arts and humanities, social sciences, each of which break down into individual disciplines despite a growing preference for inter-disciplinary research. In other institutions, STEM, STEAM,[2] as well as Law, Medicine and Education, compete for space, resources and status with Computer Science, Nursing, Physiotherapy and other disciplines. University College Dublin (UCD), for example, claims to be "Ireland's global university" while making a more traditional contribution to "nation building". Similarly, the University of Oslo, founded in 1811, at a critical juncture in the nation's history, has traditionally been concerned about the nation, while it's more outward-looking orientation is to address the world's most pressing problems such as climate change – to play a leading role on the international stage (Sutphen, Solbrekke & Sugrue 2018).

Such statements may be imbued with a spirit of tradition or innovation and entrepreneurialism, while each posture is underpinned by different value commitments, rendering it difficult to hold competing orientations at once. The more significant concern here is that orientations matter in several respects, both internally and externally: the latter in terms of how an institutional mission is perceived and regarded by funding agencies, and governments, while internally the particular mélange of orientations indicates significant priorities that in turn shape the working conditions of employees. Consequently, from the perspective of leading education, we regard it as particularly important to connect institutional orientations to workplace conditions, to teaching, learning and leading.

Public good and deliberative communication

Chapter 3 elaborates on public good and deliberative communication and, here also, we indicate its relation with praxis. Public good is frequently contrasted with private good, two longstanding concepts from liberal political philosophy and political economy. Sen (2009) describes public good as something that is for the benefit of all, while private good, by comparison, is competed for, thus exclusive and manifestly a commodity not available to all. The concept is at the centre of contemporary debates regarding university organisation, governance, resource allocation, access, autonomy, and legitimacy (Marginson, 2007; Pusser, 2006). Such considerations pave the way for the following question: How do contemporary universities teach values, beliefs and moral responsibilities in ways that are consistent with promoting public good? And how do universities lead teaching and learning practices that encourage education as, and for, public good? The Bologna agreement entered into two decades ago by almost 400 universities, committed to the Magna Charta Universitatum, a document that indicated membership of an international network of institutions sharing the same academic values and purposes, as well as principles of academic freedom and institutional autonomy, as a basis for good governance and self-understanding of universities. As indicated above, a recent convocation to deliberate on these commitments strongly suggests a considerable disparity between such rhetoric and the lived reality of university employees. The timeliness of a reconvening of the Bologna forum strongly suggests the necessity for deliberative communication, another tool for thinking.

The idea of deliberative communication stems from classical pragmatism articulated by John Dewey (1916/1966, 1897/2005) and more recently the work of Jürgen Habermas (1991), with roots stretching back to the work of Aristotle, particularly his notion of praxis (Dunne, 1993). Deliberation implies carefully balanced consideration of different alternatives. Participants in deliberative communication in higher education settings include academics who may be leaders, teachers or administrators as well as students at undergraduate and postgraduate levels while each comes to the deliberative process with different knowledge, experience as well as different positional authority both formal and informal. In a socio-political and cultural context where "fake news" and the notion of "alternative facts" seek to undermine more traditional notions of "truth" and social media platforms enable keyboard warriors to create their own networked ideological echo chambers, the necessity to engage in deliberative communication has taken on increased urgency, while also calling into question the purposes and responsibility of universities when such intellectual "barbarism" lurks at the portcullis of the academy or has already penetrated the "ivory tower". Suffice to say at this point that deliberative communication, as will be demonstrated in later chapters, has the capacity to contribute significantly to debate, decision-making, the cultivation of professional dispositions attuned to reflective engagement and refined judgement that is respectful of the "other" while pursuing and promoting public good. However, we readily recognise that adopting a deliberative disposition implies a capacity and orientation towards compromise, not as capitulation but rather finding solutions to otherwise intractable problems. An extension of the deliberative process therefore is the necessity to consider "legitimate compromise" as another conceptual tool.

Professional responsibility: legitimate compromise in a web of commitments

The terms "legitimate compromise" and "web of commitments" have been coined by Larry May (1996); we find them particularly useful to illustrate the complexity of leading higher education and the need for legitimate compromises between different logics embedded in professional responsibility. The metaphor "web of commitments" is a version of a communitarian, or group-oriented, perspective that facilitates acknowledgement of the complexity of the practice of leading education/teaching and learning in a twenty-first-century public university. The metaphor of a web includes the multiple civic, personal, professional, collegial and social commitments included in leading higher education as, and for, public good. We suggest that an acknowledgement of the web of commitments is the first step for improving leading and teaching practices. This is the focus of Chapter 4. We situate it within competing logics that in many respects have a significant shaping influence on higher education institutions and the lives of their employees. Reference was made above to the Bologna agreement and the university charter signed two decades ago. Writ large in that manifesto was institutional autonomy. Yet, in the intervening decades, there has been significant external policy encroachment; prescriptions from Brussels (EU), OECD and other international agencies, as well as national governments, to hold higher education to account, to demonstrate in a variety of ways that public funding is being disbursed in a manner consistent with public policy. This call to be accountable, perceived by those in the higher education sector to be anathema to more traditional notions of autonomy, has its own particular logic, and in Chapter 4, this is elaborated on and contrasted with the concept of responsibility (Solbrekke & Englund, 2011). In general, the language and logic of accountability requires conformity and compliance, while the language and logic of professional responsibility insists on space and opportunity for agency, deliberation and professional judgement as intimates in the formation of professionals. To behave in a professionally responsible manner is to take action that is consistent with the values and codes of conduct of one's profession and disciplinary home. Consequently, whether one is acting alone or in consort with colleagues, there is an obligation to mediate between the interest of a society and an individual citizen's interest while upholding and promoting professional standards. Chapter 4 describes how these competing logics create considerable tensions and dilemmas for professionals, while May's "legitimate compromise" suggests that within the competing logics professionals are committed to and obliged to avoid being compromised, thus not simply complying with the logic of accountability, but to seek solutions that legitimately uphold professional standards while simultaneously demonstrating that professional responsibility is evidently present in decisions and actions.

It is important to acknowledge that there is legitimacy to the insistence by national governments that its higher education institutions be accountable, to vindicate the legal rights of employees and students alike. However, to provide higher education as, and for, public good depends as much on a social and moral responsibility implying responsiveness to the needs of all students and staff – beyond answering to predetermined, transparent and quantifiable quality criteria for education. Rather, it is about helping students to see and nurture *their* capacities to live in the world and to encourage them to deliberate on what professional responsibility and active citizenship implies. It includes a capacity to cope with tensions between societal concerns and individual interests and capacity to juggle commitments in private life with the diverse and multiple requirements of working life (May, 1996). Consequently, "responsibility must precede and supersede accountability" (Hargreaves and Shirley, 2009, p. 101), requiring professionals to cultivate proactively responsible praxis, not merely reactive compliance to external demands.

Leading higher education: the contribution of academic developers

Since the book's title is *Leading Higher Education As and For Public Good*, we have some responsibility to indicate what we have in mind when using the term leading education and how such responsibilities are shared. Chapter 2 advances the argument that the leading praxis of ADs has emerged with increasing significance given the nature of university orientations. In Chapter 2 we distinguish also between leading an organisation or institution, and leading education. Much of the literature on higher education focuses on leading the organisation. As societies and institutions slip their moorings of tradition and orthodoxy, propelled by a variety of internal and external change forces, there are renewed calls for new leaders and leadership to create new visions, new possibilities and to create sustainable, viable and vital futures. Consequently, the rectors, presidents and senior leaders of higher education institutions are increasingly expected to be "entrepreneurial", seeking out "competitive advantage" and "best practice" in leading, frequently focusing on governance, finance, international rankings, overseas campuses and hiring celebrity academics, often privileging the winning of prestigious research grants over the quality of teaching and learning, which is often reflected also in criteria for promotion.

Surrounded by these many competing and potentially conflicting considerations that constitute our webs of commitments, responsibility for leading education is often one of many delegated tasks, or maybe even neglected. It is most likely that responsibility for leading education is reliant on a version of "distributed leadership" even if this is delegation rather than wholehearted embrace of a distributed perspective (Gronn, 1999, 2003; Spillane, 2006; Youngs, 2017). Nevertheless, leading education has become a much more visible activity in higher education to develop and support student engagement through active learning while attracting international students, an important measure of international standing, as well as a major source of revenue for institutions, thus also dealing with a much more diverse student body, linguistically and culturally. As higher education has expanded exponentially, it has become a requirement in an increasing number of institutions to provide pedagogical professional support for newly appointed academics in particular. Responsibility for designing and providing such programmes is the particular responsibility of ADs (Gaebel et al., 2018). Their remit, has also been expanded over time to provide support to academic staff in order to learn about or improve the scholarship of teaching and build awareness of praxis, as well as contribute to the qualification of educational leadership (Stensaker et al., 2017). As a consequence of this more visible and public role, ADs are frequently expected to broker between senior leaders' vision, frequently expressed in strategic plans, and their academic peers across all disciplines, a more political role requiring considerable expertise as well as finely attuned antennae that enable them to navigate vertically and horizontally within their respective institutions. Navigating such potentially choppy institutional waters, while taking their responsibilities seriously, there are growing tensions between being protective of their professional autonomy, mediating institutional education policies, modelling legitimate compromises and simultaneously building capacities in leading education. While it may be suggested that all employees of higher education institutions have some responsibility for leading education, and certainly for contributing to it, ADs, with considerable variation, as will be more evident in Chapter 4, are in the spotlight for leading education, while an integral element of their remit is to convince their academic colleagues in particular that they too have a significant role to play in leading education. The webs of commitments, agency and capacity of ADs to lead education in their respective institutions are all influenced considerably by the nature of its orientation(s).

We emphasise leading as an activity while not ignoring the existence of an extensive and growing literature on leadership in higher education (Black, 2015; Youngs, 2017). "Super-complexity" is increasingly accepted as an accurate descriptor of HE institutions and their positioning in the higher education landscape, due to a raft of influences: internationalisation, greater diversity among staff and students, intensification of research activity, impact of technology, governance, international rankings and so on.

In the present globalised, marketised competitive climate in which higher education institutions function, in general they seek to present different "faces" of the twenty-first-century public university to different audiences, a variation on the Hydra of Greek mythology, capable of morphing into yet another representation of itself when a combination of internal and external influences suggest another "head" (or "face"!) is necessary.

How might "legitimate compromise" (May, 1996) be identified, agreed and promoted in the tensions between competing interests and needs, which increasingly become polarised discourses on meanings and values? The rather glib retort may be to assert simplistically: "with great difficulty!" Nevertheless, as Thorvald Stoltenberg (former Norwegian foreign minister and UN Envoy in the Balkans) asserts: "'compromise' is one of the most beautiful words we have", and, as a consequence, it is necessary to accord it "much greater status than it has today". Such an orientation towards compromise leaves some room for agency, individual and collective. As Tony Judt remarks, due to "the way we live now" "our moral sentiments have indeed been corrupted" (Judt, 2010, p. 23). We need to hold ourselves to account by distinguishing between what may be considered legitimate compromise, while not falling victim to being compromised. In such circumstances, "we need to re-learn how to criticize those who govern us. But in order to do so with credibility we have to liberate ourselves from the circle of conformity into which we, like they, are trapped" (p. 161).

Despite competing interests and potential conflicts, there is common ground that conversation, deliberation, reflection, resistance and dissent even are important dimensions of our workplace realities, influenced by these various internal and external forces and mediated by leadership, formal and informal. In this maelstrom of competing and conflicting interests and differential power relations, it is preferable that such conversations are characterised by "civility", which, according to Hall, "is important because it allows disagreement to take place without violence and regularizes conflict so that it can be productive" (Hall, 2013, p. 4). We recognise "that words are our masters as well as our servants" (Collini, 2012, p. 95). This constellation of considerations points towards the necessity to recognise that the high-blown rhetoric of "the idea of a university" needs to be tempered "by the daily experience in any actual university" (p. 102). Arguably, it is in the interstices of such considerations that deliberative communication is best deployed to make a telling contribution; situations that ADs are obliged to navigate, brokering those legitimate compromises as, and for, public good.

The web of commitments in contemporary higher education institutions is extensive but with considerable variation depending on roles and responsibilities within a particular institution, each with its own institutional history, trajectory and positioning. Until relatively recently, it was probably accurate to state that professionals were identified as high status and self-governing, while in the contemporary world most of them work in organisations which are influenced and governed by complex external as well as internal interests, a situation increasingly recognisable among contemporary academics (Solbrekke & Sugrue, 2014). More recently, the reality of workplace conditions are more likely to be "governed by complex external as well as internal interests", thus increasingly "no one is free from multiple commitments and the influence of varied interests of other colleagues, leaders … nor from the challenges of differing professional identities and even incompatible epistemic traditions and moral priorities" (ibid., p. 6). Without wishing to be overly dramatic in coming to terms with leading education in such a landscape, it may be suggested that professional landmines abound, necessitating very careful navigation if conflicts or worse are to be avoided, and positive working relations forged and maintained while contributing to one's own formation as an educational leader, and those with whom regular engagement is integral to such responsibilities.

Conclusion

Our purpose in this initial chapter of the book has been to orient you as reader. We have indicated the book's purpose, as well as provided an initial map of the higher education landscape as we read it. While signalling its increasing complexity, we have introduced a number of concepts we have found most useful in getting to grips with its intricacies, while, in the process, indicating also our own positioning within this territory. We have revealed also that the purpose of the book is not merely to espouse theoretical and conceptual understandings, but to take seriously the issue of a praxis of leading education as, and for, public good. In taking the task of getting to grips with that praxis, we focus, particularly in Part II of the book, on the efforts of five ADs to use deliberative communication as a pedagogical tool as part of their efforts to lead education in a variety of settings. We understand these concepts, not in hierarchical relation to each other, but rather in a dynamic interplay where all are interacting simultaneously, and the task of leading education as, and for, public good is to find legitimate compromise between the tensions these create, in the shadow of institutional orientations, while seeking to do so in a professionally responsible manner.

In the next three chapters, these various concepts and their interconnectedness are elaborated on further, as we understand them within the higher education landscape, before turning attention to their importance for leading education praxis in Part II. We trust that, in doing so, we have set the scene sufficiently for you to continue this odyssey with us in pursuit of leading higher education as, and for, public good. In the final chapter of the book we will revisit much of this agenda in a retrospective and prospective manner, putting emergent insights and understanding on the prospectus of leading higher education, a praxis as, and for, public good; advocating for deliberative leadership as a catalyst for sustainable futures for higher education.

Notes

1 The book's orientation is a result of a shared interest in the normative mandate of public universities. As part of the international collaborative research and competence building project Formation and Competence Building of University Academic Developers (project number 246745/H20) funded by the Norwegian Research Council from 01.092015–31.05.2020, the authors had the opportunity to meet in both face-to-face and cyberspace meetings to negotiate and reach a common conceptual framework. To read more about this project, which involves academic developers and researchers from six public comprehensive universities in Norway, Sweden, Ireland and the USA, see: http://www.uv.uio.no/iped/english/research/projects/solbrekke-formation-and-competence-build ing/. The project is approved by the Norwegian Centre for Research Data and all the individual institutions.
2 The acronym STEAM is an attempt to imbue Science, Technology and Mathematics with the benefits of Arts and the Humanities – thus the "A" being added to STEM. While this may have laudable intent, it is open to the criticism of reducing the Arts to some kind of subordinate role, as an add-on, a "gadfly" to these disciplines rather than a valuable contribution to education in and off themselves. For a comprehensive discussion of this important issue see Small (2013).

References

Alvesson, M., & Skölberg, K. (2000). *Reflexive Methodology: New Vistas for Qualitative Research*. London: Sage Publications.

Appiah, K. A. (2006). *Cosmopolitanism Ethics in a World of Strangers*. London: Penguin Books.

Barnett, R. (2011). *Being a University*. London: Routledge.

Barnett, R. (2016). *Understanding the University: Institution, Idea, Possibilities*. London: Routledge.

Barnett, R. (2018). *The Ecological University: A Feasible Utopia*. London: Routledge.

Benhabib, S., with Waldron, J., Honing, B. & Kymilcka, W. (2008). *Another Cosmopolitanism*. Oxford: Oxford University Press.

Black, S. A. (2015). Qualities of effective leadership in higher education. *Open Journal of Leadership, 4*, 54–66. Published online June 2015 in SciRes: http://www.scirp.org/journal/ojl http://dx.doi.org/10.4236/ojl.2015.42006

Collini, S. (2012). *What Are Universities For?* London: Penguin.

Deem, R. (2008). Producing and re/producing the global university in the 21st century: researcher perspectives and policy consequences. *Higher Education Policy, 21*, 439–456.

Dewey, J. (1897/2005). *My Pedagogic Creed*. Michigan: Michigan Historical Reprint Series.

Dewey, J. (1916/1966). *Democracy and Education*. Newark: Plain Label Books.

Dunne, J. (1993). *Back to the Rough Ground: 'Phronesis' and 'Techne' in Modern Philosophy and in Aristotle*. Notre Dame: University of Notre Dame Press.

Gaebel, M., Zhang, T., Bunescu, L., & Stober, H. (2018). *Trends 2018: Learning and Teaching in the European Higher Education Area*. Brussels: European University Association. https://eua.eu/downloads/publications/trends-2018-learning-and-teaching-in-the-european-higher-education-area.pdf

Gronn, P. (1999). *The Making of Educational Leaders*. London: Cassell.

Gronn, P. (2003). *The New Work of Educational Leaders Changing Leadership Practice in an Era of School Reform*. London: Paul Chapman Publishing.

Habermas, J. (1991). *The Theory of Communicative Action* (Vol. *1*): *Reason and the Rationalization of Society*. Oxford: Polity Press.

Habermas, J. (1991). *The Theory of Communicative Action* (Vol. *2*): *The Critique of Functionalist Reason* (translated by Thomas McCarthy). Oxford: Polity Press.

Hall, J. (2013). *The Importance of Being Civil: The Struggle for Political Decency*. Princeton: Princeton University Press.

Hargreaves, A., & Shirley, D. (2009). *The Fourth Way: The Inspiring Future for Educational Change*. Thousand Oaks: Sage.

Judt, T. (2010). *Ill Fares the Land: A Treatise on Our Present Discontents*. New York: Penguin Books.

Kandlbinder, P. (2007). The challenge of deliberation for academic development. *International Journal for Academic Development, 12*(1), 55–59.

Karseth, B., & Solbrekke, T. D. (2016). Curriculum trends in European higher education: the pursuit of the Humboldtian University ideas. In S. Slaughter & J. T. Barrett (eds), *Higher Education, Stratification, and Workforce Development: Competitive Advantage in Europe, the US, and Canada* (pp. 215–233). Cham: Springer.

Macfarlane, B. (2012). *Intellectual Leadership in Higher Education: Renewing the Role of the University Professor*. London: Routledge.

Marginson, S. (2007). The public/private divide in higher education: A global revision1. *Higher Education, 53*, 307-333. doi:10.1007/s10734-005-8230-y

May, L. (1996). *The Socially Responsive Self: Social Theory and Professional Ethics*. Chicago: Chicago University Press.

McArthur, J. (2011). Reconsidering the social and economic purposes of higher education. *Higher Education Research & Development, 30*(6), 737–749.

Moffitt, B. (2017). *The Global Rise of Populism: Performance, Political Style, and Representation*. Stanford: Stanford University Press.

Pusser, B. (2006). Reconsidering higher education and the public good: the role of public spheres. In W. Tierney (ed.), *Governance and the Public Good*. Albany: State University of New York Press.

Said, E. (1994). *Representations of the Intellectual: The Reith Lectures*. New York: Pantheon.

Sen, A. (2009). *The Idea of Justice*. London: Allen Lane.

Small, H. (2013). *The Value of the Humanities*. Oxford: Oxford University Press.

Solbrekke, T. D., & Englund, T. (2011). *Bringing Professional Responsibility Back in Studies in Higher Education, 36*, 847–861.

Solbrekke, T. D., & Sugrue, C. (2014). Professional accreditation of initial teacher education programmes: teacher educators' strategies – between 'accountability' and 'professional responsibility'? *Teachers and Teacher Education, 37*, 11–20.

Spillane, J. (2006). *Distributed Leadership*. San Francisco: Jossey Bass.

Stensaker, B., Bilbow, G. T., Breslow, L., & Van Der Vaart, R. (eds). (2017). *Strengthening Teaching and Learning in Research Universities: Strategies and Initiatives for Institutional Change*. Cham: Palgrave Macmillan.

Sugrue, C., & Solbrekke, T. D. (2011). Professional responsibility: new horizons of praxis. In C. Sugrue& T. Dyrdal Solbrekke (eds), *Professional Responsibility: New Horizons of Praxis* (pp. 177–196). London: Routledge.

Sutphen, M., & de Lange, T. (2015). What is formation? A conceptual discussion. *Higher Education Research and Development, 34*(2), 411–419.

Sutphen, M., Solbrekke, T. D., & Sugrue, C. (2018). Toward articulating an academic praxis by interrogating university strategic plans. *Studies in Higher Education, 44*(8), 1–13. doi:10.1080/03075079.2018.1440384

Taylor, C. (1989/1992). *Sources of the Self: The Making of Modern Identity*. Cambridge: Cambridge University Press.

Thorp, H., & Goldstein, B. (2018). *Our Higher Calling Rebuilding the Partnership between America and Its Colleges & Universities*. Chapel Hill: University of North Carolina Press.

Tight, M. (2013). *Researching Higher Education*. Milton Keynes: Open University Press.

Walker, M. (2018). Dimensions of higher education and the public good in South Africa. *Higher Education*, 555–569. doi:10.1007/s10734-017-0225-y

Youngs, H. (2017). A critical exploration of distributed leadership in higher education: developing an alternative ontology through leadership-as-practice. *Journal of Higher Education Policy and Management*, *39*(2), 140–154. doi:10.1080/1360080X.2017.1276662

2

LEADING HIGHER EDUCATION

Putting education centre stage

Ciaran Sugrue and Tone Dyrdal Solbrekke

Introduction

In many instances the following was a seminal moment in our childhood "education":

> We all learned back on the playground that whoever makes the rules of the game stands a better chance of winning it. It's an uncomfortable lesson, one that requires us to accept that norms are fluid, that expectations shift, …
>
> *(Gibbs, 2019, p. 8)*

These words about standards and norms to be upheld and promoted in public spaces and places at first sight may appear disconnected from leading higher education as, and for, public good. However, the workplace conditions created in higher education public institutions are the "playgrounds" of both staff and students. These spaces have rules and norms about teaching, learning, research and assessment, overlaid with codes of professional conduct and ethical behaviour, and there are appeal processes when disputes or conflicts arise. Similarly, for those of us who are privileged to make a living from our many and varied contributions to shaping the contours of our respective higher education workplaces, it would be difficult to find any colleague who would not readily attest that fluidity of norms and policy shifts have significant consequences for our working conditions. Changing norms, different conceptions of how to fulfil the societal mandate of higher education, lead to new orientations of universities (Barnett, 2011). In such circumstances, some suggest that the anchoring influence of established norms and routines on university orientations are rapidly eroded, jettisoned as an encumbrance, supplanted by an apparent instrumentalist entrepreneurialism that privileges competitiveness, internationalisation and rankings (Pearce, Wood & Wassenaar, 2018; Swartz, Ivancheva, Czerniewicz & Morris, 2019). Alternatively, universities are faced with competing and possibly conflicting orientations where choices have to be made regarding vision and values that cultivate an "ecological professionalism" and a sustainable future (Barnett, 2011, 2016, 2018).

This is the "field" of higher education, a landscape in which contemporary public universities are situated, and our modus operandi are bound in various ways by "the rules which define the ordinary functioning of the field" (Bourdieu & Wacquant, 1992, p. 101).[1] Those of us who inhabit public universities, staff and students alike, are all "social agents" (p. 115) in the "social game". Whatever position we occupy within this landscape it is important to recognise that we are playing the game in "an open system of dispositions that is constantly subjected to experiences, and therefore constantly affected by them in a way that either reinforces or modifies its structures" (p. 133). Consequently, experience of higher education may be either as a "conceptual straight-jacket that provides no room for modification or escape" or alternatively as a "mediating ... concept which introduces a degree of free play, creativity, and unpredictability in social action" (p. 132). Throughout this book, we adopt the latter view, notwithstanding how contexts in higher education vary enormously through the "technologies of control" (Ball, 2003) that are intertwined in contemporary discourses of educational change, laced with aspects of New Public Management (NPM), all of which harbour consequences for a sense of social agency. Nevertheless, as will become more apparent in subsequent chapters, that agentic sense, both courage and capacity to be proactive,[2] is shaped considerably by career stage, and thus also location within one's institutional milieu (see Fremstad, Bergh, Solbrekke, & Fossland, 2019). Within the higher education landscape, and in public universities in particular, our overarching focus is on how the mandate to provide education as public good and for public good is understood, led and enacted. Inevitably this will vary from an international, national and institutional perspective, even if there is a general homogenising tendency in terms of international influences as evidenced recently by the Paris Communique on the Bologna process (2018).[3]

Amidst these policy statements there is recognition that what distinguishes societies from mere economies is a sense of shared, common purposes and values that act as a glue to which we adhere voluntarily. Such adherence imbues practices with a sense of collective fairness and justice that finds solidarity in difference and diversity. Nevertheless, there is concern regarding the tension between providing a "good education"[4] (Biesta, 2010) and an increasing vocationalisation of higher education as preparation for the world of work (Tam, 2013).

Our purpose in this chapter is to put education centre stage in the leadership of higher education. First, as a means of capturing succinctly key features of the higher education landscape, we indicate dominant institutional orientations. We suggest also that when these are combined with the implicit leadership theories (ILTs) of the senior leaders of institutions, they create a force field in which their employees and students are obliged to play the game. Second, against this backdrop of prominent features of the higher education landscape, we trace the evolution of leadership literature from emphasis on individuals, positional authority, and from "heroic" (Lowney, 2003) leadership to a more "distributed" perspective (Gronn, 1999; Spillane, 2006). In doing so, we identify significant elements in the changing landscape of higher education: internationalisation and competitiveness. We indicate that it is necessary also to distinguish between formal and informal leadership, thus the necessity to pay attention to a practice-based perspective, in recognition of the agency of all actors within the academy (Stensaker, Bilbow, Breslow, & Van Der Vaart, 2017; Stensaker, van der Vart, Solbrekke, & Wittek, 2017; Youngs, 2017). Third, as part of a more distributed perspective on leadership we describe the emerging roles and responsibilities of academic developers (ADs) and situate these within the wider landscape of a rapidly evolving higher education field. We indicate that leading higher education, evident in selected literature, has particular significance for the manner in which pubic good is framed with consequent implications for the book's subsequent chapters, the insights they contribute regarding the challenges entailed in maintaining a focus on as well as promoting public good. A fourth and final section draws the threads of the foregoing sections together with leading higher education, public good and web of commitments in mind.

University orientations

While analysis of orientations in this section has a primary focus on universities, we consider them to be analytical tools, with more general application within the higher education landscape. Although often opaque and written by committees of senior leaders, strategic plans nonetheless are public documents describing the purposes a university has defined for itself, ideals, general goals and lightly described strategies. As such, they are indicative of the directions they set for actions, and the general routes chosen to attain these ends (Barnett, 2011). Inspired by Ron Barnett's historical analysis and identification of different university orientations, we have earlier developed characteristics of orientations found in some selected contemporary public universities. Initial analysis was undertaken in five universities: University College Dublin (UCD), Oslo (UiO), Helsinki, (UH), Uppsala (UU), and University of North Carolina at Chapel Hill (UNC-CH), and this enabled us to identify four prominent orientations: traditional, scientific, entrepreneurial and bureaucratic (Sutphen, Solbrekke, & Sugrue, 2018). However, institutions do not conform to one orientation exclusively. Rather, orientation boundaries are porous, enabling universities to project multiple orientations simultaneously, convenient for appealing to as well as appeasing different stakeholders. Nevertheless, institutions give priority to some orientations more than others. Selected by institutions' most senior leaders, the orientations are compass readings with implications for all who work within their precincts. Table 2.1 provides a summary statement regarding the dominant characteristics of four orientations and their underpinning values.

Although these descriptions are not exhaustive,[5] they enable us to claim that universities, while different and distinct, are increasingly obliged through a variety of media to create a preferred image or images to present to their many constituencies, publics and stakeholders. Moreover, the different orientations and

TABLE 2.1 Four university orientations: characteristics and underpinning values

Traditional	The traditional orientation describes policies or programmes designed to transform individuals, as well as support a community of scholars and peers who uphold the ideal of academic freedom and create knowledge for its own sake. Values associated with the orientation include being independent, intellectual, and critical.
Scientific	The scientific orientation describes policies or programmes that create a community of scholars driven to solve problems, by generating new and applied knowledge, using reasoning that is sceptical in the absence of empirical evidence. Such endeavours aspire to exploit new knowledge. Values associated with the orientation include being rigorous, cutting edge, and useful.
Entrepreneurial	The entrepreneurial orientation describes policies or programmes that seek to commercialise a university's knowledge breakthroughs and contribute to economic and social development, while allowing the university to measure regularly its goals. Values associated with the orientation include being innovative, flexible, and internationally competitive.
Bureaucratic	The bureaucratic orientation describes policies or programmes that privilege the application of rules, procedures and the accumulation of data. To achieve these ends, universities use technologies of control to ensure high quality. Values associated with the orientation include being transparent, predictable, and accountable.

Source: Sutphen, Solbrekke & Sugrue 2018, p. 4

universities priorities, how they address internal and external expectations, have a significant shaping influence on the working conditions and learning environment for staff and students.

Institutional orientations do not emerge into the world fully formed. Rather, they are a work in progress, influenced by institutional history and tradition, as well as the leadership influences, in particular of those at the helm. Understanding this important connection, "life historians examine how individuals talk about and story their experiences and perceptions of the social contexts they inhabit" in order to "gain a recognizable impression of how particular lives are lived and expressed in a day-to-day context" (Goodson & Sikes, 2001, pp. 1 and 3). When we recently engaged in data analysis of pro-rectors (vice-presidents or deans) for education on their perspectives on the purpose of their university, and the role of ADs in contributing to, and fulfilling, this purpose, what emerged with significance was their ILTs (Eden & Leviatan, 1975).[6] The significance of ILTs stems from little systematic training for academic leadership to date, thus there are no "scripts" for these roles with the burden largely on the individual to define and find their "texts" for themselves (Henkel, 2002). Given their implicit influence, Bennis and Nanus (1985, p. 21) assert that "leadership is like the Abominable Snowman, whose footprints are everywhere but who is nowhere to be seen" (quoted in Bolden, Petrov, & Gosling, 2008, p. 358). As Schyns, Kiefer, Kerschreicher and Tymon (2011, p. 397) make clear: "Implicit leadership theories (ILTs) are lay images of leadership, which are individually and socially determined". These "implicit leadership theories develop early ... children already have implicit leadership theories" and they remain "relatively stable when the context changes" (Schyns et al., 2011, p. 399). Birnbaum (1989, p. 130) concluded based on analysis of interviews with 32 senior leaders in colleges and universities: "*College and university presidents in general define leadership as a process of influence directed towards the achievement of goals*" (italics original). He highlights the fact that such perspectives frequently overlook the following questions: "First, what is the source of the goals to be pursued? And second, by what process is influence to be exerted?" (p. 131). The combination of institutional orientation and ILTs is a pretty potent cocktail of considerable consequence for those who work in the shadow of these influences. In this manner, the ILTs of senior leaders and the vigour with which they pursue their preferred institutional orientation(s) are contextually connected to the work of those who follow their lead in both formal and informal leadership roles, including ADs, their leadership, agency and responsibilities.

With these orientations as compass readings on the landscape of higher education, we turn attention to aspects of leading higher education.

Leading higher education institutions

The book's introductory chapter has already rehearsed our normative stance that public universities are mandated to do education as public good and for public good, however that may be construed in the contemporary landscape of higher education. There is no shortage of literature on leading higher education institutions, their complexities, tensions and "crises" from a variety of perspectives—ethnicity, gender, as well as a plethora of conceptualisations including transformative, distributed and collaborative leadership with different foci, such as administrative or intellectual leadership (Macfarlane, 2012; Youngs, 2017).[7] Challenges to higher education, while evident with considerable variation, are addressed in Marginson's (2016) book *The Dream Is Over* referring to the "Master Plan for Higher Education in California", created by visionary University of California President Clark Kerr and his contemporaries. He says of the plan that its "equality of opportunity policy brought college within reach of millions of American families for the first time and fashioned the world's leading system of public research universities". More than that, its influence has had significance internationally: "The California idea became the leading model for higher education across the world and has had great influence in the rapid growth of universities in China and East Asia". Despite its undoubted success, due to a considerable change in political conditions he remarks, "Universal access is faltering, public tuition is rising, the great research universities face new challenges", while such observations are in many respects a bellwether for higher education internationally, despite contextual, cultural and historical variation (Marginson, 2016). For example, from Scandinavia to South Africa and China there are issues of funding and the consequence of a shift in emphasis from teaching and research to a more entrepreneurial culture that potentially re-orients universities as quasi-business enterprises that may also distract from public mandates to act in the interest of public good rather than private gain (Barnett, 2011, 2016; Stensaker, Bilbow, et al., 2017; Tian & Liu, 2019; Walker, 2018).

An electronic search of literature with the terms "leading higher education as and for public good" or "for public good", yields a "zero" score in both instances. An electronic search of literature with the terms "public good and higher education" yielded a modest return of 620 hits. These forays into an extensive literature on higher education strongly suggests that approaches to leading higher education from a public good perspective is relatively neglected as a research focus in higher education. While we begin this chapter with selective engagement on a wide-ranging literature on leading higher education, its purpose is to situate leading higher education as and for public good within this wider landscape. Our emphasis on leading educational processes (teaching and learning) and what that may entail in the promotion of public good through engagement with colleagues and students serves as a reminder that educational leadership is enacted in—and as—a web of commitment.[8]

From a methodological perspective, there are many intersecting literatures that make up the mosaic of leading higher education. We have endeavoured to be thorough and rigorous, yet highly selective given the vast array of materials that collectively lay claim to being a contribution to understandings of leading higher education. Consequently, our bias has been to focus on recently published literature, predominantly in peer-reviewed journals, while also including more seminal contributions based on our knowledge of the field and possibilities suggested to us during the process of reading for and writing this chapter.

Bryman's (2008, p. 694) literature review on effective leadership in higher education covered two decades (1985–2005) in part because he was persuaded that "Many writers on higher education make it clear that they view the higher education setting as having changed greatly in the last two decades, …". Acknowledging that the pace of change has accelerated, he also identified another challenge that was evident then but continues to persist in leadership literature, namely a general tendency or failure "to distinguish activities that are distinctively associated with leadership from managerial or administrative activities" (ibid.). For this reason, we appropriate three different perspectives to clarify aspects of what leading entails.

Leadership definitions

Although it describes school rather than higher education contexts, a definition that we consider helpful states:

> Irrespective of how these terms are defined, … leaders experience difficulty in deciding the balance between higher order tasks designed to improve staff, student and school performance (Leadership), routine maintenance of present operations (management) and lower order duties (administration).
>
> *(Dimmock, 1996, p. 137)*

Helpful as these distinctions may be, they warrant the following caveat that "although leadership has consumed the bulk of writing in education over the past decade or so, we believe that management is also critical"; it is difficult if not impossible "to lead without managing" (Spillane, Camburn, & Pareja, 2009, p. 88). This perspective may be extended further to suggest that very good administrative systems are often the cornerstone of quality management, but perhaps this is what we have come to describe in more recent years as bureaucracy (Sutphen et al., 2018). Remaining with the term leadership, while recognising that it may well benefit from being underpinned by solid administration and management, Gardner distinguishes between *ordinary, innovative* and *visionary* leaders (italics original) (Gardner, 1995, pp. 10–11). The ordinary leader "does not seek to stretch the consciousness of his contemporary audience" thus maintains the status quo, perhaps more accurately described as a "competent manager". By contrast, innovative leaders, through a combination of "timing", considered vital for "policy success" (Schmidt, 2008, p. 307) and imagination, are able to capture an aspect of an existing narrative that has lain dormant or neglected and breathes new life into it.[9]

The visionary leader, "by far the rarest individual" is someone who actually "creates a new story" (p. 11) thus apparently embracing what more recent leadership literature terms "transformative", such that "deep structures" of our world views are transformed, while suggesting simultaneously that this is a collective, participatory process rather than being entirely dependent on the "great man" or visionary (Montuori & Donnelly, 2018). However, such 'influencers' may be pedalling old narratives dressed in "different discourses" that "are simultaneously invoked in the ongoing production of organisational truths" while the opaque language used to appeal to several stakeholders at once may be ambiguous regarding actual "direction and hence the space of action for organisational actors" (Crevani, Ekman, Lindgren, & Packendorff, 2015, p. 148). This space of action is of particular interest in leading education as a contribution to as well as enactment of public good. An important consideration throughout the book's chapters is the necessity and timeliness to create spaces in which staff and students may critically interrogate the purposes of higher education as well as deliberate[10] on the directions of university education. Part II of the book provides descriptions of the contributions of ADs as they lead education in partnership and collaboration with colleagues in their specific institutional and policy contexts while seeking simultaneously to vindicate their university's public mandate. Thus, it is necessary to move beyond notions of leadership as being vested exclusively in the most senior personnel in higher education organisations to greater recognition of leadership, both formally and informally enacted across the whole organisation, in vertical as well as horizontal relational dynamics.

External influences: hybrid discourses on leadership

In discussing hybridity as a concept in the leadership literature, an increasing "adjectivalism" has been suggested with "distributed leadership as a new leadership kid-on-the-block" (Gronn, 2009, p. 18). As an element of this hybridisation, Chapter 1 has already indicated the increasing trend for international organisations (the EU and OECD to name but a couple), politicians, policy-makers and bureaucrats to seek increasingly to "steer" the activities of higher education institutions, frequently advocating "that universities ought to operate like market or quasi-market organizations striving to become entrepreneurial in their approach to teaching and research" (Bleiklie, 2007, p. 392). The Bologna process has been to the fore in this regard in a European context and beyond, whereby restructuring in terms of semesterisation and modularisation of programmes has also facilitated internationalisation, and coupled with qualifications frameworks adopted (inter-) nationally are indicative of participatory compliance on the part of many in the higher education sector. As Robson & Wihlborg (2019, p. 128) assert: "Globalisation, expansion, massification and privatisation have contributed to internationalisation policies and processes that have radically changed national HE systems". Additionally, it may be suggested that participation in international rankings of higher education institutions is further evidence of both competitiveness and compliance resulting in a general homogenisation, with more institutions claiming to be "research intensive" as well as being players in the global game of higher education (Stensaker, Bilbow, et al., 2017). For example, University College Dublin (UCD) in its Strategic Plan (2015–2020), a document that contains less than 5,000 words, includes the word international (14 times), internationally (five times) global (12 times) and globally (twice), while in its broad appeal to its many stakeholders it indicates that, as a community, it will engage "with all sectors of society and with all regions of the world, and in doing so "will be distinctive in our agility, innovativeness, commitment to justice, inclusiveness and friendliness" (p. 9). Clearly, there are many constituencies to be served, not all of which are mutually compatible, strongly suggesting that pursuit of "legitimate compromise"[11] is most likely to be a perennial challenge to leaders at all levels of the organisation as they, along with their colleagues, seek to live out commitments in the institution's vision and values in a manner that is resonant and congruent with their personal and professional value commitments. These wider policy influences, in addition to a decade of austerity, where, despite massification of higher education on an unprecedented scale, governments' neo-liberal leanings, encouraged by EU policy, have emboldened, out of necessity, the pursuit of private sources of funding for the sector.

Leading and internationalisation

Consequently, recruitment of international students and staff, as well as creation of a larger footprint by means of out-reach and overseas campuses, virtual or real, have fuelled the more entrepreneurial thinking and practice of the sector; a deployment of instrumental reason that runs counter to more traditional considerations of the role and contribution of the university to society. As one author indicates: "The internationalization of education has been rationalized as a response to globalization, as a means for institutions to 'cope with or exploit globalization' (Altbach, 2004, p. 3)" (Garson, 2016, p. 21). There is sufficient evidence to support the view that the influences are now ubiquitous. For example, South Africa, with its own unique historical trajectory and attendant inequalities, its elite universities seek private funding as well as "rankings and reputation" by benchmarking themselves against the Russell Group of elite universities; as one such leader put it: "If you want marketing language you need to be contextually relevant and globally competitive" (Swartz et al., 2019, p. 575). For others, such as Walker, also writing in the same context, she prioritises:

> If just one foundational public-good capability had to be chosen and one corresponding indictor I would propose epistemic contribution because ... it is distinctively what higher education in any university, including the public-good post-colonial university, ought to be fostering for all students from whatever backgrounds.
>
> *(Walker, 2018, p. 567)*

Similarly, as China rapidly expands access to higher education, it has moved away from "pure public good" to "quasi-public good" in an effort to continue to "serve society" while simultaneously doing so as a contribution to "global public good" (Tian & Liu, 2019, p. 624). In this more fluid and "liquid" (Bauman, 2000/2006) atmosphere it is important to acknowledge that it is "the discourse of educational policy" in context where "a major role of all public higher education institutions is to foster the public good" that shapes institutional orientations, while such discourses also meld into leadership narratives that, in turn, fuse with institutional orientations and the ILTs of the most influential leaders in particular (Letizia, 2016, p. 282). For these and other reasons, Garland (2019, p. 59) argues that the rise of populism as manifest in the behaviour of the current US president and the UK's "Brexiteers" may be regarded as the "aestheticization of politics", whereby the influence of these powerful forces are intended to induce "passivity and inertia of those responsive to it", thus rendering it more difficult to proactively engage with education in a climate of muddied uncertainty (see also Brubaker, 2017).

Competitiveness: teaching, research and resource allocation

Such forces are both real and consequential, as academics of all hues will readily attest. Since the advent of international rankings (Shanghai, 2003), an important dimension of which is the "measurement" of publications and bibliometric data, there is increasing pressure to be more research productive—thus publishing more frequently in the most highly ranked journals in your disciplinary field. Such expectations are frequently linked also to "winning" research funding (a significant proportion of which the institution sequesters to feed its appetite for additional resources), while tenure, promotion and status are increasingly dependent on them (O'Donovan, 2019). In such circumstances, leading teaching and learning is more challenging, and generally perceived by many academics as being demanding while increasingly less recognised, even if these activities contribute significantly to engagement and levels of job satisfaction (Biggs, 2013; Knight, 2002). As a senior leader in Uppsala University indicated to us in an interview (2016), when institutional efforts were made to insist on completing a course in university teaching "in order to get promotion to become a good professor to get a job in the first place, that has been contested at every stage". These observations reveal how being research intensive has consequences for teaching and resource allocation.

It is frequently asserted in research intensive universities that teaching is research led, but research indicates that while "many presume that excellent researchers will make excellent teachers, research evidence shows that there is no significant relationship between faculty's research productivity and the quality of their teaching" (Grunefeld et al., 2017, p. 76). Consequently, they argue, "the quality of educational leadership is very important for the quality of teaching" in all HE institutions, but particularly "in research-intensive universities" where the status of teaching may be considered lower than the kudos accruing to research (ibid.).

Increasingly therefore, it is necessary to ask: what does leading higher education entail? In the first instance, part of putting leading education centre stage is to recognise that "educational leadership should be provided at various levels of the organization" not merely senior leaders who are often more concerned with policy, strategy and resource allocation (Grunefeld et al., 2017, p. 76). Nevertheless, at the most senior level commitment to leading education requires stimulation of "university-wide discussion on quality teaching and … the development of a culture in which education is accepted as 'core business' and not merely the responsibility of adjunct, contract or the most junior academic staff" (ibid.). There is, of course, a reciprocal responsibility on department and unit leaders as well as their academic colleagues to "ensure bottom-up innovation and quality improvement of teaching and learning practices" (ibid.). In this general sense: teaching is leading and leading is teaching, and requires a wide-ranging set of competencies that include, but not confined to, being knowledgeable about epistemic traditions and research, as well as possessing the capacity to mobilise these, a "thorough awareness of the context", the personal characteristics of "self-control and resilience", as well as particular expertise in "the design, deliverance, and evaluation of teaching activities and curricula, and in their evaluation and analyses" complemented by a capacity to "motivate and involve others" (Grunefeld et al., 2017, p. 74).

The precise nature of educational leadership will vary from one institution to the next, but what emerges with increasing clarity is the necessity for and importance of educational leadership. While Macfarlane (2012) draws attention to intellectual leadership, wittingly or otherwise, he argues that this is a particular responsibility of professors when such endeavours are more widely shared among all members of the academic community. More recently he has expressed concerns about the academic freedom of students and a necessity to protect it against a more proforma approach to learning outcomes, modularisation and assessment, consequences of the homogenising influence of the Bologna process (Macfarlane, 2017). In this regard, he is in general agreement with a more widespread critique, if not preoccupation with student "satisfaction", identified as a "more consumeristic notion of satisfaction from services received, than to the sense of achievement or enjoyment associated with learning" (Elwick & Cannizzaro, 2017, p. 205). Such "learnification"

(Biesta, 2010) within the academy is what others have labelled the "negligence of cognitive formation" whereby "academically adrift HEIs are producing graduates who lack the critical thinking skills that are actually required to enter the graduate labour market and make informed life choices" (Spence, 2019, p. 768). Biesta (2010, p. 18) contrasts learning, which is *individualistic*, "even if it is couched in such notions as collaborative or cooperative learning", with "the concept of '*education*' that always implies a *relationship*: someone educating someone else and the person educating having a certain sense of purpose of his or her activities" (italics original). Thus, while education has responsibility to provide credentials, through its "*socialization*" function it "inserts individuals into existing ways of doing and being" while exposing students to "culture and tradition ... its desirable and its undesirable aspects" (p. 20). In a Western cultural context, where a competitive individualism has taken hold, these aspects of education have potential to crowd out and marginalise what Biesta identifies as "subjectification"—"the process of becoming a subject" whereby, unlike a socialisation function, becoming "your own person" is more than becoming a member of a group or society but extends to being enabled "to become more autonomous and independent in ... thinking and acting" (p. 21). His concern, one we share, is that if education is confined to certification and socialisation only there is the "real risk that data, statistics and league tables will do the decision making for us", an issue to be addressed appropriately at all levels of education (Biesta, 2010, p. 27). There is need to critically investigate and deliberate on how to take students' (and staff's) holistic formation seriously (Sutphen & de Lange, 2015; Walker 2018), but how is this to be achieved?

Leading teaching and learning

There is no blueprint. Rather, advancing this agenda is highly context specific, dependent on the dynamics of each institution, its history, traditions, leadership (formal and informal), but nevertheless requiring a combination of top-down and bottom-up educational leadership (Grunefeld et al., 2017). Given contemporary workplace conditions in public universities in particular, a concerted effort to lead education requires leadership from below and above to raise awareness of and expertise in leading education—at institutional, programme and individual levels. And, while such responsibilities need to be taken seriously by leaders at each and every level, particular responsibilities reside with ADs who are assigned the task of supporting academic colleagues to improve the quality of education. However, their responsibilities become more challenging in a context where the dynamics of higher education are altering. In this regard, Beckman points out:

> Fung & Gordon (2016, p. 6) note that "the reward for committing seriously to education [and] education leadership is perceived to be very much less than that gained through commitment to and success in research" and that "promoting education-focused staff to the most senior grades" was a particular challenge in research-intensive universities.
>
> *(Beckman, 2017, p. 156)*

For these and other reasons, the spirit if not the letter of distributed leadership has been invoked, despite trenchant criticisms of it being "blind" to power relations (Lumby, 2013), so that leading education is a shared responsibility, one whereby cultures and structures are created that "encourage individuals to be: accountable for change and development; empowered and motivated to take responsibility for change; and, engaged with others in the emotional work of building collaborative, trusting relationships (Harris, 2005)" (Carbone et al., 2017, p. 185). Despite its blind spots regarding power, " *'distributed leadership' draws attention to the large number of actors involved in leadership, and the importance of organizational processes in shaping their engagements*" (Gosling, Bolden, & Petrov, 2009, p. 299; italics original). However, in complex organisations such as higher education institutions, there is also an emerging literature that expresses frustration with the slow pace of change if there is over-reliance on bottom-up, more collegial innovation, thus the role of senior leader teams as "'orchestration' of change" and the role of vice-chancellor as "that of a strategic director and change agent" has also resulted in "traditional academic leadership of institutions … being replaced by a more managerial-oriented culture" (Boyadjieva & Llieva-Trochkova, 2018, p. 265). Such tensions are multiplied when accompanied by "the adoption of private sector management practices" (p. 266). These are the waters that academic developers are obliged to swim in.

Leading higher education: roles and responsibilities of ADs

In a systematic literature review of the field of academic development in higher education as it has evolved during the past two decades (including previously conducted reviews), trends were identified that have become integral element of the roles and responsibilities of ADs variously referred to in the literature as: instructional development, faculty development, educational development and academic development. At a general level, this literature underscores the increasing significance being attached to leading education, with considerable institutional variation (Sugrue, Englund, Solbrekke, & Fossland, 2017). Other themes that contribute gossamer threads to ADs' growing webs of commitments include, not surprisingly, technology (see also Chapter 4). In this regard the paper concluded: "In an internationally competitive HE environment wherein many contexts funding of mass tertiary education is contested, there is fear and anxiety (as well as optimism) that technology is facilitating a 'race to the bottom' while fuelling 'creative destruction' (Schumpter 1943/2010)" (Sugrue et al., 2017, p. 6). Since this review was completed, we argue that the influence of quality assurance policies, internationalisation and increasing diversity among students have intensified a focus on educational quality; teaching, learning and assessment resulting in greater demands on ADs for their support and expertise. This intensified focus has challenged public university leaders to provide the educational leadership that is now deemed (from a policy perspective) most apposite to promote and support education in the academy. Such conclusions are consistent with the view that internal as well as external influences have "increased demands for accountability of higher education institutions, as well as demands for universities and academics to critically reflect on and develop teaching, learning and assessment strategies" (Mårtensson & Roxå, 2016, p. 247). As evidenced by the recent Trend report on European higher education: "More than 85% of the institutions have developed teaching and learning centres, 50% have established formal requirements regarding teaching experience, and 77% provide academic development courses of which 37% are compulsory" (Gaebel et al., 2018).

In this general climate additional challenges to the status, identity and expertise of ADs have accrued since there is

> a shift towards AD as a more adaptive, collaborative partnership where ADs work in partnership with academic leaders to influence and change educational practice. It may be argued therefore that the evolution of the field of AD, and the agency of ADs as actors has brought their work more into the mainstream, whereby new relationships are being forged with institutional leaders, while there is potential too for the autonomy of ADs to be eroded as they become more instrumental in the implementation of institutional plans regarding teaching, learning and leading within HE.
>
> *(Sugrue et al. 2017, p. 7)*[12]

Nevertheless, despite evidence of a maturing of the field of academic development, there is recognition also that, as Kensington-Miller, Renc-Roe, and Morón-Garcia (2015, 279) assert: "For many years the status of academic development as a coherent field of practice has been of concern to both developers and their critics" (quoted in Sugrue et al., 2017, p. 7). Apart from the challenge to status, identity and claims to expertise, given the widening remit of ADs, there is a growing necessity to work in teams, to pool expertise. They are increasingly positioned in the crosshairs of their respective institutions with growing recognition that "teaching (and its development) [is] ... a collegial and collective responsibility" (Mårtensson & Roxå, 2016, p. 248) while readily recognising also that "mainstream higher education research on leadership largely overlooks the educational (teaching and learning) leadership role of both informal, distributed leaders ... and formal leaders in universities" (ibid.). What has emerged with an abundance of clarity is that there is:

> a new language of leadership ... already in existence, and it continues to evolve, even if as yet it is somewhat underdeveloped. It includes aspects of leadership, awareness of organisational cultures, of educational change, the necessity to model leadership, to advocate for sustainable innovations, to be strategic, to be politically aware, aware of values, of power and positioning within the organisation. This is a much more visible, vulnerable and challenging role; responsibilities no longer confined to teaching and learning only.
>
> *(Sugrue et al., 2017, p. 11)*

Despite this multi-level distributed consideration of leading higher education, in contradistinction to versions of leadership that are vested in individuals in positions of power and authority only, a particular responsibility falls on the shoulders of ADs, while this, in turn, is shaped considerably by institutional leaders, and the particular melange of orientations that they create for their universities.

Leading as brokering: negotiating legitimate compromises

As indicated above, academics are increasingly expected to "account" for quality teaching, as well as being "research productive", and ADs are progressively being called upon to be "brokers" (Brew & Cahir, 2014), occupying the role of "third space" professionals (Whitechurch, 2013). Such responsibilities strongly suggest agency and relative autonomy to forge new alliances and collaborative networks, to reach out and create common ground and mutual interest where these did not previously exist. Consequently ADs are increasingly expected to have a broad perspective on the university landscape to "approach new initiatives with an element of detachment" and while they'll continue to be knowledgeable about teaching and learning, their leadership remit will also extend to challenging the "underlying assumptions about the role of the higher education teacher, ... and the role and function of universities and how these relate to broader societal trends" (Brew and Cahir, 2014, p. 350). ADs' work, however, varies enormously from one institutional context to another, and while there is some research on how context matters (Fremstad et al., 2019), these contextual disparities have been absent to a significant extent from previous international publications on ADs' roles and responsibilities (Sugrue et al., 2017). Due to tensions created by competing orientations, and their underlying value positions, Barnett (2018, p. 184) argues that it is necessary to engage simultaneously with "*the university as an institution and the university as an idea*" (italics original) to find ways of leading higher education as and for public good.

In the shadow of an institution's orientations, ADs, as leaders and brokers, are obliged to determine legitimate compromises between the institution and the idea of a university, while simultaneously "translating" their knowledge of teaching, learning and leading. ADs take part in transformative engagements with colleagues that are imbued with their value commitments, whether or not they resonate with institutional prioritised orientations. Thus, when leaders' orientations (their ILTs) and ADs' leading are considered through the lens of orientations, their "interconnectedness" becomes more apparent. In their turn, the challenge to ADs is to encourage colleagues to take ownership of that responsibility, whereby "each member should feel responsible for what the other members do" (May, 1992, p. 10). This challenge is far from being a fait accompli. Rather, it is the outcome of an ongoing deliberative process, thus fulfilling their brokerage responsibilities. Orientations serve a useful purpose in surfacing crucial threads in this tapestry of responsibilities, while they reveal also that institutional senior leaders' ILTs are an additional twist in this complex tapestry of interconnectedness that operates on a horizontal as well as a vertical organisational axis, requiring ADs to undertake sophisticated readings of the landscape, its tensions and contradictions (Sugrue et al., 2019).[13]

Conclusions

We have endeavoured in this chapter to indicate and illustrate the changing nature of the higher education landscape, with a particular focus on the necessity to bring the purpose of university teaching and leading higher education as and for public good into discourses on leadership in higher education. We have described it as a complex web of commitments,[14] in which external forces influence internal priorities with important variation whereby each institution differs due to history, tradition, national policies and, increasingly also, internationalisation wrought by globalisation, as well as the nature of institutional orientations. While there is considerable evidence of creeping homogenisation due to various global forces and external policies, for this reason it is increasingly necessary to think in terms of global, national and local contexts. Collectively they constitute a "web of commitments", or what Letizia (Letizia, 2016, p. 283) describes as "a continuous circuit" whereby "scholars … envision the public good as a constellation of various ideas, institutions, criticisms, bridging structures, and goods interwoven together" in a spirit of "openness, participation, transparency, and a more collective sense of social cohesion for citizens across glo-na-cal frontiers".

Given the scale of the multiple challenges facing higher education, and public universities in particular, it is necessary to recognise just how daunting it is, Sisyphean even, to embrace the situation and move "beyond working only with individual teachers, [to] an understanding of organisational change and leadership … [as] vital"(Gibbs, 2013, p. 11). Clearly, in the process, it is vitally necessary to recognise that leading higher education is a relational and collective responsibility. For public universities, it is necessary to understand educational leadership as a dynamic process that is unapologetic about its commitment to public good. It requires leaders who are willing to prioritise time to critically investigate together with staff and students what such a mandate entails with consequence for the web of commitments in which leading higher education is enacted. Such perspective calls for leadership approaches that engage staff and students in interactive dialogue on the purpose of higher education. We identify this as "deliberative leadership" and elaborate on it in the concluding chapter.

Notes

1 Bourdieu (1992, footnote 57, p. 104) asserts that "the concept of field can be used at different levels of aggregation: the university … the totality of disciplines or the faculty of the human sciences" or indeed "relatively autonomous unit[s]".
2 To act in a professionally responsible manner necessitates being both proactive and courageous. This is elaborated on in Chapter 4.
3 For further information on the Paris Communique see the European University Association (EUA) website: https://eua.eu/news/106:bologna-process-paris-communiqu%C3%A9-adopted.html

4 Biesta (2010, p. 94) recognises, and we concur, that even when seeking to determine what constitutes a "good" education, "in any given curriculum the interests of some are always better served than the interests of others".

5 For a comprehensive account of how these orientation descriptors and their under-pinning value commitments were developed see Sutphen, Solbrekke & Sugrue (2018).

6 The term "implicit leadership theory" was first coined by Eden and Leviathan in 1975, and has been subsequently developed by various authors; see Sugrue, Solbrekke, Bergh, Sutphen & Fossland (2019).

7 Entering "leadership in higher education" into one search yields almost one million hits, far too numerous to be included here. Similarly, entering "leading higher education" into the same search engine provides in excess of 1.8 million hits.

8 The idea of—and experiences with—leading in a web of commitments receives focused attention in Chapter 4.

9 Gardner identifies both Thatcher and Reagan as leaders who were innovative suggesting that "it was their particular genius to have identified stories or themes that already existed in the culture but had become muted or neglected over the years" (p.10). Nevertheless, it should also be noted both of these "leaders" had an abundance of critics since they had major polarising influences on their respective societies, legacies that have filtered into discourses of reform in higher education also in terms of becoming more "entrepreneurial" (see, for example, Barnett, 2011, 2016).

10 Deliberative communication is presented and described in Chapter 3 where its principles are commended as an approach to leading and teaching for promoting public good as well as an enhancement of leading and pedagogical praxis.

11 Legitimate compromise, a term used by Larry May (1996), suggests that from a professional responsibility perspective compromise is necessary and unavoidable, while seeking to avoid being compromised in terms of personal and professional values. This idea is elaborated further in Chapter 4.

12 The case studies presented in Part II of this book indicate the struggle to reach legitimate compromises between instrumental needs and more time-consuming investments of time, expertise and resources that build pedagogical capacities to lead education as, and for, public good.

13 For a more extensive account of the significance of implicit leadership theories on university senior leader's orientation and leader's practice, see Sugrue et al., 2019, pp. 11–15.

14 See Chapter 4 for an elaboration of what such webs of commitments may entail.

References

Ball, S. (2003). The Teacher's Soul and the terrors of performativity. *Journal of Education Policy, 18*(2), 215–228.

Barnett, R. (2011). *Being a University*. London: Routledge.

Barnett, R. (2016). *Understanding the University: Institution, Idea, Possibilities*. London: Routledge.

Barnett, R. (2018). *The Ecological University: A Feasible Utopia*. London: Routledge.

Bauman, Z. (2000/2006). *Liquid Modernity*. Cambridge: Polity Press.

Beckman, E. A. (2017). Leadership through fellowship: distributed leadership in a professional recognition scheme for university educators. *Journal of Higher Education Policy and Management, 39*(2), 155–168. doi:10.1080/1360080X.2017.1276663

Bennis, W., & Nanus, B. (1985). *Leaders: The Strategies for Taking Charge*. New York: Harper Business.

Biesta, G. (2010). *Good Education in an Age of Measurement: Ethics, Politics, Democracy*. Boulder: Paradigm Publishers.

Biggs, G. (2013). Reflections on the changing nature of educational development. *International Journal for Academic Development, 18*(1), 4–14. doi:10.1080/1360144X.2013.751691

Birnbaum, R. (1989). The implicit leadership theories of college and university presidents. *The Review of Higher Education, 12*(2), 125–136. doi:doi:10.1353/rhe.1989.0025

Bleiklie, I. (2007). Systemic integration and macro steering. *Higher Education Policy, 20*, 391–412. doi:10.1057/palgrave.hep.8300166

Bolden, R., Petrov, G., & Gosling, J. (2008). Tensions in higher education leadership: towards a multi-level model of leadership practice. *Higher Education Quarterly, 62*(4), 358–376. doi:10.1111/j.1468-2273.2008.00398.x

Bourdieu, P., & Wacquant, L. J. D. (1992). *An Invitation to Reflexive Sociology*. Chicago: University of Chicago Press.

Boyadjieva, P., & Llieva-Trochkova, P. (2018). From conceptualisation to measurement of higher education as a common good: challenges and possibilities. *Higher Education*. doi:10.1007/s10734-018-0319-1

Brew, A., & Cahir, J. (2014). Achieving sustainability in learning and teaching initiatives. *International Journal for Academic Development, 19*(4), 341–352. doi:10.1080/1360144X.2013.848360

Brubaker, R. (2017). Why populism? *Theory and Society, 46*(5), 357–385.

Bryman, A. (2008). Effective leadership in higher education: a literature review. *Studies in Higher Education, 32*(6), 693–710. doi:10.1080/03075070701685114

Carbone, A., Evans, J., Ross, B., Drew, S., Phelan, L., Lindsay, K., … Ye, J. (2017). Assessing distributed leadership for learning and teaching quality: a multi-institutional study. *Higher Education Policy and Management, 39*(2), 183–196.

Crevani, L., Ekman, M., Lindgren, M., & Packendorff, J. (2015). Leadership cultures and discursive hybridization: on the cultural production of leadership in higher education reforms. *International Journal of Public Leadership, 11*(3–4),147–165. doi:10.1108/IJPL-08-2015-0019

Dimmock, C. (1996). Dilemmas for school leaders and administrators in restructuring. In K. Leithwood, Chapman, J., Corson, D., Hallinger, P. & Hart, A. (eds), *International Handbook of Educational Leadership and Administration* (Vol. 2, pp. 135–170). Dordrecht: Kluwer.

Eden, D., & Leviatan, U. (1975). Implicit leadership theory as a determinant of the factor structure underlying supervisory behavior scales. *Journal of Applied Psychology, 60*(6), 736–741.

Elwick, A., & Cannizzaro, S. (2017). Happiness in higher education. *Higher Education Quarterly, 71*(2), 204–219.

Fremstad, E., Bergh, A., Solbrekke, T. D., & Fossland, T. (2019). Deliberative academic development: the potential and challenge of agency. *International Journal for Academic Development*, 1–14. doi:10.1080/1360144X.2019.1631169

Gaebel, M., Zhang, T., Bunescu, L., & Stober, H. (2018). *Trends 2018: Learning and Teaching in the European Higher Education Area*. Brussels: European University Association. https://eua.eu/downloads/publications/trends-2018-learning-and-teaching-in-the-european-higher-education-area.pdf

Gardner, H. with Laskin, E. (1995). *Leading Minds: An Anatomy of Leadership*. London: HarperCollins.

Garland, C. (2019). Taking back control of nothing: elites denouncing elites to mobilize populism. *Fast Capitalism, 16*(1), 51–68. doi:10.32855/fcapital.201901.006

Garson, K. (2016). Reframing internationalization. *Canadian Journal of Higher Education, 46*(2), 19–39.

Gibbs, G. (2013). Reflecting on the changed nature of educational development. *International Journal of Academic Development, 18*(1), 4–14. doi:10.1080/1360144X.2013.751691

Gibbs, N. (2019). Whose standards will Democrats embrace? *Time*, 25 April, 8–11.

Goodson, I. F., & Sikes, P. (eds). (2001). *Life History Research in Educational Settings*. Buckingham: Open University Press.

Gosling, J., Bolden, R., & Petrov, G. (2009). Distributed leadership in higher education: what does it accomplish? *Leadership, 5*(3), 299–312. doi:10.1177/1742715009337762

Gronn, P. (1999). *The Making of Educational Leaders*. London: Cassell.

Gronn, P. (2009). Hybrid leadership. In K. Leithwood, B. Mascall & T. Strauss (eds), *Distributed Leadership According to the Evidence* (pp. 17–40). London: Routledge.

Grunefeld, H., Prins, H., Tartwijk, J. V., Van Der Vaart, R., Loads, D., Turner, J., … Wubbles, T. (2017). Faculty development for educational leadership. In B. Stensaker, G. T. Bilbow, L. Breslow & R. Van Der Vaart (eds), *Strengthening Teaching and Learning in Research Universities Strategies and Initiatives for Institutional Change* (pp. 73–102). London: Palgrave Macmillan.

Henkel, M. (2002). Emerging concepts of academic leadership and their implications for intra-institutional roles and relationships in higher education. *European Journal of Education, 37*(1), 29–41.

Knight, P. (2002). *Being a Teacher in Higher Education*. Buckingham: SHRE and Open University Press.

Letizia, A. J. (2016). Dissection of a truth regime: the narrowing effects on the public good of neoliberal discourse in the Virginia performance-based funding policy. *Discourse: Studies in the Cultural Politics of Education, 37*(2), 282–297. doi:10.1080/01596306.2015.1015966

Lowney, C. (2003). *Heroic Leadership Best Practices from a 450 Year-Old Company that Changed the World*. Chicago: Loyola Press.

Lumby, J. (2013). Distributed leadership: the uses and abuses of power. *Educatinal Management Administration & Leadership, 41*(5), 581–597.

Macfarlane, B. (2012). *Intellectual Leadership in Higher Education: Renewing the Role of the University Professor*. London: Routledge.

Macfarlane, B. (2017). *Freedom to Learn: The Threat to Student Academic Freedom and Why It Needs to Be Reclaimed*. Abingdon: Routledge.

Marginson, S. (2016). *The Dream Is Over: The Crisis of Clark Kerr's California Idea of Higher Education*. San Francisco: University of California Press.

Martensson, K., & Roxa, T. (2016). Leadership at a local level – enhancing educational development. *Educational Management Administration & Leadership, 44*(2), 247–262. doi:10.1177/1741143214549977

May, L. (1992). *Sharing Responsibility*. Chicago: University of Chicago Press.

May, L. (1996). *The Socially Responsive Self. Social Theory and Professional Ethics*. Chicago: Chicago University Press.

Montuori, A., & Donnelly, G. (2018). Transformative leadership. In J. Neal (ed.), *Handbook of Personal and Organizational Transformation* (pp. 1–31). New York: Springer.

O'Donovan, O. (2019). What is to be done about the enclosures of the academic publishing oligopoly? (Editorial). *Community Development Journal, 54*(3), 363–370. doi:10.1093/cdj/bsz014

Pearce, L. M., Wood, B., & Wassenaar, C. L. (2018). The future of leadership in public universities: is shared leadership the answer? *Public Administration Review, 78*(4), 640–644. doi:10.1111/puar.12938.

Robson, S., & Wihlborg, M. (2019). Internationalisation of higher education: impacts, challenges and future possibilities. *European Educational Research Journal, 18*(2), 127–134.

Schmidt, V. A. (2008). Discursive institutionalism: the explanatory power of ideas and discourse. *The Annual Review of Political Science, 11*, 303–326. doi:10.1146/annurev.polisci.11.060606.135342

Schyns, B., Kiefer, T., Kerschreiter, R., & Tymon, A. (2011). Teaching implicit leadership theories to develop leaders and leadership. *Academy of Management Learning and Education, 10*(3), 397–408.

Spence, C. (2019). 'Judgement' versus 'metrics' in higher education management. *Higher Education, 77,* 761–775. doi:10.1007/s10734-018-0300-z

Spillane, J. (2006). *Distributed Leadership.* San Francisco: Jossey Bass.

Spillane, J., Camburn, E. M., & Pareja, A. S. (2009). School principals at work: a distributed perspective. In K. Leithwood, B. Mascall & T. Strauss (eds), *Distributed Leadership According to the Evidence* (pp. 87–110). London: Routledge.

Stensaker, B., Bilbow, G. T., Breslow, L., & Van Der Vaart, R. (eds). (2017). *Strengthening Teaching and Learning in Research Universities Strategies and Initiatives for Institutional Change.* London: Palgrave Macmillan.

Stensaker, B., van der Vart, R., Solbrekke, T. D., & Wittek, L. (2017). The expansion of academic development: the challenges of organizational coordination and collaboration. In B. Stensaker, G. T. Bilbow, L. Breslow & R. Van Der Vaart (eds), *Strengthening Teaching and Learning in Research Universities: Strategies and Initiatives for Institutional Change* (pp. 19–41). London: Palgrave Macmillan.

Sugrue, C., Englund, T., Solbrekke, T. D., & Fossland, T. (2017). Trends in the practices of academic developers: trajectories of higher education? *Studies in Higher Education, 43*(12), 2336–2353. doi:0.1080/03075079.2017.1326026

Sugrue, C., Solbrekke, T. D., Bergh, A., Sutphen, M., & Fossland, T. (2019). University leaders' talk about institutional missions and academic developers' contributions. *European Educational Research Journal,* 1–17. doi:10.1177/1474904119866520

Sutphen, M., & de Lange, T. (2015). What is formation? A conceptual discussion. *Higher Education Research and Development, 34*(2), 411–419.

Sutphen, M., Solbrekke, T. D., & Sugrue, C. (2018). Toward articulating an academic praxis by interrogating university strategic plans. *Studies in Higher Education, 44*(8), 1400–1412. doi:10.1080/03075079.2018.1440384

Swartz, R., Ivancheva, M., Czerniewicz, L., & Morris, N. P. (2019). Between a rock and a hard place: dilemmas regarding the purpose of public universities in South Africa. *Higher Education, 77,* 567–583. doi:10.1007/s10734-018-0291-9

Tam, M. (2013). Increasing professionalization and vocationalization of continuing education in Hong Kong: trends and issues. *International Journal of Lifelong Education, 32*(6), 741–756. doi:10.1080/02601370.2013.774066

Tian, L., & Liu, N. C. (2019). Rethinking higher education in China as a common good. *Higher Education, 77,* 623–640. doi:10.1007/s10734-018-0295-5

Walker, M. (2018). Dimensions of higher education and the public good in South Africa. *Higher Education, 76,* 555–569. doi:10.1007/s10734-017-0225-y

Whitechurch, C. (2013). *Reconstructing Identities in Higher Education: The Rise of Third Space Professionals.* London: Routledge.

Youngs, H. (2017). A critical exploration of distributed leadership in higher education: developing an alternative ontology through leadership-as-practice. *Journal of Higher Education Policy and Management, 39*(2), 140–154. doi:10.1080/1360080X.2017.1276662

3

HIGHER EDUCATION AS AND FOR PUBLIC GOOD

Past, present and possible futures

Tomas Englund and Andreas Bergh

Introduction

In recent educational discussions, the concepts public and private good have often been used to describe tensions in the higher education sector. There is little doubt that what many researchers have described as a shift from public to private good has challenged central and classical academic and educational values as well as the autonomy of higher education. To contribute to this discussion, we will explore how these two concepts can be used as intellectual and rhetorical resources to analyse and discuss potential contributions to and challenges in elaborating the meaning of public good today.

Rather than representing a clear dichotomy, the concepts of public and private good, as we will show, in many ways have historically overlapped and been intertwined. Here, we argue that an open-minded approach to what public good and private good in higher education might mean can provide a deeper understanding of different, often contested, ideas of the university. We do not propose distinct and fixed definitions of the two concepts. Rather, we provide an overview of different attempts to define and use them, especially the concept of public good, in different contexts of public universities. Our focus here is universities and higher education in general, but public universities in particular that, historically, have been state-financed, and which have "undergone a seemingly unending series of reforms designed to make them more responsive both to markets and to government priorities" (Shore & Wright 2017, p. 2).

But although dominant discourses and governing structures have a great influence on higher education institutions, it is also important to remember that there would be no institutions without the people, the academics and students, who are responsible for the actions taken. What means do they have to encourage the public good, and in what ways and with what tools do academics who lead different activities consider their choices? These questions lead us to formulate the following aims for this chapter: (a) to make use of the concept of *public good* and its complement *private good* as dynamic criteria against which proposals and ongoing activities within contemporary higher education can be interpreted; and (b) to show ways in which *deliberative communication* may be used as a tool to identify and analyse "different *rationalities*, different meaning-creating contexts based in different choices of content with which teaching can be arranged" (Englund, 1996, p. 19). Our expectation is that deliberation using these concepts of public and private good will enable academics generally to be more conscious, more articulate morally and politically about the role of higher education as, and for, public good. It is anticipated also that such an approach will cultivate deliberative attitudes and virtues as means of promoting public good, thus providing academics with tools to consider their choices and their consequences.

In this chapter, we present a chain of arguments on the need to develop communicative reason among academics within universities, creating a foundation for deliberative communication that will strengthen public good. We consider that this is necessary since public universities today, as Chapters 1 and 2 indicate, face many societal and democratic challenges. At the same time, higher education institutions have a great potential for critical analysis and to point out directions for future actions by embracing democratic values such as sustainability, integrity, openness, social justice and public good. Our argument is organised in four sections, as follows.

In the first section the main focus is on the concept of public good. Different definitions and ways of understanding the concept, historically and contextually, are presented. We show that, historically, reforms seeking to strengthen access to higher education for all, thereby creating social mobility and better-informed citizens, are a central dimension of the public good. Here, the role of public financing of universities is crucial (Shore & Wright 2017). Additionally, we show how different conceptions of knowledge and moral formation can be combined in different ways with the question of access to higher education and social mobility as expressions of public good.

Second, the chapter deals with the challenge posed by the ongoing transformation of universities from public good towards private good. We refer to Barnett (2011), who shows, in terms of shifting and struggling university rationalities, how instrumental reason has gradually colonised the lifeworld of both universities as institutions and the actors within them. More precisely, Barnett argues that today the entrepreneurial university's rationale has been built into and integrated with the bureaucratic rationale, with a sense of the university as a corporation being a strong expression of higher education for private good.

Third, we problematise and examine in greater depth this recent development from the perspective of public good. We believe that Habermas (1987; see Barnett 2011) has provided some basic starting points for analysis of the relationship between society and education within a perspective of normative rationalisation, i.e. transformation of the source of the sacred into communication as collective will-formation. With Habermas (1996, 2001) we understand communicative reason as significant for a possible future for the communicative rationality of the twenty-first-century public university, consistent with a university for public good. This also represents an opportunity and a responsibility for universities and their academics to develop communicative activities that strengthen public good.

Fourth, we concretise this communicative rationality within universities by elaborating the idea of deliberative communication as a practice of communicative reason, turning to leaders in universities and other academics with a specific interest in ADs (see Chapter 1) and their responsibility to lead higher education as and for public good. Here we combine the idea of deliberation with the classical idea of critical thinking, which we consider important, but not sufficient, when it comes to developing each individual's capacity for analysis of societal questions and for participation.

Public good in retrospect

The idea that higher education has an obligation to promote public good, based on public financing, dates back to the earliest European universities, and public funding of them was justified on the grounds that they served the public good (Collini, 2012). Historically, Kant (1798/1979) articulated that universities could provide "a public good through acting as a critical ally to national governments, the professions and society more broadly" (Williams. 2016, p. 620).[1] In the Victorian era, proponents such as John Stuart Mill (1873/1981; see Small 2013, p. 123) and Cardinal Newman (1852/1959) saw the knowledge produced in universities and other educational institutions as a public good. This view of knowledge itself as a public good, as we will see, has long been a central dimension of the concept of public good, in views developed by the sociologist Émile Durkheim and the philosopher Hannah Arendt. They both indicate that universities and their educators have a social and moral responsibility to problematise and question the knowledge transmitted if it is to qualify as a public good (cf. Walker 2018).

An important meaning of public good related to a modern society with a mass education system, following Durkheim and Arendt (1954) is Marginson's (2011, p. 416) rather broad definition of the concept as referring to activities, benefits or resources accessible to all and reaped through participation in higher education. This form of public good includes better-informed citizens, leading to improved democracy, a more inclusive society and knowledge conceived of as an end-in-itself. This way of defining public good is closely related to and goes back to a Durkheimian tradition of understanding (higher) education, with the inherent authority of its academic disciplines, making educated professionals human and socially responsible through its moral and cultural training towards a moral individualism (see Durkheim, 1899/1992, 1938/1977; Cladis, 1992).[2] This Durkheimian public-good perspective on education is developed further by Arendt, who stresses its "role in preserving and transmitting society's accumulated collective knowledge and understanding of the world for future generations" (Williams 2016, p. 621; see also, Arendt, 1954).

One central theme of the development of knowledge within higher education in this Durkheimian tradition is its gradual secularisation (Durkheim, 1912/1961). Another is the importance of the freedom to reason, upheld especially by the philosophy faculty. As Williams also stresses:

By the end of the nineteenth century, Durkheim could confidently assert that the capacity for individuals to reason was the unique quality that made people human and this formed the basis for the society's collectively held objective knowledge of the world. At this time one form of public good of HE was assumed to occur through the moral and cultural training of a social elite in preparation for leadership in society.

(Williams, 2016, p. 623)

This era implied an inherent authority of the academic disciplines, especially the humanities, which remained "unquestioned as the best way of preparing men of the appropriate lineage to reach positions of power at home and abroad" (Muller & Young, 2014; quoted in Williams, 2016, p. 623). This view remained largely unchallenged until the Second World War, an era termed by Delanty (2001, p. 34) "the liberal modernity". In spite of the experience of the Nazi challenge, and later the dominance of Nazism and the Second World War, during the twentieth century "public good was considered to be inherent in the very existence of universities as places of learning and advancing knowledge" (Williams, 2016, p. 623). In the decades after the war, universities were also increasingly expected to play a role in scientific advance and technological development.

In line with this view, the economist Paul Samuelson (1954) developed an economic definition of public good(s) which questioned the conception of knowledge and public good as ends in themselves. However, the main problem or actual weakness with this economic definition is its often unsophisticated, quantified characterisation of knowledge. This view of knowledge as quantifiable, together with attempts to make learning more practically meaningful to students and more directed towards individual outcomes, has proven to be quite influential in recent decades. It is easy to criticise this development, but it is necessary also to realise that universities have to develop science, technology, engineering and mathematics for public good. In contrast to Samuelson's narrow economic definition of public good, we prefer, in consort with many critical researchers such as Daviet (2016), to understand "education for and as public good" primarily as a philosophical concept.[3]

In Williams's analysis of government policy documents in England from the last 50 years she finds a redefining of the public good of higher education, "away from knowledge towards economic and social outcomes; and from public benefits to more individual gains" (Williams, 2016, p. 622). The public good, she says, is now more frequently defined as social justice, which is considered to emerge from higher education providing the conditions for individual social mobility. This shift in the meaning of public good, stressing access to higher education for disadvantaged groups and a weaker and vaguer relationship to knowledge, however much the latter was stressed by many traditionalists, opened up new perspectives on public and private good. Fisher (2005) argued that it was not enough for universities to promote social mobility simply by widening access policies: "Graduates are likely to become the 'advantaged' in society even if they come from a 'disadvantaged' background, and thus the university, if it is serving the public good, should be equipping graduates to advance social justice" (East et al., 2014, p. 1620).

But even if reforms that strengthen access for disadvantaged social groups, or what is called greater social mobility, tend to be of central importance as, and for, public good, it remains crucial what kind of knowledge is chosen, and for what purposes and how it is communicated in higher education (see, Walker, 2018). This is particularly the case when contemporary higher education is part of a mass education system and is educating professionals of different kinds in large numbers.[4]

Professionals educated in higher education have long been seen as an essential contribution to public good, but already in the early 1990s this view was questioned in the light of their growing orientation to private gain (Brint, 1994; Sullivan, 2005). Thus, the unquestioned orientation of professions "to the public good is no longer taken for granted" (East et al., 2016, p. 1619), while many professionals are increasingly conflicted due to being positioned between two different logics, the logic of accountability and the logic of responsibility (Solbrekke & Englund, 2011). So how is public good to be characterised now, challenged as it is by private good? That is the theme of the following sections.

The shift towards private good

During the last decades of the twentieth and the first decades of the twenty-first century, there have been obvious signs, observed by many critical researchers, of a gradual shift of universities from public to private good. However, there are different understandings of how this shift is to be characterised. Slaughter and Leslie (1997) call it academic capitalism, while others use terms such as commodification, corporate culture (Grace, 1989; Giroux, 2002; Naidoo, 2003) and marketisation (Nixon, 2011).

That said, the general trend in recent decades can be described in terms of a gradual move from higher education as public good to higher education as private good, with universities characterised by commercialisation, commodification, competition and classification (Nixon 2011), producing good that is increasingly privately financed and geared to private/individual benefits and marketing.

Furthermore, this shift means that the authority to decide the content and forms of education is moving away from academics doing research and teaching to administrative units, resulting in an amalgamation of what we have earlier referred to, with reference to Barnett, as the entrepreneurial and the bureaucratic university rationalities. This also means, as Barnett develops the argument, that these two rationalities today create a mixed, dominant rationality. From an entrepreneurial rationality perspective, it endeavours to commercialise universities' knowledge, and from the bureaucratic characterised by "a *generalized* form of surveillance" (Barnett, 2011, p. 48; italics original). The consequences of this mixed rationality are that "instrumental reason is tending to colonise the 'lifeworld'; that getting things done to fulfil ends comes to be more important than arriving at a deep interpersonal understanding of matters" (Barnett 2011, p. 49, quoting Habermas, 1987).

In line with these two rationalities and the four characteristics of private good mentioned by Nixon, higher education is becoming marketised (more of a private good), and in accordance with that the university itself, its academics and students, becomes more oriented towards goals, other than public good. Characteristics and efforts in line with the public-good values of supporting democracy, equality and social justice are becoming progressively weaker and higher education has less and less room for humanistic studies and social sciences (see Nussbaum, 2010). At the same time, we can see universities being directed more to preparing a majority to be employable in the labour market rather than preparing politically engaged, communicative and participatory citizens as in a more explicit public-good perspective, our focus in the next section.

Possible futures of *and* for public good

In relation to what has been stated so far it may be legitimate to ask: Does the increasing presence and prominence of bureaucratic and entrepreneurial rationality marginalise or even preclude communicative rationality? Is this challenge primarily a question to be addressed by leaders of higher education institutions and academics or by politicians, policy-makers and public? There are of course powerful influential forces beyond the inner life of universities that prioritise different logics, but historically the more or less dominant direction of the university has been left to all staff and students to reflect and act upon. At the same time, making room for open communication (Dewey, 1916/1980), aimed at achieving public good through communicative reason and pluralism, represents a communicative rationality. This rationality does not sit comfortably with nor is it supported by entrepreneurial and bureaucratic rationalities. Rather, it has to be argued for on different levels.

To be more specific about higher education as a public good, certain democratic values are stressed, values that underpin each student's political awareness and an education and a society that promote a civic and professional responsibility (Sullivan, 2005, 1986). In this perspective, we suggest that there is a need for a communicative rationality in universities striving for public good that may be characterised in the following terms: a university built on communicative rationality maintains policies and programmes that are designed to widen civic participation and responsibility to promote public good. Higher education within this communicative perspective opens up the possibility of collective and collegial analysis of and deliberation on democratic values. Values associated with the communicative rationality include sustainability, integrity, critical communication, openness and social justice.

We relate communicative rationality to a broad pragmatic tradition, both classical (Dewey 1916/1980, 1927/1984) and neo-pragmatic (Habermas, 1981/1987, 1992/1996; see also Englund, 2000/2005), a tradition that has been revitalised by many authors stressing the democratic potential of deliberation and deliberative democracy.[5] One representative of deliberation in relation to universities is the Dewey-inspired Amy Gutmann (1987), who proposed as early as 1987, in her classic work *Democratic Education*, that:

learning how to think carefully about political problems, to articulate one's views and defend them before people with whom one disagrees is a form of moral education to which young adults are more receptive and for which universities are well suited.

(Gutmann 1987, p. 173)

Ten years later, Martha Nussbaum, in her book *Cultivating Humanity* (1997), asserted that the noble kind of liberal education as a base for the cultural dimension had not been fully realised in colleges and universities, but rather subordinated to instrumentalism, to technical and vocational education. Nussbaum's perspective leads us to see higher education institutions as public spaces for advanced mutual communication, reflection and deliberation, and not primarily as predestined curriculum routes preparing people for different vocations. Her development together with Sen (1999) of a theory of capabilities (Nussbaum, 2000) affords a conceptual way to analyse public good from a perspective of personhood and self-formation (Walker, 2018).

While the dominant tendency regarding the role of the universities has been to underline "the idea of excellence" and a kind of "academic capitalism" in contrast to Nussbaum's ideas, one can also observe attempts to deepen higher education as a place for dissensus, where:

the point is to institutionalize dissensus and to make university a site of public debate ... that the central task of the university is to become a key actor in the public sphere and thereby enhance the democratization of knowledge.

(Delanty, 2001, pp. 7 & 9; see also, Englund, 2008)

This idea goes back to Habermas's argument that "in the last analysis it is the communicative forms of scientific and scholarly argumentation that hold university learning processes in their various functions together" (Habermas, 1992, p. 124).

Thus, Habermas places the realisation of deliberative policy in the institutionalisation of procedures, from which an intersubjectivity on a higher level is expected to emerge; public discourses meet with a good response only under circumstances of broad participation. This in turn "requires a background political culture that is egalitarian, divested of all educational privileges, and thoroughly intellectual" (Habermas, 1996, p. 490).

This also leads us to Nixon's (2011) elaboration of what he calls collective reasoning as a public good that needs to be central in higher education:

There is no other way of being reasonable in a plural world, no other way of doing reason. We reason other-wise – or not at all. To define reason in this way – as a collective resource – is to claim it as a public good; and to claim it as a public good is to acknowledge that it is a part of "what we owe to each other": so, for example, "when we say, in the course of some collective decision, that a person is being unreasonable, what we often mean is that he or she is refusing to take other people's interests into account".

(Nixon, 2011, p. 84, citing, Scanlon, 2000, p. 33)

So, in order to reason, we need to engage with one another's reason:

That is what reasoning together means. Moreover, we need to exercise responsive understanding within our *worlds of difference* and in relation to *different worlds* – the differences that characterise and inform our knowable world and those that define other worlds as unknowable. Such understanding is central to the deliberative process.

(Nixon, 2011, p. 94; italics original)

Consequently, in the light of recent developments within theories of democracy and education, in the next section we propose and test the idea of deliberative communication as an expression of public good for the twenty-first century.

Deliberative communication as, and for, public good

Deliberative communication stands for an idea about how to lead and practice communication in which different opinions and values are set against each other. It implies an endeavour by each individual to develop his or her view by listening, deliberating, seeking arguments and valuing, coupled with a collective and cooperative undertaking to find values and norms which everyone may find acceptable, reflective of a plurality of perspectives. Current advocates of deliberative democracy stress the presence of different views and arguments, which are to be put against each other (Dryzek, 2000). Different views on a subject are proffered by individuals who confront each other, but with an openness in the argumentation, thus though readily "acknowledging that we are destined to disagree, deliberative democracy also affirms that we are capable of deciding our common destiny on mutually acceptable terms" (Gutmann & Thompson, 1996, p. 361). For these writers, deliberation puts particular emphasis on responsibility and consequences, implying that the focus must be on formation for citizenship and the exercise of citizenship.

The challenge of deliberation for academic developers has been addressed by Peter Kandlbinder (2007) where he explores and proposes how academic development practices may be rethought, enacted and evaluated in a process of deliberation. His underlying argument is that universities, historically, have been deeply involved in the support of public deliberation and, moreover, that the university ideally is itself a site of democratic processes (Delanty, 2001). This is modelled not only in institutional governance, referring to Habermas (1989a), but also in the leading of higher education, where academics and students engage in critical inquiry, practise the questioning of assumptions and "argue their case toward conclusions based on the best available evidence" (Kandlbinder, 2007, p. 56; quoting

Barnett, 1997). Thus, Kandlbinder, describing what we understand as representing a communicative interest and rationality, maintains that the

> university contributes to the very foundations of deliberative democracy – as Young (2000) argued, it is important for people to *experience* democratic processes if there is any hope of building collective social responsibility. Academic developers can contribute to this process by ensuring that within the academic community there are active and inclusive debates on student learning, for example, as well as opportunities for deliberations on the nature of university teaching.
>
> *(Kandlbinder, 2007, p. 56; italics original)*

Pursuing his argument further on how to develop deliberation among academics, Kandlbinder refers to investigations of urban planners by Forester (1999) and the need to work between independent but conflicting parties to develop the key skills of deliberative practice: "The deliberative practitioner learns, from conversation and argument, the actual interpretations and reconstruction of what parties working together say and do. In deliberative practice, critical listening, reflection-in-action, and constructive argument all interact" (Forester 1999, p. 12; quoted in Kandlbinder, 2007, p. 57).

Evident here is the occurrence of value conflicts or difference in views as the constitutive starting point for deliberation, and also the need for procedural qualities such as critical listening. These dimensions are also stressed in an earlier attempt by Englund (2006b) to set out the most important characteristics of deliberative communication (originally aimed at schools):

Deliberative communication implies communication in which:

a   different views are confronted with one another and arguments for these different views are given time and space to be articulated and presented (Habermas, 1987, 1996; Gutmann and Thompson, 1996);

b   there is tolerance and respect for the concrete other and participants learn to listen to the other person's argument (Habermas, 1987, 1996; Benhabib, 1992);

c   elements of collective will-formation are present, i.e. an endeavor to reach consensus or at least temporary agreements or to draw attention to differences (Habermas, 1987, 1996; Gutmann and Thompson, 1996);

d   authorities or traditional views (represented, for example, by parents and tradition) can be questioned, and there are opportunities to challenge one's own tradition (Gutmann, 1987; Nussbaum, 1997); and

e   there is scope for students to communicate and deliberate without teacher control, i.e. for argumentative discussions between students with the aim of solving problems or shedding light on them from different points of view (Hoel, 2001).[6] *(Englund 2006b, p. 512)*

The first point to be understood is a substantive one, in the sense that the precondition for starting a deliberative process, deliberative communication, is the emergence of a situation of conflicting views or different perspectives. As argued by Englund:

The presence of different views is one of the fundamental elements in deliberative communication and in creating, in spite of the differences, a common ground for discussion. This common ground can be called a *discursive situation* ... The dimension of conflict and confrontation (of different views) is substantially central to, and constitutive of, deliberative communication as a procedural phenomenon. This dimension implies both openly conflicting views and a search for and attempt to expose relatively minor differences, which are seen in deliberative communication as crucial to investigate and possibly to resolve.

(Englund, 2006b, pp. 513–514; *italics original*)

While this first point opens the way for the crucial value of argumentation, the second point stresses, in relational terms, respect for the concrete Other – the other person(s) actually present and deliberating – as well as the need for transactional listening. Such listening is a human gift that can be nurtured and realised in and through respectful communication (Waks, 2011). Transactional listening can also be facilitated and shaped by what is going on in the communicative situation, especially in the way academic developers act, build relationships, and communicate with colleagues and students. A conclusion from these two points is

that nobody who could make a relevant contribution may be excluded; (ii) that all participants are granted an equal opportunity to make contributions; (iii) that the participants must mean what they say; (iv) that communication must be freed from external and internal coercion so that the "yes" or "no" stances that participants adopt on criticizable validity claims are motivated solely by the rational force of the better reasons.

(Habermas, 1998, p. 44; *see Englund, 2010, pp. 29–30*)

The third point, the endeavour to reach collective will-formation through rational deliberation, has been both stressed and questioned (Sanders 1997, Young 2000). However, differences between perspectives and values are central to, and constitutive of, deliberation (Erman, 2009).[7] Further, whether or not consensus is reached is an empirical question. While collective will-formation leads to mutual agreement or at least to mutual understanding of what the conflict is about, which is the ideal, it is not the only acceptable result. Another might be greater clarity about differences.

It should also be noted, however, that the collective will-formation process implies that the seminar room can be viewed as a weak public sphere, in which different views occurring in public debate will also be highlighted, even if they challenge the values people participating in the deliberation bring with them (see Fraser, 1992; Giroux, 2002). Thus, the fourth point stresses the public character of deliberative communication, in the sense that universities are potential public spaces in which there is a preference for pluralism of views. This implies that "the principle of pluralism becomes a fundamental and crucial element of deliberative communication" (Englund, 2006b, p. 514). The pluralist principle further implies that an educational institution will not "be a companion to the values students bring with them, rather it will be pluralistic" (ibid., p. 514) and that "authorities and traditional views may be challenged" (ibid., p. 515) in deliberations with peers and while "teachers' opinions – especially if they leave no space for pluralism – may of course be questioned" (ibid., p. 515). In short, from a public-good perspective, it is the task of academics within educational institutions to liberate every individual from his or her private life into a public world.

Collectively, the four points stress the pivotal role of academics as deliberative professionals, since it is their responsibility to create and make use of the discursive situation of conflicts, or indeed different views on any issue, as they seek to realise the characteristics of deliberative communication. This is implied in the fifth point, concerning the need for and pursuit of a deliberative culture: that is to say, preconditions for further deliberative communication among participants, even without the formal guidance or presence of the academic. Central to this is a meaning-creating process among "equals". Developing such learning communities requires not only the will to deliberate, but also an investment of time and a spirit of humility. Building learning communities, and societies, that rest on the ideas of deliberative democracy is a long-term project: "democratic deliberation requires *equal opportunity of access to political influence*" (Knight and Johnson, 1997, p. 280; italics original). Higher education institutions and their academics can play a central role in such a democratically oriented project, with potential to lay the foundations for developing deliberative capacities and attitudes in line with the hope expressed by Gutmann and Thompson (1996, p. 359): "In any effort to make democracy more deliberative, the single most important institution outside government is the educational system".

As noted above, the main area for the use of deliberative communication is when conflicts, controversies, confrontations or different views on any issue arise or are observed and pointed out. These discursive situations can be distinguished along a continuum, from scarcely observable differences to highly explicit conflicts. Drawing attention to very small differences in views on a given issue, where there is a learning potential and the possibility of developing a more nuanced analysis of what the differences imply, is one way to initiate and foster deliberative communication. This means that almost any kind of difference between perspectives might be constitutive of deliberation. The part played by academics is crucial, since they (usually) have both the real authority (in terms of the necessary knowledge and perspectives) to determine the discursive conditions for dealing with the problem in question, and the formal authority to do so, although the latter is open to misuse. Here perhaps is the crucial key to the contingency and the possible realisation of the practice of deliberative communication. Creating a discursive situation, having intuition and knowledge about whether such a situation exists, and knowing how to handle it mainly hinges on the capabilities and judgement of members of the academic community, and the extent to which their work climate facilitates or constrains such engagements.

Deliberative communication, then, is a process in which different opinions and values can be set against each other and evaluated, such as tensions between public and private good in education. This implies an endeavour by each individual to develop his or her view and judgement by listening, deliberating, seeking arguments and valuing, coupled to a collective and cooperative endeavour to find values and norms which everyone can accept, at the same time as pluralism is acknowledged. As Kandlbinder summarises with particular reference to the contribution of academic developers: "The deliberative academic developer will be involved in a discussion of the processes of collaboration and thus, at the very least, will need skills that are relevant to the complexities of community building: negotiation, mediation, facilitation, and consensus building" (Kandlbinder 2007, p. 57). Kandlbinder (2007, pp. 57–58) ends his article by putting the central question that is also ours: "To what extent do academic developers enable and facilitate participatory, discussion-based processes within the academic community?"

In his comments on Kandlbinder, Stephen Rowland (2007) stresses the importance of the former's ambition of going beyond the uncertainties of the academic development identity and instead presents a case for the nature of this work being to develop deliberation, understood as creating an arena for the contestation of public opinion.

Conclusion: deliberative communication, critical reflection and public good

Critical thinking and reflection are widely regarded as important dispositions to cultivate as intrinsic to higher education. However, we consider that, for twenty-first-century higher education, these are necessary but not sufficient conditions. Rather, they are strengthened considerably when combined with deliberative communication with greater potential to cultivate and promote public good (see Solbrekke et al., 2016).

This necessitates shifting the frame of reference from Kant's solitary moral consciousness to Habermas's (1992) idea of a community of moral subjects developing a shared moral consciousness through communicative action in dialogue and deliberation. Thus, critical thinking as an individual capacity benefits from being combined with deliberative communication: encouraging the ability to listen to others, while also considering communal concerns in the interests of democracy and public good. Deliberative communication enhances critical thinking enabling the participants to make nuanced moral judgements and decisions consistent with public good (see Englund, 2016). We argue that this encouragement of public good could be promoted even more through the cultivation of communicative reason and deliberation, contesting and balancing the dominance of bureaucratic and entrepreneurial rationality in higher education, sufficient to re-orient higher education more reflective of and committed to public good.

Notes

1 In this first historical part, examining the use of the concept of public good, we are inspired by Joanna Williams's (2016) historical overview.
2 Moral individualism requires an education that shapes our vision to see "unjust social relations" as contrary to our understanding of human dignity (Cladis 1992, p. 195).

3 For a thorough critique of Samuelson's definition of public good as being too rooted in neoclassical economic theory, see Daviet (2016) and Kaul (2001). It should be noted that Samuelson later came to regret his narrow definition (Daviet 2016, note 8).
4 While this chapter primarily deals with an academic view of public good, it should be noted that, already in the 1990s, neoliberalism gave the concept of public, and also public good, a rhetorical meaning according to which it "increasingly becomes a metaphor for public disorder" (Giroux, 2002, p. 428; see also Giroux, 2001).
5 The concept of deliberation was first explicitly developed in the ethics and rhetoric of Aristotle and has been revitalised mainly within American East Coast liberalism (Bohman & Rehg, 1997) and by Habermas (1996); see also, Englund 2006a, with reference especially to Dewey, 1927/1984. The close relationship between democracy and deliberation is stressed by the authors mentioned and many others.
6 Originally developed by Englund (2000) in Swedish; see also Englund (2002, 2008) on deliberation in higher education, and Solbrekke (2008).
7 See Englund (2016, pp. 68–71), on the challenge of agonism versus deliberation.

References

Arendt, H. (1954). *Between Past and Future*. London: Penguin.

Aristotle (1991). *On Rhetoric: A theory of civic discourse*. New York: Oxford University Press.

Barnett, R. (1997). *Higher Education: A critical business*. Buckingham: Society for Research into Higher Education & Open University Press

Barnett, R. (2011). *Being a University*. Buckingham: Society for Research into Higher Education & Open University Press.

Benhabib, S. (1992). *Situating the Self: Gender, community and postmodernism in the global era*. Cambridge: Polity Press

Bohman, J., & Rehg, W. (eds) (1997). *Deliberative Democracy: Essays on reason and politics*. Cambridge, MA: MIT Press.

Brint, S. (1994). *In an Age of Experts: The changing role of professionals in politics and public life*. Princeton: Princeton University Press.

Cladis, M. (1992). *A Communitarian Defense of Liberalism: Emile Durkheim and contemporary social theory*. Stanford: Stanford University Press.

Collini, S. (2012). *What Are Universities For?*London: Penguin.

Daviet, B. (2016). Revisiting the principle of education as a public good. *Education Research and Foresight Series*, No. 17. Paris: UNESCO. Available at http://www.unesco.org/new/en/education/themes/leading-theinternational-agenda/rethinking-education/erf-papers/

Delanty, G. (2001). *Challenging Knowledge: The university in the knowledge society*. Buckingham: Society for Research into Higher Education & Open University Press.

Dewey, J. (1916/1980). Democracy and education. In *The Middle Works 1899–1924: Volume 9, 1916*, ed. J. A. Boydston. Carbondale: Southern Illinois University Press.

Dewey, J. (1927/1984). The public and its problems. In *The Later Works 1925–1953: Volume 2, 1925–1927*, ed. J. A. Boydston, pp. 235–372. Carbondale: Southern Illinois University Press.

Dryzek, Have . (2000). *Deliberative Democracy and Beyond: Liberals, critics, contestations*. Oxford: Oxford University Press.

Durkheim, E. (1938/1977). *The Evolution of Educational Thought*. London: Routledge.

Durkheim, E. (1899/1957/1992). *Professional Ethics and Civic Morals*. London: Routledge.

Durkheim, E. (1912/1961). *The Elementary Forms of the Religious Life*. New York: Collier Books.

East, L., Stokes, R., & Walker, M. (2014). Universities, the public good and professional education in the UK. *Studies in Higher Education*, *39*(9), 1617–1633.

Englund, T. (1996). The public and the text. *Journal of Curriculum Studies, 28*(1), 1–35.

Englund, T. (2000). Rethinking democracy and education: Towards an education of deliberative citizens. *Journal of Curriculum Studies, 32*(2), 305–313. Also in: W. Carr (ed.) (2005). *The Routledge Falmer Reader in Philosophy of Education*, pp. 135–142. Abingdon: Routledge.

Englund, T. (2002). The university as a place for deliberative communication: An attempt to apply Habermas's discourse theory on higher education. Paper presented at the ASHE-conference in Sacramento, USA, November.

Englund, T. (2006a). Jürgen Habermas and education. *Journal of Curriculum Studies, 38*(5), 499–501.

Englund, T. (2006b). Deliberative communication: A pragmatist proposal. *Journal of Curriculum Studies, 38*(5), 503–520.

Englund, T. (2008). The university as an encounter for deliberative communication: Creating cultural citizenship and professional responsibility. *Utbildning & Demokrati/Education & Democracy, 17*(2), 97–114.

Englund, T. (2010). Educational implications of the idea of deliberative democracy. In M. Murphy & T. Fleming (eds), *Habermas, Critical Theory and Education*, pp. 19–32. New York: Routledge.

Englund, T. (2016). On moral education through deliberative communication. *Journal of Curriculum Studies, 48*(1), 58–76.

Erman, E. (2009). What is wrong with agonistic pluralism? Reflections on conflict in democratic theory. *Philosophy & Social Criticism, 35*(9), 1039–1062.

Fisher, S. (2005). Is there a need to debate the role of higher education and the public good? *Level, 3*(3), 1–29.

Forester, J. (1999). *The Deliberative Practitioner: Encouraging participatory planning processes.* Cambridge, MA: MIT University Press.

Fraser, N. (1992). Rethinking the public sphere: A contribution to the critique of actually existing democracy. In C. Calhoun (ed.), *Habermas and the Public Sphere*, pp. 109–142. Cambridge, MA: MIT Press.

Giroux, H. (2001). *Public Spaces, Private Lives: Beyond the Culture of Cynicism.* Lanham: Rowman & Littlefield.

Giroux, H. (2002). Neoliberalism, corporate culture, and the promise of higher education: The university as a democratic public sphere. *Harvard Educational Review, 72*(4), 425–469.

Grace, G. (1989). Education: Commodity or public good? *British Journal of Educational Studies, 37*(3), 207–221.

Gutmann, A. (1987). *Democratic Education.* Princeton: Princeton University Press.

Gutmann, A., & Thompson, D. (1996). *Democracy and Disagreement.* Cambridge, MA: Belknap Press.

Habermas, J. (1981/1987). *The Theory of Communicative Action, Vol. 2: Lifeworld and System: A critique of functionalist reason.* Boston: Beacon Press.

Habermas, J. (1967/1988). *On the Logic of the Social Sciences.* Oxford: Polity Press.

Habermas, J. (1962/1989a). *The Structural Transformation of the Public Sphere.* Cambridge: MIT Press.

Habermas, J. (1985/1989b). *The New Conservatism: Cultural criticism and the historian debate.* Cambridge, MA: MIT University Press.

Habermas, J. (1985/1990). *The Philosophical Discourse of Modernity: Twelve lectures.* Cambridge: Polity Press.

Habermas, J. (1983/1992). *Moral Consciousness and Communicative Action.* Cambridge: Polity Press.

Habermas, J. (1992/1996). *Between Facts and Norms: Contributions to a discourse theory of law and democracy.* Cambridge: Polity Press.

Habermas, J. (1996/1998). *The Inclusion of the Other: Studies in political theory*. Cambridge, MA: MIT Press.

Habermas, J. (2001). *Communicative Action and Rationality*. Cambridge, MA: MIT Press.

Hoel, T. L. (2001). *Skriva och samtala: Lärande genom responsgrupper* [Writing and conversing: Learning through response groups]. Lund: Studentlitteratur.

Kaul, I. (2001). Public goods: taking the concept to the 21st century. In D. Drache (ed.), *The Market of the Public Domain*, pp. 255–273. London: Routledge.

Kandlbinder, P. (2007). The challenge of deliberation for academic developers. *International Journal of Academic Development*, *12*(1), 55–59.

Kant, I. (1798/1979). *The Conflict of the Faculties*. New York: Abaris Books.

Knight, J., & Johnson, J. (1997). What sort of political equality does deliberative democracy require? In J. Bohman & W. Rehg (eds), *Deliberative Democracy: Essays on reason and politics*, pp. 279–319. Cambridge, MA: MIT Press.

Marginson, S. (2011). Higher education and public good. *Higher Education Quarterly*, *65*(4), 411–433.

Mill, J. S. (1873/1981). Autobiography and Literary Essays. In *Collected Works*, vol *1*, ed. J. M. Robson &J. Stillinger. Toronto: University of Toronto Press, Routledge & Kegan Paul.

Muller, J., & Young, M. (2014). Disciplines, skills and the university. *Higher Education*, *67*, 127–140.

Naidoo, R. (2003). Repositioning HE as a global commodity: Opportunities and challenges for future sociology of education work. *British Journal of Sociology of Education*, *24*(2), 249–259.

Newman, C. (1852/1959). *The Idea of a University*. New York: Image Books.

Nixon, J. (2011). *Higher Education and the Public Good: Imagining the university*. London: Continuum.

Nussbaum, M. (1997). *Cultivating Humanity: A classical defense of reform in liberal education*. Cambridge, MA: Harvard University Press.

Nussbaum, M. (2000). *Women and Human Development*. Cambridge: Cambridge University Press.

Nussbaum, M. (2010). *Not for Profit: Why democracy needs the humanities*. Princeton: Princeton University Press.

Rowland, S. (2007). Academic development: A site of creative doubt and contestation. *International Journal of Academic Development*, *12*(1), 9–14.

Samuelson, P. (1954). The pure theory of public expenditure. *The Review of Economics and Statistics*, *36*(4), 387–389.

Sanders, L. (1997). Against deliberation. *Political Theory*, *25*(3), 347–376.

Scanlon, T. (2008). *What We Owe to Each Other*. Cambridge, MA: The Belknap Press of Harvard University Press.

Sen, A. (1999). *Development as Freedom*. Oxford: Oxford University Press.

Shore, C., & Wright, S. (2017). Privatizing the public university. In S. Wright & C. Shore (eds), *Death of the Public University? Uncertain futures for higher education in the knowledge economy*, pp. 1–24. New York: Berghahn.

Slaughter, S., & Leslie, L. (1997). *Academic Capitalism: Politics, policies and the entrepreneurial university*. Baltimore: Johns Hopkins University Press.

Small, H. (2013). *The Value of Humanities*. Oxford: Oxford University Press.

Solbrekke, T. D. (2008). Educating for professional responsibility: A normative dimension of higher education. *Utbildning & Demokrati/Education & Democracy*, *17*(2), 73–96.

Solbrekke, T. D. & Englund, T. (2011). Bringing professional responsibility back in. *Studies in Higher Education*, *36*(7), 847–861.

Solbrekke, T. D., Englund, T., Karseth, B., & Beck, E. (2016). Educating for professional responsibility: From critical thinking to deliberative communication, or why critical thinking is not enough. In F. Trede & C. McEwen (eds), *Educating the Deliberate Professional: Preparing for future practices*, pp. 29–44. Berlin: Springer.

Sugrue, C., Englund, T., Fossland, T., & Solbrekke, T. D. (2018). Traditions, trends and trajectories in the praxis of academic developers: a twenty-year literature odyssey. *Studies in Higher Education, 43*(12), 2336–2353.

Sullivan, W. (1986). *Reconstructing Public Philosophy*. Berkeley: University of California Press.

Sullivan, W. (2005). *Work and Integrity: The crisis and promise of professionalism in America.* Second edition. Stanford: Jossey Bass.

Sutphen, M., Solbrekke, T. D., & Sugrue, C. (2018). Toward articulating an academic praxis by interrogating university strategic plans. *Studies in Higher Education, 44*(8), 1400–1412.

Waks, L. (2011). John Dewey on listening and friendship in school and society. *Educational Theory, 61*(2), 191–205.

Walker, M. (2018). Dimensions of higher education and the public good in South Africa. *Higher Education, 76*(3), 555–569.

Williams, J. (2016). A critical exploration of changing definitions of public good in relation to higher education. *Studies in Higher Education, 41*(4), 619–630.

Wright, S., & Shore, C. (eds) (2017). *Death of the Public University? Uncertain futures for higher education in the knowledge economy*. New York: Berghahn.

Young, I. M. (2000). *Inclusion and Democracy*. Oxford: Oxford University Press.

4

LEADING IN A WEB OF COMMITMENTS

Negotiating legitimate compromises

Tone Dyrdal Solbrekke, Ciaran Sugrue and Molly Sutphen

The last two and a half years, and as part of the quality assurance system, I have worked closer and closer with the university leadership and worked less and less as an academic developer. We have got more and new assignments from the university leadership, especially international assignments like starting up academic development units or providing supervision courses in African universities. This means less contact with faculty staff on the faculty level or department level.

(Leader of academic development unit, Uppsala)

I am also the chair of the committee evaluating teachers. That is very hot at our university as we have got the meriting system for 'elite' teachers.

(Leader of academic development unit, Örebro)

Introduction

There is increasing pressures on twenty-first-century universities to demonstrate both high- quality research and high-quality education (Spence, 2019). While traditionally public reputation relied primarily on the production of research, more recently the quality of teaching has gained public attention also. Students expect to be recognised as active members of a university community, and require their rights (educational, political and social) to be vindicated within their respective universities. For example, the European Students' Union's mission statement indicates the intention to "work for sustainable, accessible and high quality higher education in Europe" (ESU, 2011). Politicians govern more directly insisting that public universities align with and deploy standardised systems to evaluate the quality of teaching and educational leadership (Gaebel et al., 2018). Similarly, a recent Norwegian White Paper states: "the Government will provide more of the tools and guidelines required to raise the quality in higher education", and "educational quality must be the responsibility of the academic environment as a whole, including the academic leadership" (Ministry of Education and Research, 2016–2017, p. 2).

Collectively, these expectations to engage more actively with improving education are intended to influence all academics with responsibility for educational programmes. Nevertheless, academic developers (ADs) have a particular remit since they are responsible for developing and leading the academic development programmes within their respective institutions. However, as the quotations from the leaders of two academic development units (ADUs) in Sweden cited above indicate, the expectations regarding the contributions of ADs are changing and expanding while also being aligned more closely with formal educational leadership work. Such experiences are consistent with what recent international research has documented; namely, that institutional leaders increasingly expect ADs to shape and influence how their university meets the increased and sometimes contradictory expectations from (external as well as internal) higher education policy makers and other stakeholders (Fremstad et al., 2019; Stensaker et al., 2017; Sugrue et al., 2019). While such expectations bring recognition to ADs' work, these accrued responsibilities expand ADs' professional portfolios and place increasing demands also on their time and expertise, as well as change their relationship with academics with teaching responsibilities. For example, expectations regarding international collaboration, or giving AD leaders responsibility for coordinating evaluation of university teachers, not only intensify demands on time and expertise, but have potential to create tensions between evaluation and support. In May's terms (1996), ADs' webs of commitments continue to expand. Consequently, their capacity to negotiate legitimate compromises is both vital and under scrutiny, while simultaneously they are obliged to be attentive to the overall purpose of higher education as public good and for it.

In this chapter we draw on the testimony of five leaders of AD units to indicate key constituent elements of commitments evident in all five webs of commitments, despite institutional and individual contextual variation. While ADs have specific responsibilities regarding teaching and learning on campus, the common responsibility they hold in common with all academic colleagues is the necessity to determine their commitments.

Consistent with research findings on ADs' responsibilities, all five ADU leaders indicate that they are being asked to take on additional obligations (Gibbs, 2013; Stensaker et al., 2017; Sugrue et al., 2017). This expanding portfolio extends to providing research-based courses in university pedagogies and undertaking consultancy work with individual academics and whole schools or departments, as well as faculties or units. Additionally, university leaders more frequently request support with implementing internationally driven policy reforms, such as supporting academics to develop local learning outcomes "aligned" with predefined (trans) national qualification frameworks (Handal et al., 2014). Similarly, university leaders expect ADs to take a leading role in integrating digital technologies into teaching and learning strategies and to develop systems for student and teacher evaluations (Sugrue et al., 2017). Consequently, academic development is high on the agenda in most contemporary public universities. As reported by *Trends 2018*, more than

85 per cent of 303 institutions (in 43 countries) agree that academic development is important to improve the quality of higher education and ADs are important resources for the development of dynamic institutional learning and teaching communities (Gaebel et al., 2018).

The increased and increasing responsibilities have several consequences for ADs. As already indicated, they are being drawn closer to political governance and the university leadership. These new relationships may have implications for their interactions with academic colleagues (Solbrekke & Fremstad, 2018). There are increasing expectations among institutional leaders that ADs "broker" with academic peers policies espoused by institutional leaders and the praxes[1] such new requirements may spawn (Brew & Cahir, 2014). These additional responsibilities are reflective of new expectations for twenty-first-century universities and the consequent metamorphosis of university orientations (see Chapter 2). Others arise from aspects of New Public Management (NPM) that challenge traditional academic governance and leadership ideals as well as ideas concerning public good. As ADs observe their assigned responsibilities accumulate, they must review their webs of commitments, navigating and negotiating legitimate compromises in changed and changing circumstances.

Although ADs as well as their academic colleagues face new responsibilities that do not necessarily originate with NPM, it has had a major influence on the strategic priorities and orientations of higher education (see Chapter 2) with consequences also for how educational programmes are understood as and for public good (Pinheiro et al., 2019). In light of such influences, the next sections of this chapter focus on relational aspects of leading higher education as and for public good in increasingly complex webs of commitments. We begin with a brief indication of how the contemporary landscape of higher education influences webs of commitments and this is followed by a focus on the logics of responsibility and accountability, the latter as it has evolved shaped by NPM. The argument we advance contends that professionally responsible educational leadership is enacted with autonomy, discretionary judgement and integrity, and requires the capacity to negotiate legitimate compromises in the tension between the competing logics of responsibility and accountability. It involves proactive decisions and actions that move beyond mere compliance required by the strictures of NPM. Subsequently, these logics are deployed as analytical tools to gain insight into how leaders of five academic development units, Norway (two), Sweden (two) and the USA (one), (re-)negotiate legitimate compromises within their respective webs of commitments. We indicate their struggles when additional tasks are assigned to them by institutional leaders to recalibrate their commitments within the demands and constraints, personal, professional and institutional; how they arrive at legitimate compromises within their particular webs of commitments. The concluding section reflects on the challenges faced by academic staff in contemporary public universities, and attendant difficulties in negotiating legitimate compromises in and between their webs of commitments; and the demands of the institutional workplace as well as its external policy mandates while seeking to serve the public as a distinct contribution of higher education.

Contemporary higher education: changing webs of commitments

As indicated in the introduction, May's (1996) "web" metaphor describes the responsibilities and commitments that we have in our work and lives.[2] For academics, such commitments include teaching and research in a discipline and/or a profession. Academics have commitments also to ideals and individuals outside of the university that include families, friends, and, community organizations. As May suggests, academics' commitments are a tangled web. And each web of commitments is unique to each person, and, while some commitments may be shared, individuals do not configure in precisely the same ways. What differentiates one individual's web of commitments from another's is shaped by personal values, professional ideals, local working conditions that include an institution's mandate to serve public good and its commitment to honour such a remit. How we designate time, attention, and resources become proxies for our values and priorities that, in turn, influence how we engage with professional responsibilities and determine commitments to their enactment.

NPM and transnational higher education policy, such as the Bologna[3] process, have changed higher education significantly and thus also webs of commitments. Part of NPM ideology is to deregulate public institutions and to move away from policy steering by rules to a process of "soft governance", an approach to regulation that is designed for political convergence through implicit discursive mechanisms such as language use, knowledge making and meaning making in general (Le Bianic & Svensson, 2008, p. 573). In the current context of public universities, their leaders have the freedom to define their strategies as long as they "comply with" tools and suggested ways of implementing the Bologna process defined in national policy, frequently transposed from European higher education policy by national agencies or national policy-making bodies (Karseth and Solbrekke, 2010). Consequently, university leaders are granted autonomy to decide how to lead their institutions while simultaneously they are increasingly regulated through soft governance and the transnational standardisation of higher education, political expectations and workplace needs (Ekman, Lindgren & Packendorff, 2018). Although the Bologna process does not prescribe rules, the creation of formal follow-up mechanisms, according to Ravinet (2008, p. 365), "leads to a series of intermediate obligations linked to the idea of playing a part in a collective whole, such as the national reports and the stocktaking".

As a result of new roles and responsibilities that accrue from NPM, the webs of commitments for all agents within universities change, and so too does the decision-making that facilitates the determination of legitimate compromises. For example, due to an increased focus on quality assurance systems, administration, documentation and reporting there are additional requirements on academic staff to comply with pre-defined programmes, learning outcome descriptions, cross-disciplinary work, as well as more collaboration with employers, all of which are characteristics of an accountability logic (Solbrekke & Sugrue, 2014). Many academics report that these new commitments allow little room to decide how to serve society and public good. They report that their sense of intellectual leadership and academic capital is devalued, and their academic freedom diminished (Macfarlane, 2012). In many contexts, academics resist what they interpret as new requirements that suggest their academic and pedagogical capacities are no longer trusted (Di Napoli, 2014). Recent research indicates how academics develop different coping strategies within contemporary public universities. Senior academics may ignore new requirements or develop resistance strategies while more junior academics feel greater compunction to comply with a more entrepreneurial orientation, thus increasing pressure to be excellent in both research and teaching (Ese, 2019).

New governance of higher education creates tensions within academic communities around what counts as 'good' university pedagogy. Such tensions are often left to ADs to de-escalate (Deem, 2008). For example, institutional leaders call on leaders of AD units to support them in the implementation of new approaches to teaching and assessment, development of online and blended learning, engagement in cross-disciplinary programmes, or collaboration with external professionals or industry. Such new practices are typically embraced by some, ignored or resisted by others. In such circumstances, wise reasoning and the capability to reach legitimate compromises on the part of leaders of AD units become an indispensable element of expertise, particularly if the continuing commitment is to lead in a way that promotes public good. Increasingly, therefore ADs need to cultivate brokering capabilities, vertically on behalf of their colleagues with institutional leaders and horizontally between and across all disciplinary and professional programmes (Sugrue et al., 2019). Such brokering requires the capacity to analyse how institutional policies, plans and orientation(s) (see Chapter 2) influence the aims of higher education, and how structural and cultural conditions impact academics' webs of commitments. It implies agency and knowing when and why to comply and account to policy-makers and leaders at a macro level, and when to resist (Peseta, 2014; Fremstad et al., 2019). While academics in general cannot escape from such pressures and demands, ADs are very much in the eye of the storm, positioned at the institutional intersection where vertical and horizontal brokering meet and sometimes collide.[4] Although the increased responsibilities assigned to ADs may be indicative of trust in their leading and pedagogical capacities (Solbrekke & Fremstad, 2018), they are also illustrative of how university leaders cope with their more complex and intensive webs of commitments, namely by delegating or "distributing" additional responsibilities to others in the organisation, and ADs in particular regarding leading education.

Although not a requirement in every institution, in Europe there is increased policy focus on professional support for academic staff. In many countries the number of pedagogical course hours for all newly appointed academics has increased with immediate consequences for the workload of ADs (Gaebel et al., 2018). For example, the Norwegian government recently legislated that all higher education institutions provide a basic pedagogy course of 200 hours (an increase from 150 hours) for all newly appointed academics in permanent positions within a period of two years following initial appointment (Ministry of Education and Research, 2016–2017). Similarly, since criteria for promotion now require more explicit documentation of teaching and qualifications in educational leading, those who wish to advance their careers turn to ADs in increasing numbers for support. In this manner, the very requirement of insisting on all having a "basic" pedagogical qualification spawns an emergent need for follow-up, more advanced courses to meet these newly minted criteria. In research-intensive universities promotion typically hinges on quantification of peer-reviewed papers in highly ranked journals, as well as high-quality teaching, measured against predefined learning outcomes and students' evaluation of teaching. Consequently, both newly appointed academics and those pursuing promotion often feel squeezed between research and teaching commitments, and ADs are called upon to help juggle what frequently appear as unrealistic and impossible demands. As the AD leader in Oslo commented: "we get a lot of feedback from academics in the courses that they really want to do more with the teaching, but they are so pressed doing research. The public rhetoric is that teaching is important, but when it comes to what is appreciated, it is research which really matters"; a refrain that is being heard more frequently in many jurisdictions.

In the shadow of NPM, ADs and their leaders as *professionals* are subject to a moral and societal mandate to serve both public and their individual needs (Solbrekke, 2007; Sullivan, 2005). They do not simply flit from course to course teaching pedagogy and informing academic staff of new university policies. Rather, ADs, along with their leaders and colleagues, share responsibility for the overall mission of the university. In order to gain further insights into how ADs in particular arrive at professionally responsible decisions, we provide an account of the two logics: of accountability and responsibility. We consider that navigating between these often competing logics is necessary within the webs of commitments in which, as professionals, academics are obliged to function, in order to broker legitimate compromise.

Tensions between accountability and responsibility: necessitating negotiated legitimate compromises

To cope with the many new expectations and commitments from NPM and the Bologna process that characterise the working conditions of many academics, whether they occupy formal education leadership positions or not, a first step is to acknowledge the complex tensions of leading in a web of commitments. A second is to be able to parse the differences between being accountable and being responsible in different situations. Accountability is associated with answerability, blame, liability and obligation, and relates to counting, building on legal and economic rationales bound to contractual obligations, as defined by politicians or bureaucrats, thus emphasising the "duty" to answer for actions to others or to society in terms of meeting the goals defined by others rather than by the profession itself. The accountability logic implies an obligation to adhere, and be accountable, to prescriptive policy standards of quality (Solbrekke & Englund, 2011).

Responsibility connotes trustworthiness, capacity, dependability, reliability, judgment and choice (ibid.). Responsibility highlights moral and social obligations and relies on the ability to deploy discretionary specialisation (Freidson, 2001)

based on professional standards and expert knowledge, as well as critical deliberation on the overall purpose of, and moral obligations inherent in, professional
work. Thus, in the context of leading higher education as and for public good, we
posit that professional responsibility reflects a leader's[5] integrity and values in
dynamic interplay with specified professional (academic) standards and norms in
light of the overall purpose of higher education. It is about justifying decisions and
actions in a specific setting from a professional point of view based on a holistic
approach in which science- and experience-based knowledge integrate with moral
reasoning. The possibility to live out such responsibility depends on the social
contract whereby a certain autonomy is assigned by society to all professionals, and
in this case academics, who as professionals are both trusted and committed to act
for public good. With greater autonomy comes greater responsibility. However,
within this logic, actions taken cannot always be predicted and their outcomes are
not always measurable in terms of clear and predefined descriptors or indicators.
Inherent moral evaluations move beyond predefined codes, thus relying on judgement (Solbrekke, 2007).

These competing logics are summarised in Table 4.1 developed from Solbrekke
and Englund (2011).

In twenty-first-century public universities, all academics are obliged to answer to
both logics. Thus being employed in public universities necessitates the capacity to
cope in the "field of force" between the two logics. It is legitimate that the state
requires public universities to account for use of taxpayers' money. It is legitimate
that politicians and university leaders insist on being provided with information
about the quality of teaching and learning. However, the extent to which what is
measurable has come to dominate what counts as quality in higher education is
increasingly perceived as problematic (Solbrekke & Sugrue, 2014). Providing
higher education as and for public good depends on a social and moral responsibility
broader than reporting on predetermined, transparent and quantifiable quality criteria.
It depends on reflection on the complexity of one's web of commitments and whether decision-making is merely accountable rather than being professionally

TABLE 4.1 The logics of professional responsibility and accountability

Responsibility	Accountability
• based in professional mandate	• defined by current governance
• situated judgement	• standardised by contract
• trust	• control
• moral and epistemic rationales	• economic and legal rationales
• internal evaluation	• external auditing
• negotiated standards	• predetermined indicators
• implicit language	• transparent language
• framed by professions	• framed by political goals
• relative autonomy and personally inescapable	• compliance with employer's/politicians' decisions
• proactive	• reactive

responsible. Such reflection may facilitate being and becoming more aware of decisions for action and provide a "moral compass" (Taylor 1989) for reaching legitimate compromises in the tension between the two logics, recognising also that it is possible to be accountable without necessarily being professionally responsible.

Leaders of AD units: their webs of commitment and legitimate compromises

In this section, we provide examples of how ADs experience their web of commitments, while also indicating the possibilities and challenges they encounter in their efforts to contribute to developing higher education as and for public good. The evidence we provide draws on semi-structured interviews with each leader of the AD units at the universities of Oslo, Tromsø, Örebro, Uppsala and North Carolina at Chapel Hill, completed during March–April 2016 and an online focus group with the same five leaders in December 2018. In the interviews, we asked about the mission of contemporary public universities and ADs' roles and responsibilities in contributing to this mission.[6] All interviews followed an insider–outsider and abductive approach moving between theory and data. The analysis is consensus based inspired by the abductive and deliberative communication research approach (see Chapter 5). Interview extracts enable us to demonstrate how university priorities and institutional leadership approaches impact on ADs' webs of commitments, and consequent tensions between the logics of responsibility and accountability as they struggle to find legitimate compromises.

Figure 4.1 depicts the constituent elements of AD unit leaders' webs of commitments when interviewed during March–April 2016. Although webs of commitments depend on the context and time in which the leaders of the AD units work or have worked, the constituent elements in Figure 4.1 are those shared by these leaders at the time of the initial interviews. For example, the leaders had commitments to teaching university pedagogies to academic staff. In their differing circumstances, this may entail introducing academic staff to new pedagogies or deploying existing pedagogies differently. Or it may be helping a department or programme leader find ways of coping with changes in budgets by increasing class

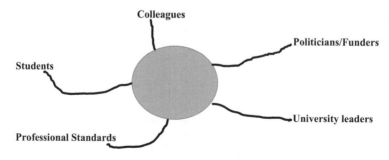

FIGURE 4.1 Example of a web of commitments for a leader of an AD unit.

sizes, which, in turn affects how academics teach. In order to teach university pedagogies, ADs must be up to date on research in higher education, and learn new pedagogies through collaborating with colleagues, engaging with as well as contributing to research, national and international organisations of ADs. In Figure 4.1 these commitments are depicted by multiple, overlapping interactions with colleagues. For example providing support to academics who struggle with their teaching is a central element of AD unit leaders' webs of commitment, while how such support is enacted may vary, as illustrated by the AD leader at Chapel Hill who said: "I do have faculty who come to me and say: 'I am on a one-year contract, my student evaluations have not been very good, I am worried about having my contract renewed, can you please help me?' And so I will spend time with that faculty member …"

The quotation exemplifies the experiences ADs have of bearing witness to the increased uses of student evaluations to determine the quality of an academic's teaching. Those on short-term contracts may be particularly vulnerable to poor student evaluations, a vulnerability that may be exploited by students and faculty. When student evaluations of teaching are based on predetermined criteria (typical in an accountability logic), this may create a culture in which there is less room for unanticipated and emergent learning[7] that is less amenable to easy measurement. In this regard, an additional responsibility that accrues to ADs in such a climate and context is to explain to academics the uses and pitfalls of student evaluation.

All five leaders struggled with how they and their AD colleagues should use their time, whether to commit to the needs of individual academics or more collective oriented needs, maximising potential benefits of available resources. One obvious tension here is between an economic rationale and moral obligation to the individual. The moral rationale that imbues the logic of responsibility calls for an immediate response to the individual academic. However, pedagogical and professional dimensions of the responsibility rationale oblige the AD to find a legitimate compromise that embraces these concerns while being cognisant of the economic obligation to use allocated resources in an "accountable" manner. The AD leader in Oslo indicated that her strategy was to make such individual needs more collective, and thereafter engage with department leaders to collaborate and find ways to develop a seminar or course for a larger group of academics in their home department. In her view that may be a modest effort to make academic development work a public rather than a private good for the individual academic.

Another tension frequently mentioned was the one which arises when ADs are asked to provide a course on how to teach more effectively. From an accountability perspective, the answer to such requests lies in an instrumental approach that demonstrates "best practice" delivered to groups of academics who expect ADs to give them tips and tricks of the trade that have predetermined criteria for "good teaching" with general measurement indicators. But, as the AD leader from Chapel Hill remarked, when ADs resist such overtures from overburdened academics for "recipes for busy kitchens" the latter are disappointed (Huberman, 1983). Even if ADs were to capitulate to such instrumentalism, it is not possible for them to provide academics with quick pedagogical solutions applicable to every discipline and teaching situation. Instead, ADs make suggestions and help academics figure out how to tailor pedagogical possibilities to their discipline, students, teaching environments and a whole host of other local conditions – a strategy that follows the logic of responsibility. It is labour intensive and time consuming for both the ADs and their colleagues, yet in the long run more efficient from a teaching and learning perspective. As the AD leader in Chapel Hill indicated, such encouragement to reflect on one's teaching, perhaps speaking with students and helping to analyse their feedback, is worth the effort since she sees it as a vindication of the university's commitment to students: "The goals are for students ... to aspire to be curious, to be prepared for their lives, as workers and citizens". These goals do not lend themselves to tips and tricks. Instead they require academics to reflect on what it means to be curious in open-ended ways and to be a citizen now and in the future. To settle for less would be to compromise one's professional commitments.

The leaders of the AD units also have commitments to university leaders at various levels within their organisation. For example, there is intensified pressure on AD units to commit to follow their institutional leaders' decisions to integrate digital technologies into teaching, learning and assessment approaches. The leader from Chapel Hill worried that the emphasis and time devoted to digital tools might eclipse the efforts of ADs to help academics continue to improve all the pedagogies they use, not simply the ones that lend themselves to digital tools. She stated:

> But this gets at academic development because it is just not enough to come in and say, "'I can help you with your teaching by helping you set up your learning management system site (IT platform) and using all the tools and the bells and the whistles on the site". That to me is a different thing than what I consider academic ... development to be.

Because ADs have limited time, expectations to follow their institutional leaders' priorities and policies can press against what ADs' consider to be important to live up to the standards of their disciplinary knowledge and professional experience as an AD. The leader of the AD unit in Tromsø addressed this pressure by saying:

> It has been an issue [in the ADU] because the university is focusing on the technology. They have a pressure on us as a [teaching and learning] centre so how can it be shown here that we take it further. And we are trying, it is three years ago we got established [as a centre] and it is more and more like we do a lot of cooperation ... but it is also about the pressure on the academic development group because we have so many requests for things we should be doing and we don't manage to do everything so it is hard to find time.

Such pressures and tensions are magnified since ADs have become part of a larger centre with different professional groups and epistemic traditions. The presence of different "tribes" within the university (Becher & Trowler, 2001), such as librarians and instructional or educational technologists in more centralised centres where the ADU may constitute one of more subgroups becomes a basis for further tensions.

Additionally, such configuration complicate the prospects of negotiating legitimate compromises while protecting professional integrity and simultaneously taking additional responsibilities seriously – reconfiguring webs of commitments.

Unit leaders, in common with many middle leaders, have commitments also to university administrators, such as those who are responsible for booking teaching rooms or for reconciling budgets. Or as the leader in Oslo remarked, "it is also necessary to negotiate the demands in light of the allocated resources". In Nordic countries unit leaders face the difficulties of meeting government requirements for academic staff for whom it is compulsory to complete prescribed pedagogical programmes as indicated above. University leaders increasingly follow the accountability logic to comply with politicians or *other* funders of higher education. And, although ADs may be obliged to make such pedagogical provision, they are resistant to the assumption that more pedagogical hours necessarily improve either teaching quality or pedagogical competence. The AD leader in Tromsø stated:

> [We have] a lot of autonomy about how we develop our programmes, but in the last couple of years there has been increasing pressure to deliver more, more focus on how many courses, how many people can you get in. And I think there is a tension between … delivering courses, and we want to have a focus on how we should run this course, how do we enhance teaching and learning at the university, how do we develop the programme? How can we be better? And if it is too much pressure and too much focus on delivering several courses we are losing some of the focus on quality and enhancements of teaching and learning.

A policy adoption to raise the status of teaching within this university to be on an equal footing with research, as well as the government's increased prescription regarding basic pedagogical courses for recently appointed academics, means that the research time of ADs is sacrificed in order to commit to additional teaching (Sugrue et al., 2019). This tension is evident in the following remarks that provide testimony of commitment to research communities that focus on teaching and learning in higher education as a research field. The leader continues:

> And I think it is impossible not to have ADs with that [research] background. Because it is about, I hate that word, legacy for the rest of the academic staff of the university. That is one of the reasons that we should do research. It is also that we are into higher education and talking about the necessity for teaching to be research-based and, if our teaching is not research based, … I think it is impossible. That is one of the main challenging parts of this work, I think, because it is a pressure being in service, delivering, responding. One department contacts us, "can you have a seminar about blah, blah, blah, and we say, yes of course". Then it is too much of that, then you lose time to do research and focusing on research.

Due to a particular confluence of competing interests, and in particular the tension between increasing demands to teach more pedagogical courses and to greater numbers of newly appointed academics, this leader's time for research is considerably curtailed, to the point where finding a legitimate compromise is seriously challenged. Thus, as the web of commitments extends to university leaders as well as politicians or other funders arriving at legitimate compromises may prove elusive. In response to a combination of national policy and internal policy pressures, she says:

> So last year we increased the intake into the programme to 30 and that was too many for us. And this year the board for the centre said that they wanted us to put a lot of resources into this programme because of the frustration around the university from those who didn't get into it. So I pushed to have one programme running from September and one from January, so now we have 50 persons, plus the other courses running and that is too much. And I have reported back to the board that we can do that now but it is not sustainable. So we are doing this to help the long queue of people getting into it but it can't be like this next year ...

Such demands, even in the short term, have major consequences while serving as a clear indication that when external policies shift, and are taken up internally by senior leaders, they frequently are shifted into other's webs of commitments where the struggles to find legitimate compromise are all too real, particularly in the absence of increased allocation of resources. When, or if, additional responsibilities go unrecognised, finding legitimate compromise within newly configured webs of commitment may be unattainable, resulting in degrees of moral injury, defined as "psychological consequence of a betrayal of what's right by someone who holds legitimate authority in a high stakes situation" (Shay, 2011, p. 179). While the leader in this context was subsequently compensated or rewarded with sabbatical leave in order to undertake research, it is clearly evident from the above that the circumstances in which she sought to find legitimate compromise was not sustainable, and certainly not without adequate additional resource allocation that would render legitimate compromise more attainable. It may be argued that the "soft governance" in this instance was coercive, thus creating conditions whereby being compromised was a definite possibility. Leaders at various levels in such circumstances need to be challenged to reflect more carefully on their responsibilities and webs of commitments and how these have implications for colleagues, intended or otherwise.

As indicated above, leaders of AD units (and their colleagues) have commitments, in various measure: to research, colleagues, university leaders, politicians, funders, students and university administrators. They must balance resources of time, money, expertise and space to answer to accountability logics common in twenty-first-century universities, including being transparent, reacting to government policies and using an economic/legal rationale. As the leader at Tromsø put it:

The workload and the feeling that we are running to deliver courses – and the pressure is increasing, and because of the workload you lose empowerment and you try to deliver what you are expected to. You need to prove your activity and also your existence by delivering courses.

There is obvious tension if not direct conflict between the logic of responsibility and accountability. Responsibility requires the courage and capacity to enact proactively, where leaders of AD units broker among institutional leaders, policy agenda and their own professional commitments to research, whereas the logic of accountability expects leaders of units to be loyal and react to top-down decisions that may restrictive, thus preventing them from doing what they believe is necessary to maintain their professional integrity, in this instance, by doing research. To cope in such circumstances, the leaders of the AD units must remain true to their professional responsibilities, including their autonomy, judgement and standards. As they make decisions about how to use their resources to ensure higher education as and for public good, ADs have to consider both the logics of professional responsibility and accountability, and how to negotiate with themselves and with their colleagues to find compromises that they consider legitimate in specific circumstances.

Concluding reflections: leading in webs of commitments for public good

Contemporary universities increasingly privilege an ethos of measurement to verify high-quality teaching and pedagogy in pursuit of competitive advantage in a global higher education market (Spence, 2019). However, relying too heavily on an entrepreneurial orientation and the economic rationale embedded in the accountability logic runs the considerable risk that the moral and social commitments of making higher education a public good are compromised (Sugrue et al., 2019; Walker, 2018). As ADs are expected to take a leading role in developing new strategies to promote high-quality teaching, they are likely to struggle to find legitimate compromise between the demands of university leaders and their shared responsibilities and commitments to academic colleagues' and students' needs. Amid such competing and potentially conflicting tensions, it becomes more urgent to deliberate critically on how to negotiate legitimate compromises in an ongoing changing higher education context without compromising one's professional integrity.

The metaphor of the web of commitments we have found to be a useful means of understanding how it is possible to deal in a professionally responsible manner with the tensions manifest in the contemporary higher education landscape. The gossamer threads of our commitments are rather like our values, they "are not independent but must form a coherent system with the metaphorical concepts we live by" (Lakoff & Johnson, 1980, p. 23). However, neither commitments nor values are unbreakable, or imply "having a point of no return". We are all part of the ecology in which we work and live, and commitments may vary in intensity throughout an individual's career. Our professional selves and what we believe in, are not unshakeable, and as May (1996, p. 25) argues: "The holes in the web are as important as the strands, for the holes tell us quite a bit about how previous and adaptable to changing context a particular self is likely to be". Consequently, he maintains: "What we must do, though – and this is not an easy matter at all – is to comprehend commitments within a sea of often conflicting value orientations that exist within a single self" (ibid., p. 25).

If leading higher education has as its major purpose to promote public good, then not just ADs, but all academics, must search for and live by values and attendant strategies that they consider promote public good. In the fast-paced, more turbulent and uncertain surroundings of higher education, finding legitimate compromise to retain coherence (at least temporarily) with one's core values and commitments is always a work in progress, and, depending on circumstances, not something to be taken lightly or for granted.

Given the scale of the challenge, it is inappropriate that responsibilities should rest solely on individuals. Rather, we suggest a more public (collective and inclusive) deliberative conversation among all staff and students as well as other stakeholders on what public good entails, and how we may lead and develop pedagogies that encourage public good in higher education. As individual academics, we must look beyond our personal webs of commitments to avoid retreating into cocoons of our own making where we develop ritualised routines inured to the commitments of colleagues, and to the wider mandates of our respective higher education institution (Day et al., 2007). In a wider context of social media, where various platforms have become echo chambers for our own prejudices, it is even more important that we continue to deliberate openly on the importance of professional autonomy and judgement as well as professional responsibility and to do so with "civility" (Hall, 2013). Although there is no silver-bullet solution to the complex set of challenges embedded in making higher education a public good (Walker, 2018), it is necessary to deliberate and negotiate legitimate compromises on how higher education may contribute to public good.

The next part of the book takes key concepts, concerns and tensions, and documents through a series of five case studies how ADs deploy deliberative communication, as research method and pedagogy in pursuit of public good through their teaching, while simultaneously indicating just how challenging leading education is as a praxis for public good.

Notes

1 The term praxis, as elaborated in Chapter 1, brings into productive tension critical and ethical reflection, disciplinary knowledge, expertise, humanity and finesse.
2 Larry May (1996) discusses how to understand the consequences of living in a "web of commitments" in light of a person's whole life situation and which makes it necessary to reach "negotiated compromises" of multiple professional obligations and also commitments in the private sphere (Solbrekke, 2007). Following May, it is argued that compromising one's moral stances or principles does not necessarily mean that a professional

acts irresponsibly (May, 1996, p. 120). Rather, it is argued, negotiated compromises, if based on reflective awareness of core professional values, and legitimate negotiations of the multiple expectations and inevitable dilemmas at work, may be more responsible than blind loyalty to predefined codes of conduct. However, if these compromises are made without a profound commitment to professional values and knowledge, as is the case here where there is a mandate to lead higher education as and for public good, there is a risk that such compromises may become "illegitimate" solutions and irresponsible actions. While acknowledging the private dimension in ADs' lives, in this book we concentrate on the multiple demands and commitments in their work as ADs.

3   While the Bologna process (1999) was a European initiative on the part of ministers for education among the EU members at the time, in the intervening twenty years it has had influence well beyond the geographical European area.

4   It is possible also that in some institutions, perhaps where AD units are less well developed that the coercive force of central, top-down policy making is exercised through heads of departments and deans rather than ADs, in which case ADs continue to play a more horizontal role, while others engage in the vertical deliberations.

5   As Chapter 1 elaborates, within a distributed leadership perspective, all who are engaged in leading or doing teaching are enacting leadership, whether they are in formal or informal leadership roles in a university.

6   For more other published papers that draw on these data, see Fremstad et al. (2019); et al. (2019).

7   See Chapter 1 for an elaboration on the distinction between education and learning (Biesta, 2010) which is indicative of why this AD leader wants to encourage teaching that creates space for the unanticipated as important for holistic student formation (see also Sutphen and de Lange, 2015) for an elaboration on the concept of formation).

References

Becher, T., & Trowler, P. R. (2001). *Academic Tribes and Territories: Intellectual enquiry and the cultures of discipline*. Buckingham: The Society for Research into Higher Education and Open University Press.

Biesta, G. (2010). *Good Education in an Age of Measurement Ethics, Politics, Democracy*. Boulder: Paradigm Publishers.

Day, C., Sammons, P., Stobart, G., Kington, A., & Gu, Q. (2007). *Teachers Matter: Connecting Lives, Work and Effectiveness*. Maidenhead: Open University Press.

Deem, R. (2008). Producing and re/producing the global university in the 21st century: researcher perspectives and policy consequences. *Higher Education Policy*, *21*, 439–456.

Di Napoli, R. (2014). Value gaming and political ontology: between resistance and compliance in academic development. *International Journal for Academic Development*, *19* (1), 4–11.

Ekman, M., Lindgren, M. & Packendorff, J. (2018). Universities need leadership, academics need management: discursive tensions and voids in the deregulation of Swedish higher education legislation. *Higher Education*, *75*, 299–321

Ese, J. (2019). *Defending the University? Academics' reactions to managerialism in Norwegian higher education*. Doctoral thesis, Karlstad University.

European Students' Union (2011). Mission statement: https://www.esu-online.org/about/ (accessed 26 September 2019).

Freidson, E. (2001). *Professionalism: The third logic*. Cambridge: Polity Press.

Fremstad, E., Bergh, A., Solbrekke, T. D., & Fossland, T. (2019). Deliberative academic development: the potential and challenge of agency. *International Journal for Academic Development*, 1–14. doi:10.1080/1360144X.2019.1631169

Gaebel, M., Zhang, T., Bunescu, L., & Stoeber, H. (2018). *Trends 2018: Learning and teaching in the European Higher Education Area.* Report, European University Association. http s://eua.eu/resources/publications/757:trends-2018-learning-and-teaching-in-the-europea n-higher-education-area.html (accessed 26 June 2019).

Gibbs, G. (2013). Reflections on the changing nature of educational development. *International Journal for Academic Development, 18*(1), 4–14.

Hall, J. (2013). *The Importance of Being Civil: The Struggle for Political Decency.* Princeton: Princeton University Press.

Handal, G., Lycke, K. H., Mårtensson, K., Roxå, T., Skodvin, A., & Solbrekke, T. D. (2014). The role of academic developers in transforming Bologna regulations to a national and institutional context. *International Journal for Academic Development, 19*(1), 12–25.

Huberman, M. (1983). Recipes for busy kitchens: a situational analysis of routine knowledge use in schools. *Knowledge, Diffusion, Utilization, 4,* 478–510.

Karseth, B. & Solbrekke, T. D. (2010). Qualifications Frameworks: the avenue towards the convergence of European higher education? *European Journal of Education, 45*(4), 563–576.

Lakoff, G., & Johnson, M. (1980). *Metaphors We Live By.* Chicago: University of Chicago Press.

Le Bianic, T. & Svensson, L. G. (2008) European regulation of professional education: a study of documents focusing on architects and psychologists in the EU, *European Societies, 10,* 567–595.

Macfarlane, B. (2012). *Intellectual Leadership in Higher Education: Renewing the Role of the University Professor.* Abingdon: Routledge.

May, L. (1996). *The Socially Responsive Self: Social Theory and Professional Ethics.* Chicago: University of Chicago press.

Ministry of Education and Research. (2016–17). Quality culture in higher education. *Meld. St. 16.* Report to the Storting (white paper). https://www.regjeringen.no/contentassets/a ee30e4b7d3241d5bd89db69fe38f7ba/en-gb/pdfs/stm201620170016000engpdfs.pdf (accessed 26 June 2019).

Peseta, T. L. (2014). Agency and stewardship in academic development: the problem of speaking truth to power. *International Journal for Academic Development, 19*(1), 65–69.

Ravinet, P. (2008) From voluntary participation to monitored coordination: why European countries feel increasingly bound by their commitment to the Bologna Process, *European Journal of Education, 43,* 354–367.

Pinheiro, R., Geschwind, L.Hansen, H. F., & Pulkkinen (eds) (2019). *Reforms, Organizational Change and Performance in Higher Education: A comparative account from the Nordic countries,* pp. 269–298. Cham: Palgrave Macmillan Springer (eBook). https://doi.org/10. 1007/978-3-030-11738-2

Shay, J. (2011). Casualties. *Daedalus, 140*(3), 179–188.

Solbrekke, T. D. (2007). *Understanding Conceptions of Professional Responsibility.* Doctoral thesis. Universitetet i Oslo (University of Oslo).

Solbrekke, T. D., and Englund, T. 2011. Bringing professional responsibility back in. *Studies in Higher Education, 36,* 847–861.

Solbrekke, T. D., & Fremstad, E. (2018). Universitets- og høgskolepedagogers profesjonelle ansvar [Academic developers' professional responsibility]. *UNIPED, 41*(3). doi:10.18261/ issn.1893-8981. UNIPED, 41(3). doi:10.18261/issn.1893-8981

Solbrekke, T. D., & Sugrue, C. (2014). Professional accreditation of initial teacher education programmes: teacher educators' strategies – between "accountability" and "professional responsibility"? *Teachers and Teacher Education, 37,* 11–20.

Spence, C. (2019). 'Judgement' versus 'metrics' in higher education management. *Higher Education, 77,* 761–775. https://doi.org/10.1007/s10734-018-0300-z

Stensaker, B., Van der Vaart, R., Solbrekke, T. D., & Wittek, A. L. (2017). The expansion of academic development: The challenges of organizational coordination and collaboration. In B. Stensaker, G. Bilbow, L. Breslow & R. Van der Vaart (eds), *Strengthening Teaching and Learning in Research Universities: Strategies and initiatives for institutional change* (pp. 19–42). New York: Palgrave Macmillan.

Sugrue, C., Englund, T., Solbrekke, T. D., & Fossland, T. (2017). Trends in the practices of academic developers: trajectories of higher education? *Studies in Higher Education, 43*(12), 2336–2353.

Sugrue, C., Solbrekke, T. D., Bergh, A., Sutphen, M., & Fossland, T. (2019). University leaders' talk about institutional missions and academic developers' contributions. *European Educational Research Journal*, 1–17. doi:10.1177/1474904119866520

Sullivan, W. C. (2005). *Work and Integrity: The crisis and promise of professionalism in America.* San Francisco: Jossey-Bass.

Sutphen, M., & de Lange, T. (2015). What is formation? A conceptual discussion. *Higher Education Research and Development, 34*(2), 411–419.

Taylor, C. (1989). *Sources of the Self: The making of modern identity.* Cambridge: Cambridge University Press.

Walker, M. (2018). Dimensions of higher education and the public good in South Africa. *Higher Education, 76*, 555–569. doi:10.1007/s10734-017-0225-y

PART II

5

LEADING HIGHER EDUCATION

Deliberative communication as praxis and method

Tone Dyrdal Solbrekke and Ciaran Sugrue

Introduction

Part I of this book (Chapters 1–4) set out to paint a picture of dominant features of the contemporary landscape of higher education, putting on the palette issues that give a particular hue to twenty-first-century universities, and how public universities in particular grapple with these conditions as they seek to serve their publics. We indicated that the manner in which external policy expectations are interpreted by institutional leaders has consequences for how they and their university colleagues cope with and strive to uphold academic and scientific values while also coping with more entrepreneurial and bureaucratic leadership demands and institutional orientations. In Chapter 1, we identified and briefly described key concepts that we have found particularly generative in reflecting on and interrogating aspects of leading higher education as, and for, public good. In Chapter 2, we argued that given the super-complexity of contemporary higher education, and its more contested and varied possible contributions, such choices necessitate leading and teaching approaches that embrace differences and encourage deliberative communication while simultaneously working in ways that have public good in mind as well as being readily identifiable as enactment of it. Chapter 3 focused on public good, how it has metamorphosed over time as well as the manner in which it is challenged and buffeted in the contemporary higher education landscape. In Chapter 4, we advocated that leading higher education (educational leadership) requires the capacity to negotiate legitimate compromises in an increasingly demanding web of commitments, and that deliberative communication is a valuable resource as well as an approach to dealing with tensions and conflicts between different perspectives on what public good entails. In particular, we averred that contemporary governance of public institutions creates tensions between the logics of responsibility and accountability and indicated how professionally responsible educational leadership requires legitimate compromises.

In this second part of the book, you are invited to engage with the implications of the normative stance espoused in Part I and how such commitments may be lived out in practice. The focus in this part is on praxis,[1] that of five academic developers (ADs) as they grapple with and reflect upon their efforts to deploy deliberative communication as part of their pedagogical repertoire as they lead educational practices. These case studies of praxis are the substance of Chapters 6–10. We like to think that they speak in various ways to all who engage in university teaching, but also to institutional leaders, academic and administrative, as well as to politicians, policy-makers and international agencies with responsibility for, as well as influence on, the governance and orientations of higher education. We also describe the case study methodology and how deliberative communication is deployed as a research approach.

Leading is teaching and teaching is leading in a web of commitments

Our approach to the investigation of educational leadership as part of ADs' work is inspired, in part, by a distributed leadership perspective. From this perspective, all academics with university teaching commitments, are leaders – whether they inhabit formal leadership roles or not (Gronn, 2018; Lumby, 2013; Youngs, 2017). Within this perspective, leading implies teaching, and teaching implies leading (Spillane 2006). Nevertheless, the nature of ADs' leading and teaching responsibilities differs from that of other academics since its focus is academic development for staff rather than teaching students. Nevertheless, their commitment to providing higher education as public good for all students is shared in common. ADs' teaching commitment comprises pedagogical courses, increasingly a requirement for newly appointed academics, and consultancy work, in which they are assigned the specific responsibility to lead processes of academic development to enhancing the quality of university teaching more broadly, working with whole teams or entire faculties. Their responsibilities serve a dual purpose, namely to make courses and consultation work a public good, while also encouraging academic colleagues to develop their teaching as public good, as well as for public good.

Understood in this manner, leading and teaching is a moral and societal responsibility, an extremely complex endeavour for all involved. Since both staff and students come to the university setting with different agentic capacities, needs, commitments and expectations, they necessitate leading approaches that build on situated judgements and legitimate compromises between competing and possibly conflicting needs. It requires the capacity to operationalise pedagogy enabling all participants to be included in the core activity in higher education; epistemic contributions (Walker 2018). There is neither a "quick fix" nor a "best practice" to apply to the very diverse and complex leadership and pedagogical challenges academics face in the context of contemporary higher education. With these considerations in mind, we interrogate the different cases in which ADs operationalise a normative ideal but first we indicate the methodologies employed across the cases and the approach adopted in their construction.

Deliberative communication: leading-teaching for public good

All five cases represent an individual and distinct effort on the part of an AD to practise deliberative communication as a means of leading teaching processes to nurture increased consciousness among academics of how to maintain and develop higher education as and for public good in their home institution. By documenting in detail their efforts to deploy deliberative communication as a teaching and leading pedagogy, we anticipate that this will stimulate reflections on how the praxis of making higher education a public good may also be enhanced in your own case, while simultaneously encouraging you to extend professional reflection with colleagues in a deliberative, sustained and sustainable manner. In the same spirit that Stake suggests that, regarding case studies, it is the function of the reader to generalise, we are relying on you to engage with the interstices of the cases in this part, to deliberate on their import for your leading and teaching, and to take up these pedagogical possibilities with colleagues (Stake, 1995).

The cases comprise ADs' leading-teaching practices, their experiences with and reflections on using deliberative communication as a means of leading different academic development activities. They are situated within two Swedish and two Norwegian public universities. While readily recognising how political, cultural and historical contexts institutional influence workplace conditions, we anticipate nevertheless that the "thick descriptions" in the cases will enable readers from other context to benefit from deliberative reflective engagement with their efforts (Fremstad et al., 2019). Two of the universities, Uppsala and Oslo, may be defined as more traditionally oriented public universities, while Örebro and Tromsø are more entrepreneurially oriented, according to criteria indicated in Chapter 2. Despite such different institutional orientations, common to all is their efforts to lead in a web of commitments – indicative also of the complexities of leading and teaching. Two of the cases demonstrate ADs' leading approaches in a session part of basic university pedagogy courses, and two of the cases are from a session in courses for more experienced academics. One of the cases is part of consultation work spanning two semesters. This variation provides examples of possibilities and challenges when using deliberative communication as a means of leading very different teaching situations. Attention is now turned to methodological considerations and the construction of the cases.

Deliberative communication: a research approach

While differing in design, the research approach is common to all cases inspired by the principles of deliberative communication. All cases are part of a larger international research project on the Formation and Competence Building of University Academic Developers[2] in which all contributors to this book participate.[3] This has provided us with a unique opportunity to spend time together to reflect on how to do deliberative communication in practice – and not only writing and talking about it as a normative ideal. Planning for this research initiative began in the autumn of 2015 and continued through 2016–17 thus allowing an extensive period of time in which to thoroughly discuss how to develop the cases and the research approach. Iterative deliberations on how to understand public good and deliberative communication to lead teaching for public good in practice were necessary. Living out our values and ideals in the very process of leading and teaching is challenging for all academics, not just ADs, particularly if our praxis is to be critically investigated by our peers. In the spirit of the idea of a community of practice (Wenger 1998) the process enabled us to develop enough trust to open up for our critical friends, and the courage to try out ideas in our different teaching and leading situations. We developed a collective and shared enterprise, though aware and tolerant of variation and contextual differences. This approach is consistent with socio-cultural perspectives acknowledging that practices are produced and reproduced through everyday interactions between individual agents and the changing socio-political environments in which they are immersed (Edwards, 2018; Gee, 1999; Wenger, 1998). Similarly, we adhere to theory on self-reflexive awareness and perspectives on formation and agency which emphasise the dialectic interplay between negotiations of meaning, values and norms, in the shadowed presence of influential historical legacies and traditions – global as well as institutional and local (Giddens, 1991; Shotter, 1984, Sutphen & de Lange, 2015; Taylor, 1989). Collectively, these perspectives enabled us to develop a common approach to developing the cases and the analyses of them. While descriptions of data sources, timeline and method are provided in each case study chapter, here we describe the general approach adopted.

Initiating deliberative conversations

All ten participants in the Formation project team took part in initial deliberations on the relational aspects of leading, teaching and deliberative communication as a means of fostering and promoting public good. Subsequently, teams for each case were formed based on the criteria of insider–outsider, and a mix of ADs and researchers. In each case the team consisted of the AD whose practice was to be studied and two partners who acted in a dual role, as "critical friends" (Handal, 1999) and "insider–outsider" researchers (Dwyer & Buckle, 2009).

Analysis of practice: methodological considerations

Each case developed as a collaborative process. It began with the AD developing a plan for the leading practice to be studied, including teaching approaches and how they were intended to promote public good. This document was circulated to the two critical friends who then individually and in partnership, either electronically or in face-to-face meetings, prepared for a pre-enactment conversation with the AD. In this conversation the partners engaged as critical friends, encouraging the AD's reflection by providing critical questions about the AD's intentions and how deliberative communication could be used as a means of leading the teaching practice to be studied. This phase was crucial in order to increase the AD's awareness of his/her role as leading education and promoting deliberative communication as a way of enhancing education as, and for, public good. In light of this feedback conversation in which we all aimed at living out a deliberative attitude, the AD edited the plan and re-sent it to the two critical friends. This document worked as a useful artefact for reflection for both the AD and the critical friends. It enabled all to sharpen the focus on what to observe from a data analysis perspective. Then the AD(s) (in one case two ADs shared the responsibility for leading the teaching situation) carried out their planned activity. This was video-recorded and distributed among the individual team members.

Data analysis: individual and collective

The video was then individually reviewed by the two critical friends who now wore the "hats" of researchers. The recorded practice of the AD was now the "research object". The researchers individually initiated a preliminary analysis of the video focused on what the AD(s) had defined as the main aim with their practice. This was followed by another conversation between the two researchers on their observations. The specific intention of this conversation was to identify questions that would enable them to engage with the AD on his/her intentions and the extent to which these were evident in the practice (video evidence). In particular, the two researchers sought out specific sequences in which deliberative communication was initiated and practiced to varying degrees. Thereafter, the two researchers and the AD(s) met (either physically or virtually) to have a post-action conversation. All three (in one case four) watched sequences of the video that the researchers had identified as being significant. The intention was to encourage self-reflection on the part of the AD(s) on his/her/their experiences in a deliberative manner. The aim was to support the AD(s) in becoming more aware of his/her formation as a leader of educational processes, and whether his/her/ pedagogical approaches contributed to public good or not. Additionally, the potential of deliberative communication was critically scrutinised among the critical friends and the AD(s). This conversation which was also recorded became an important data source for the succeeding reflection on their respective praxis. This collective conversation was followed by individual reflection notes on individual experiences from an AD perspective, a critical friend and a researcher perspective.

Trustworthiness of the research on our own praxes

The analytical lens deployed in order to interrogate the relational aspects between orientations of public universities and leading education for public good in webs of commitments has emerged in a process of deliberative and iterative communication among the authors of this book. The validation of the case study is ensured using an insider–outsider approach (Dwyer and Buckle, 2009) actively combined with an abductive approach using "reflexive interpretation" (Alvesson and Sköldberg 2000, p. 247) and deliberative communication. The insider–outsider approach ensured important contextual insight, yet also the necessary critical distance when preparing, conducting, and analysing the cases (Dwyer & Buckle, 2009; Sutphen, Sugrue & Solbrekke, 2018). To cater for the insider's bias and also to enable or facilitate the surfacing of internal tensions and politics concerning the role and actions of ADs (Hanson, 2013), the outsider's role as critical friend and researcher was essential. The person inhabiting the outsider role was able to keep a more distanced stance and ask naïve and possibly more challenging questions during the conversations. Other research carried out within the frame of the Formation project also provided useful insights into the different contexts in which the five cases are carried out.[4] The abductive approach allowed us to adapt methodologically and alter our interpretations of data alongside reading scholarly texts and research literature.

Community of praxis: deliberation and legitimate compromise

Throughout all phases of developing and analysing the cases, we committed to practising deliberative communication in the interaction with each other as ADs and researchers. We have challenged each other's stances and understandings iteratively in ways that brought us to a shared interpretation of data, while simultaneously gaining new insights into the benefits and challenges of doing international and interdisciplinary research on our own praxes. We have learnt about how difficult it may be to be open and willing to respect and tolerate conflicting perspectives on what is "good" research. We have experienced challenging and difficult negotiations to reach shared meanings of core concepts such as "leading as, and for, public good", "web of commitments", "legitimate compromise", "deliberative communication – and dispositions". Through these shared experiences over time, we have learned to appreciate more that if leading higher education as and for public good requires legitimate compromises in a web of commitments, so too does international research collaboration.

Nevertheless, our experience is that while epistemological and ontological variations may promote challenging conflicts, through returning to reflection on the principles of deliberative communication we have managed to reach legitimate compromises on how to move the work forward. We have also benefited greatly from the epistemic contributions of the team – ADs and researchers. Since members inhabit both insider and outsider roles in relation to each other, we have come to appreciate and recognise that the quality of both the analyses of the data and the writing of the cases have benefited. Being alert to the promoted ideals of deliberative communication and an abductive reflexive research approach, we developed a writing process for the book where, as partners, we engaged in each other's chapters through arranging workshops and feedback seminars to provide and receive feedback on texts in a structured yet in as open and deliberative manner as possible (Dysthe, Hertzberg & Hoel, 2010). Such processes helped us not to close interpretations of what we identified in the different cases too early. It also allowed us to refine the analytical lenses until the final writing and editing of chapters. It was advantageous that the project team included researchers and ADs from different countries and with disciplinary backgrounds from history, religion, sociology and pedagogy; a valuable resource in the writing process. While challenging and sometimes difficult, the collaborative writing has contributed new insights into the roles and responsibilities of ADs as contributing to public good through their work as leaders of academic development. The approach taken: beginning with a normative ideal and seeking to imbue our actions with it through deliberation and reflection on our experiences individually and collectively we are enabled to become more aware of our praxis. In doing so, we have greater awareness of and insight into the manner in which the values that underpin our praxis become an important influence on how we navigate our respective webs of commitments in ways that allow for legitimate compromises to be negotiated. While no missionary zeal is intended, we entertain the prospect that your engagement with the cases will be more than a momentary spark to your own deliberations on your praxis.

Notes

1 We have indicated in Chapter 1 how we use the term praxis. Here, it is appropriate to connect praxis with Habermas's notion of communicative action. As Dunne (1993, p. 194) points out: "the distinctions and relations between theory and practice have always been Habermas's central concern: what has particularly characterised his philosophy – and introduced the biggest strain into it – has been an attempt to protect the integrity of practice and *at the same time* not to foreshorten or dilute the claims of theory" (italics original). Communicative action is his means of pursuing "legitimate compromise" between theory and practice – reflecting as well as altering in certain ways Aristotle's sense of the term praxis.

2 The cases we benefit from in this book are all part of a larger international research and competence building project; Formation and Competence Building of University Academic Developers. The project (project number 246745/H20) was funded by the Norwegian Research Council from 1 September 2015 to 31 May 2020. To read more about this project, which involves academic developers and researchers from six public comprehensive universities in Norway, Sweden, Ireland and the USA, see: http:// www.uv.uio.no/iped/english/research/projects/solbrekke-formation-and-competence-building/. The project is approved by the Norwegian Centre for Research Data and all the individual institutions. Interviews and video-recordings are stored in TSD, Services for Sensitive Data, provided by the University of Oslo and accessed only by the project participants. No potential conflict of interest was reported by the project participants or colleagues who voluntarily participated in sessions that have been video-recorded.

3 Four of the project participants inhabited a triple role, both as practising AD, leader of AD units, and as a researcher in higher education. Three wore two hats, AD and researcher, while three of the participants have no experience as ADs, but are experienced researchers in the field of educational leadership and pedagogy. This mix turned out to be very productive as it challenged all ADs to become more explicit about their work, and contributed highly to reflections on formation and own praxis. The researchers without AD experience developed new insight into the world of academic development and the complex roles and responsibilities of ADs in public universities.

4 Publications that we benefit from particularly are on international trends and trajectories of the roles and responsibilities of ADs in the current landscape of higher education (Sugrue, Solbrekke, Englund and Fossland, 2017); the role of strategic plans (Sutphen,

Solbrekke and Sugrue, 2018); dominant orientations of the different universities and institutional leadership approaches (Sugrue et al., 2019); ADs' own descriptions of and experiences with work in local geographical contexts (Solbrekke and Fremstad 2018; Fremtad et al. 2019).

References

Alvesson, M., & Skölberg, K. (2000). *Reflexive Methodology: New Vistas for Qualitative Research*. London: Sage Publications.

Bolden, R. (2011). Distributed leadership in organisations. *International Journal of Management Reviews*, 13(3), 251–269

Dunne, J. (1993). *Back to the Rough Ground 'Phronesis' and 'Techne' in Modern Philosophy and in Aristotle*. Notre Dame: University of Notre Dame Press.

Dwyer, S. C., & Buckle, J. L. (2009). The space between: on being an insider–outsider in qualitative research. *International Journal of Qualitative Methods*, 8(1), 54–63.

Dysthe, O., Hertzberg, F., & Hoel, T. L. (2010). *Å skrive for å lære. [Writing to learn] forlag.* Oslo: Abstrakt Forlag.

Edwards, A. (2018). Agency, common knowledge and motive orientation: Working with insights from Hedegaard in research on provision for vulnerable children and young people. *Learning, Culture and Social Interaction*. ISSN: 2210–6561 2210–2657X; doi:10.1016/j. lcsi.2018.04.004

Fremstad, E., Bergh, A., Solbrekke, T.D., & Fossland, T. (2019). Deliberative academic development: the potential and challenge of agency. *International Journal for Academic Development*, doi:10.1080/1360144X.2019.1631169.

Gee, J. P. (1999). *An Introduction to Discourse Analysis: Theory and Method*. London: Routledge.

Giddens, A. (1991). *Modernity and Self-Identity*. Cambridge: Polity Press.

Gronn, P. (2018). Commentary silos, bunkers and their voices. In G. Lakomski, S. Eacott & C. W. Evers (eds), *Questioning Leadership New Directions for Educational Organisations* (pp. 192–201). Abingdon: Routledge.

Handal, G. (1999). Consultation using critical friends. *New Directions for Teaching & Learning*, 79, 59–70.

Hanson, J. (2013). Educational developers as researchers: the contribution of insider research to enhancing understanding of role, identity and practice . *Innovations in Education and Teaching International*, 50(4), 388–398. doi:10.1080/14703297.2013.806220

Lumby, J. (2013). Distributed leadership: the uses and abuses of power. *Educational Management Administration & Leadership*, 41(5), 581–597.

Shotter, J. (1984). *Social Accountability & Selfhood*. Oxford: Basil Blackwell.

Solbrekke, T. D., & Fremstad, E. (2018). *Universitets- og høgskolepedagogers profesjonelle ansvar.* [Academic developers' professional responsibility]. Oslo: Tidsskrift for universitets og høgskolepedagogikk.

Spillane, J. (2006). *Distributed Leadership*. San Francisco: Jossey Bass.

Stake, B. (1995). *The Art of Case Study Research*. London: Sage Publications.

Sugrue, C., Englund, T., Solbrekke, T. D. & Fossland, T. (2017). Trends in the practices of academic developers: trajectories of higher education? *Studies in Higher Education*, 43(12), 2336–2353. doi:0.1080/03075079.2017.1326026

Sugrue, C., Solbrekke, T. D., Bergh, A., Sutphen, M., & Fossland, T. (2019). University leaders' talk about institutional missions and academic developers' contributions. *European Educational Research Journal*, 18(6), 1–17. doi:10.1177/1474904119866520

Sutphen, M., & de Lange, T. (2015). What is formation? A conceptual discussion. *Higher Education Research and Development*, *34*(2), 411–419.

Sutphen, M., Solbrekke, T. D., & Sugrue, C. (2018). Toward articulating an academic praxis by interrogating university strategic plans. *Studies in Higher Education*, *44*(8), 1400–1412. doi:10.1080/03075079.2018.1440384

Taylor, C. (1989). *Sources of the Self: The Making of Modern Identity*. Cambridge: Cambridge University Press.

Walker, E. (2018). Dimensions of higher education and the public good in South Africa. *Higher Education*, *76*, 555–569. https://doi.org/10.1007/s10734-017-0225-y

Wenger, E. (1998). *Communities of Practice. Learning, Meaning, and Identity*. Cambridge: Cambridge University Press.

Youngs, H. (2017). A critical exploration of distributed leadership in higher education: developing an alternative ontology through leadership-as-practice. *Journal of Higher Education Policy and Management*, *39*(2), 140–154. doi:10.1080/1360080X.2017.1276662

6

INTELLECTUAL VIRTUES FOR LEADING HIGHER EDUCATION

Molly Sutphen, Tomas Englund and Kristin Ewins

Introduction

Notions about a university's contributions to a public good are embedded liberally throughout their strategic plans. The plans express a university's purpose and hopes to contribute to a future public good (Sutphen, Solbrekke & Sugrue, 2018). Virtues are other tropes we can find in the public documents of universities, such as curiosity and a passion for knowledge. We can also hear these tropes when Svein Stølen (2019), the University of Oslo's Rector, explained his university's purpose to graduates as a "drive to understand, explain, find answers and solutions is at the heart of the university's activities and in all education. And the best part is that this joy of finding things is the most important prerequisite for creating a better society."

Recently discussions about curiosity or courage, and other virtues have begun to creep out of speeches by rectors and glossy university publications to migrate to the current literature on the state of the university. It is about time. The shift of focus is an opportunity for researchers of higher education to consider how to align the claims in strategic plans for how universities contribute to a public good with the practices of academics who work in webs of commitments (see Chapter 3 and May, 1996). As Karlsohn (2018) notes, virtues and emotions, such as courage and hope, are part of the work in, on and of universities. Bengtsen and Barnett (2017) find that because of the current darkness in higher education, courage and hope are necessary for and in higher education. Baehr (2013) has argued that the purpose of higher education is to cultivate intellectual virtues of open-mindedness, courage, curiosity and honesty. Such virtues are those many academics use day in and day out, and they constitute attempts to form universities as a public good and for a public good (Walker, 2018).

This chapter lays out how the use of deliberative communication (Englund, 2006) can be a resource for bringing to light intellectual virtues and/or epistemic values that academics may not realise they possess, or acknowledge that they need

(Barnett, 2009; Palmer, 2011). We propose deliberative communication as a way for academic staff and leaders to articulate the intellectual virtues they draw on as they find legitimate compromises within their webs of commitments. In the midst of deliberative communication participants reflect on their biases, which may be an opportunity to engage in curiosity, humility and other intellectual virtues. In addition, deliberative communication can help participants clarify their praxes, or the ways in which they live out their values. Deliberative communication requires that one be open to the views of others and may be enacted by recognising each other's vulnerabilities. Or the courage to take intellectual risks is another virtue that may be facilitated or encouraged by the use of deliberative communication.

In this chapter, we focus on the use of deliberative communication in teaching and research because both are relevant for academic staff in their daily work, regardless of discipline or university. We will detail how conversations and reflection prompt participants to recognise their own and each other's intellectual virtues. We seek to answer two questions: How might ADs use deliberative communication to provide colleagues with opportunities for collective and individual reflection on intellectual virtues they have? Furthermore, is this a general approach that has potential for everyone, including leaders, in the university community?

We present two instances of using deliberative communication, one in a teaching situation and the other one in our research group meetings. Deliberative communication renders recognition to intellectual virtues that can in turn help advance full personhood, which Walker (2018) writes is integral to a vision of public good. To advance full personhood depends on relationships that contribute both to one's formation and to the collective project of universities for a public good. We have divided the chapter into four sections. First, we discuss further the two concepts at the heart of this chapter: deliberative communication as a reflective practice and the concept of intellectual virtue in higher education. Second, we briefly detail our methods to show how deliberative communication was used in the classroom and research meetings. Third, we present an example of using deliberative communication to show how participants engage with intellectual virtues. In the final section we speculate on the opportunities and limitations of using deliberative communication in higher education to bring to the surface virtues one uses or might need.

Concepts

Deliberative communication offers conditions wherein participants agree to have or try out a set of dispositions, including a willingness to reflect on one's biases or "blind spots"; to engage in collective will-formation; and to be open to the views of others. It is a form of communication based on the principles of John Dewey and Jürgen Habermas, and developed by Englund (2006). As Chapter 2 notes, deliberative communication's purpose is to create conditions for participants to reflect on a problem or situation and be used for a public good.

We suggest that deliberative communication provides opportunities for participants to reflect on intellectual virtues they possess or witness. Intellectual virtues are those characteristics that Roberts and Wood (2007, p. 59) define as "an acquired base of excellent functioning in some generically human sphere of activity that is challenging and important". Although there is currently a lively debate among virtue epistemologists about how to define intellectual virtue (Baehr, 2011; Pritchard, 2013; Watson, 2016; Battaly 2017), we are interested in how deliberative communication may provide opportunities to identify and enact intellectual virtues. We draw on Baehr for our definition. Intellectual virtue:

> is fundamentally rooted in a deep and abiding desire for knowledge and understanding ... [T]his fundamental motivation tends to spawn a range of more specific characteristics or virtues, including intellectual courage, diligence, determination, perseverance, ingenuity, and resourcefulness ...[T]he aim or goal of intellectual virtue is relatively broad in scope, that is, that an intellectually virtuous person is characteristically curious about a rather wide range of ideas and subject matters.
>
> *(Baehr, 2011, pp. 5–6)*

Furthermore, we agree with Baehr (2013) who argues that the cultivation of courage and several other intellectual character virtues – curiosity, open-mindedness and honesty – is the right aim of higher education.

In this chapter we focus on the virtue of intellectual courage, in part because it is a virtue that others also put front and centre in their discussions on the meaning and purpose of higher education and its role in civil society (Palmer, 2007; Palmer, Zajonc and Scribner, 2010; Barnett, 2018).

Methods

Deliberative communication is a practice that asks participants to reflect both individually and collectively. We followed an approach common to the other authors, as described in the introduction to Part II of the book, and used an abductive and reflexive insider–outsider approach inspired by the principles of deliberative communication. In our case, we used collective reflection on a course on pedagogy for academic staff at Örebro University in Sweden and during several meetings with researchers and the academic developer (AD) responsible for the course on pedagogy. The individual reflection studied is that of the authors in two different roles. One role was taken up by the AD who reflected on her use of deliberative communication in one of her course sessions. The AD and four critical friends engaged in a series of pre- and post-teaching conversations, during which the critical friends used deliberative communication to study the AD's teaching, pose questions, reflect collectively and give suggestions. Thus all used deliberative communication and reflected individually and collectively. The critical friends included a researcher from the same institution as the AD and three researchers from different universities. Throughout the process, all wrote research logs and email communications. The AD wrote her research memos and emails from her perspective as an AD trying out deliberative communication in courses for academic staff. The critical friends also wrote theirs on the process of using deliberative communication in a course session and for discussions on deliberative communication. All four critical friends also wrote reflections on what they learned throughout the research on the uses of deliberative communication.

The context for the case

The AD is relatively new to Örebro University and to academic development, having shifted from English literature to the field in 2013. Not only was she new to academic development and Swedish universities, she was new to leadership of a

TABLE 6.1 Methods and data sources

Event	What took place; who participated; and types of data sources generated	How data sources were used by critical friends
Spring 2017	AD decides on the course in which to try out deliberative communication and tells critical friends Data source(s): Notes, course documents	To prepare for observation
Fall 2017	AD and critical friends discuss AD's plans. AD uses deliberative communication in a course session with one critical friend present. AD and critical friends discuss course session Data sources(s): Notes and video recording	To find themes and examples of themes of using deliberative communication for research and teaching
Winter 2018	AD reflects on 2017 course meeting and decides to treat it as a pilot. AD discusses with critical friends and all agree that AD will teach another course session with deliberative communication with 15–17 participants from several disciplines. Data sources(s): Notes	To analyse the uses of deliberative communication for individual and collective critical reflection
Spring 2018	AD uses deliberative communication in a second course session with 5–7 participants from several disciplines. Critical friends watch digital recording of course meeting at least twice and list themes. AD and critical friends discuss AD's experiences teaching the course session Data sources(s): Video recording of course session; notes	To find themes and examples of themes of for research and teaching. To analyse the uses of deliberative communication for individual and collective critical reflection
Fall 2018	AD and critical friends answer a series of questions that invited individual reflection on our experiences over the course of the planning, implementation, and reflection on the AD's teaching sessions Data sources(s): Completed questionnaire	To analyse the uses of deliberative communication for individual and collective critical reflection

newly established unit for academic development. She first incorporated deliberative communication in a course session in autumn 2017 with two groups of 15–17 participants. She based her teaching on an exercise she had used previously in courses with academic staff, though she adapted the exercise to deliberative communication for the context of her teaching. The course, entitled Supervising Research Students, was designed for advanced researchers who currently supervise research students or who hope to do so in the future. It is held twice a year, in Swedish in the autumn and in English in the spring. It consists of six full days of presentations, seminars and workshops with an estimated additional 65 hours of self-study, for a total of about 110 hours. On the second day of the course, participants are asked to reflect on two documents on Swedish doctoral education that the AD introduced by noting that course participants would find differences in relation to 1) the aim of a doctoral thesis (social good or individual growth) and 2) the agency of the doctoral student.

The AD provided the course participants with the following prompt for their discussion:

> In this session, we're going to practise a method for collegial learning, deliberative communication, with the purpose of responding to the question: What is PhD education (good) for? So deliberative communication as a model provides concrete steps for achieving open and equal discussion among participants in a group. And as such it's a useful model for working with PhD students in different constellations. It is also a good mode of communication for learning. And by public good I mean what is good for us communally, from the perspective, not of the individual, but society. What is the PhD for, from a social or civic perspective? That is, what good do PhD theses do to a society? And what good do PhD (students) do? You may, of course, find that the private and public good intersect in (many) places.

The AD's handout also provided the academic staff in her two courses with the following description of deliberative communication, published by one of the critical friends (Englund, 2006):

a Different views are set against each other and arguments for each are presented.
b There is tolerance and respect for the "specific other" and participants learn to listen to the other person's argument.
c Elements of collective will-formation are present, in other words an endeavour to reach consensus or at least to reach temporary agreements while also acknowledging and drawing attention to differences.
d Authorities and/or traditional views may be questioned and there are opportunities to challenge one's own tradition.
e There is encouragement for students to communicate and deliberate both inside and outside of the formal course, in other words: argumentative discussions between students aiming to solve problems or shed light on issues from different viewpoints is encouraged in a range of contexts.

(Course handout, April 2018)

The AD chose to try out deliberative communication in the session entitled "What is PhD education (good) for?" because, as she noted in a pre-seminar conversation with her critical friends: "The topic to be discussed often raises animated debate that, and this is my contention, could usefully be deepened by using deliberative communication as [a] pedagogical vehicle. The topic itself is intimately concerned with questions of public good" (AD communication to critical friends, August, 2017).

However, she reported that for "practical/logistical reasons", it was difficult to use deliberative communication with 15–17 participants. "It was especially challenging," she noted, "to encourage participation by all" (written reflection by AD in December, 2018). She decided, after reflection on her own and discussions with her critical friends, to teach deliberative communication to another cohort and reduce the group size to 5–7. The AD considered the autumn 2017 session to be a pilot and found it to be an advantage to use the pilot as a guide for organising the spring 2018 session. For the course meeting in spring 2018, the AD used the same reading materials and instructions to the participants as she did in the autumn meeting. Based on her reflection on the difficulties of engaging all the participants in the autumn session, she then taught the same session in the spring term, this time with a different cohort and 5–7 participants.

Deliberative communication and courage

The purpose of the following is to focus on the opportunities that deliberative communication offer for structured self-reflection and reflection in a group. We present the use of deliberative communication to illustrate its potential for a type of reflection that can reveal to participants values and character traits that are important to them; in short what they hold dear. When we analysed the data, we found different examples of courage, an intellectual character virtue that the authors prize and consider important for the public good. Courage – and vulnerability were evident through the use of deliberative communication in the AD's course meetings and in research discussions we had before and after the course meetings.

During post-teaching conversations after the autumn 2017 session, the AD provided an example of intellectual courage that emerged from individual and group reflection.

She demonstrated the virtue by being willing first to share her doubts with her critical friends about the autumn 2017 session, specifically how she interacted with participants in her courses. In light of her relatively new position in academic development and as a leader of an academic development unit, it is possible that she felt vulnerable about sharing her doubts, which in turn underscores the courage she showed by acknowledging that the approach did not work. As she put it: "What I found though, on reflection, was that the discussion meandered too much and it lacked the energy that I often inject into the group" (written reflection by AD in December, 2018). She might have felt that she would lose her critical friends' respect for her teaching and leadership abilities. She explained to her critical friends that in her courses, she worried that she too readily jumps into discussions. No matter how accomplished, prepared or experienced the academic, it is rare that first attempts to expand a pedagogical repertoire go as hoped. The AD persisted and modified her approach, evidence of both the virtue of courage and her commitment to her teaching. The AD planned to teach the session again and be video recorded so that her colleagues could pore over it to analyse her teaching.

Despite her misgivings about repeating the session, the AD focused on what was best for the participants, as well as the improvement of her own teaching and the research goals. As she put it, she was deliberately stepping "back to enable a freer discussion among the participants" (reflection by AD in December, 2018). With fewer participants, it was easier for her colleagues to follow how the participants used deliberative communication. She noted that one of her goals was to allow the group to engage more than before and "to find a balance in my own role in facilitating the discussion. In the past I have often gone in too forcefully and taught in a way where my own standpoints – perhaps – a little too explicit?" (written reflection by AD in December, 2018). The AD's comment suggests that, as a course facilitator, one of her values is to step back and allow participants more of a role in discussions. In turn, the AD interprets this experience with deliberative communication to be an opportunity to take time with colleagues willing to explore her praxis, which in this case means how connected her values are with her actions. To use May's term (1996), part of the AD's web of commitments in her teaching is to allow participants to develop their stances on a topic rather than give her own (see Chapter 4 for more on webs of commitments and negotiated legitimate compromises). She engages in a negotiation with herself to find a compromise, where she facilitates a discussion without dominating it.

The AD hints at a sense of self-consciousness in her use of deliberative communication to study her practice, or as she noted when she reflected on the 2018 spring session: "I was very conscious of my own position in the discussion, of playing an important part in the group, without driving the discussion too intensely and thus preventing participants from fully engaging and expressing their thoughts" (written reflection by AD in December, 2018). The AD also expresses self-consciousness, even vulnerability, in her introduction to the participants in the spring 2018 session. As she explained why the session was organised as it was, she noted: "I've randomly selected one group for a filmed discussion, which I'll join. I've been in touch with those in that group and the material will be used in the project but really to study my formation as an academic developer; quite uncomfortable, but very useful!" (course handout, spring 2018). During the class session, she reinforces her sense of discomfort as she starts the session with the comment: "I'll chip in (break of several seconds) if it feels like a good idea" (video recording of class session, April 2018).

The AD's remark underscores her goal of stepping back and not jumping in to the discussion but letting it flow. To reach her goal, she must weigh whether "it feels like a good idea" in the moment and not rely on a detailed plan for when she will discuss what during the class meeting. So too during deliberative communication: conversations must be open-ended to allow for self-reflection and self-questioning as well as listening to others' points of view. Because academics report that they are overworked and have little time, an open-ended discussion can seem to be a luxury. It takes courage to invite academics to an unstructured conversation, where one challenges one's beliefs as they arise, instead of moving down a list of bullet points and arguing one's corner about each point. It all depends on the context for using or not deliberative communication.

The AD facilitated the sessions according to the premises of deliberative communication, which she had given to participants. She provided her students with documents espousing different views and asked them to compare them. She gently and repeatedly asked participants to engage more with the texts by saying, for example, "I want to push you more" or "provoke you" (video recording of class session, April 2018). In reflecting upon the session, she noted that her approach "built on a strength I have had also in the past of playfully, yet sharply, challenging participants on their assumptions, thus stimulating discussion and exchange between participants" (reflection by AD in December, 2018). In doing so, participants argued about the different views presented, and one admitted that they had changed their mind during the session.

Soon after the AD finished teaching the spring 2018 session, she and her critical friends met face-to-face in May 2018 and attempted to use deliberative communication to discuss the teaching sessions and conversations. In line with one of the premises of deliberative communication, different views were set against each other and arguments for each presented. In this instance, tensions within the research group were evident. The AD considered the tensions to have arisen in the course of deciding to treat the session in autumn 2017 as a pilot:

> I wouldn't say that all the discussions that preceded the [face-to-face meeting in May 2018] went that smoothly, but even through the more challenging conversations, I learnt a lot from having to set appropriate boundaries and standing up for myself as a professional. And despite the friction, I got some valuable feedback on how to organise the intervention itself. Just the fact of having to explain to a critical friend what I wanted to do helped me formulate my aims and intentions more clearly than I'd have been able to do on my own.
>
> *(Written reflection by AD in December 2018)*

During the face-to-face conversation in May 2018, the AD pointed out that she judges herself harshly and assumes when a conversation is difficult or contentious, she must be deferential, and it was by way of the conversation the AD and her critical friends had on deference that the topic of courage emerged. As one of the critical friends reflected after the conversation:

> What struck me was when [the AD] disagreed with one of the critical friends, she stood her ground, with both feet sound and firm. She also had the experience of not deferring or demurring when a conversation with her critical friends became testy.
>
> *(Written reflection by critical friend in December 2018)*

Several months later in December 2018, the AD and critical friends addressed the question "What was most fruitful for your learning?" in regards to teaching or using deliberative communication. The AD replied that between the autumn 2017 and spring 2018 sessions, she had found "an appropriate role for me as AD/teacher in the [spring 2018 class] discussion. From the second attempt, I learnt to adjust my practice." She goes on to say:

> The discussions with my critical friends helped me see my strengths as AD and my work with the academics more clearly. This was hugely valuable in more fairly assessing my role in the teaching context, … [and] has given me more confidence and self-insight and also helped me see the short-comings of the pilot in less self-punishing terms.
>
> *(Written reflection by AD in December 2018)*

Further, she reflected that the experiences have helped her "in a very concrete way" with a task she had to undertake in her academic development work. She explained that "I knew the task would only work if I really believed in it, and in my ability to carry it out, and I felt a new strength in holding my own during the task that really helped with the learning outcomes for the group" (written reflection by AD in December 2018). Despite feeling vulnerable, the AD had the courage to risk not only to try using deliberative communication in her course, but to be open to public scrutiny by her critical friends.

The AD's experience of teaching both sessions with deliberative communication and its use in the course of conversations with her critical friends became a guide for her subsequent work, so too with her critical friends. When using deliberative communication in our conversations, we made many references to structured self-reflection both in connection with deliberative communication and not. Although it is hard to say whether we made these references because each of us tried to use deliberative communication, and we saw the role of self-reflection everywhere, or we actually became more self-reflective and thus saw ways of becoming even more so. For example, one of her critical friends remarked:

> My interactions with the AD led me to reflect on the role of courage needed as an AD (and many other areas of academia), courage not to defer, especially when a difficult conversation involves differences in perspectives because of age, genders and temperament.
>
> *(Written reflection by critical friend in December 2018)*

Deliberative communication and intellectual virtues

The AD's willingness to share her reflections led us to consider intellectual courage, which she demonstrated in two different arenas common in academia: her teaching and in the course of research discussions. Deliberative communication is central o both situations, and we suggest that it offers participants opportunities to practice as well as to cultivate intellectual virtues. To return to the approach to deliberative communication that is advocated in chapter two, we find several intellectual virtues that Baehr (2013) has argued are at the heart of the purpose of higher education. According to Baehr, the intellectual virtues are: open-mindedness; courage; curiosity, and honesty, all of which are demanded of participants who attempt to use deliberative communication (see Table 5.2).

In one form or another, those who engage in deliberative communication enact intellectual virtues. Such virtues are of value for academics as they work in a web of commitments and try to reach negotiated legitimate compromises (see Chapter 3). Part of deliberative communication is to participate in self and collective reflection, which provides opportunities to learn how to or have the capacities to: Be open to the views and beliefs of others; curious about why one or another takes the stance they do; and honest about one's biases and beliefs. The AD and critical friends were willing to try out each of these behaviours in order to improve their capacities to reflect. In turn, these are virtues that can aid academics to make legitimate compromises when faced with competing commitments.

Concluding remarks

We have outlined how deliberative communication might be used in a course setting as well as for research meetings, arguing that opportunities for self-reflection and reflection in a group can be resources for individual and group discernment of intellectual virtues. The experiences of the AD in this chapter clarify how deliberative communication can be a resource, as a pedagogy, for those new to leading higher education or who have not considered what they do as leading. The AD

TABLE 6.2 Deliberative communication and intellectual virtues

Deliberative communication	Baehr's intellectual virtues
Different views are set against each other and arguments for each are presented	Open-mindedness, curiosity
There is tolerance and respect for the "specific other" and participants learn to listen to the other person's argument	Open-mindedness and curiosity
Elements of collective will-formation are present, in other words an endeavour to reach consensus or at least to reach temporary agreements while also acknowledging and drawing attention to differences	Honesty and courage
Authorities and/or traditional views may be questioned and there are opportunities to challenge one's own tradition	Courage, open-mindedness and honesty
Argumentative discussions between students aiming to solve problems or shed light on issues from different viewpoints is encouraged in a range of contexts, including outside of formal courses	Open-mindedness and curiosity

used the individual and collective practices of deliberative communication to find ways for her to change her teaching and receive feedback from her colleagues. For academics both to change teaching approaches, even if they consider the change will improve their teaching, and to receive feedback from colleagues require courage. In the example from this chapter, deliberative communication can be an especially important resource for a new, relatively young, female leader in one of her courses. However, it can also be used in many other situations, such as when the chair of a faculty uses it with her colleagues to solve problems that affect all. Or, when the merger of a unit with another is discussed, or when there is an increase or reduction in resources. Deliberative communication can also be a means to give feedback to a colleague who needs to make changes in their approaches to their work.

We suggest further that deliberative communication is a resource both to articulate one's beliefs and biases and to enact intellectual virtues of courage, open-mindedness and honesty. Although there is no guarantee that through deliberative communication academics will solve thorny problems, whether they be those deciding on who should be first author on a journal article, or problems that affect all academics at a university. For example, as politicians increase pressures for universities to prepare students for jobs that will contribute to short-term economic concerns, not all university leaders and academic staff are willing to heed their calls for education to be an instrument of national or local economies. Deliberative communication offers opportunities for academics, staff and students to engage in sustained discussions on their own and their colleagues' discernment of their values and goals for the education of students. Some may consider contributions to national and or local economies to be sufficient, while others may consider other types of contributions that students and academic staff make as citizens. We hold that students who are invited to learn to practise deliberative communication may take full advantage of opportunities for identifying and articulating the intellectual virtues they would like to embody long after they graduate. For leaders of higher education and academic staff deliberative communication is a bulwark against instrumental arguments for what it means for universities to contribute to a public good.

References

Baehr, J. (2011). *The Inquiring Mind: On Intellectual Virtues and Virtue Epistemology*. Oxford: Oxford University Press. http://www.oxfordscholarship.com/view/10.1093/acprof:oso/9780199604074.001.0001/acprof-9780199604074- Chapter 1.

Baehr, J. (2013). Educating for intellectual virtues: from theory to practice. *Journal of Philosophy of Education*, 47(2): 248–262.

Barnett, R. (2009). Knowing and becoming in the higher education curriculum. *Studies in Higher Education*, 34(4), 429–440. doi:10.1080/03075070902771978.

Barnett, R. (2018). The thinking university: two versions, rival and complementary. In S. Bengtsen & R. Barnett (eds), *The Thinking University. Debating Higher Education: Philosophical Perspectives*, vol. 1. Cham: Springer.

Battaly, H. (2017). Intellectual perseverance. *Journal of Moral Philosophy*, 14(6), 669–697. doi:10.1163/17455243-46810064.

Bengtsen, S. & Barnett, R. (2017). Confronting the dark side of higher education. *Journal of Philosophy of Education, 51*(1), 114–131.

Englund, T. (2006). Deliberative communication: a pragmatist proposal. *Journal of Curriculum Studies, 38*(5): 503–520.

Karlsohn T. (2018). Bildung, emotion and thought. In S. Bengtsen & R. Barnett (eds), *The Thinking University: Debating Higher Education: Philosophical Perspectives*, vol 1. Cham: Springer.

May, L. (1996). *The Socially Responsive Self: Social Theory and Professional Ethics*. Chicago: University of Chicago Press.

Pritchard, D. (2013). Epistemic virtue and the epistemology of education. *Journal of the Philosophy of Education, 47*, 236–247. doi:10.1111/1467-9752.12022.

Palmer, P. (2007). *The Courage to Teach: Exploring the Inner Landscape of a Teacher's Life* (2nd edn). San Francisco: Jossey-Bass.

Palmer, P. (2011). Higher education and habits of the heart: restoring democracy's infrastructure, *Journal of College and Character, 12*(3). doi:10.2202/1940–1639.1823.

Palmer, P., Zajonc, A., & Scribner, M. (2010). *The Heart of Higher Education: A Call to Renewal: Transforming the Academy through Collegial Conversations*. San Francisco: Jossey-Bass.

Roberts, R. and Wood, J. (2007). *Intellectual Virtues: An Essay in Regulative Epistemology*. Oxford: Clarendon Press. doi:10.1093/acprof:oso/9780199283675.001.0001.

Stølen, S. (2019). @Rector Blog, March 14, 2019.@ Celebration of 138 doctoral degrees form UIO. https://www.uio.no/om/aktuelt/rektorbloggen/2019/138-nye-doktorander-fra-uio.html

Sutphen, M., Solbrekke, T., & Sugrue, C. (2018). Toward articulating an academic praxis by interrogating university strategic plans. *Studies in Higher Education*, doi:10.1080/03075079.2018.1440384.

Walker, M. (2018). Dimensions of higher education and the public good. *Higher Education, 76*, 555–569.

Watson, L. (2016). The epistemology of education. *Philosophy Compass, 11*(3): 146–159. doi:10.1111/phc3.12316.

7

DELIBERATIVE COMMUNICATION

Stimulating collective learning?

*Andreas Bergh, Tone Dyrdal Solbrekke and
Johan Wickström*

Introduction

University teaching has great potential to promote development that serves the public
good. More specifically, teaching and learning are foundations for societal and democratic development as well as for individual growth. However, while few would disagree that good teaching may empower and encourage students to engage as citizens
and take active roles in society, it is far more challenging to describe what good teaching
actually is and how it may be achieved. From this perspective, it is most relevant to
explore what can be learned from, and with, those who are assigned a leading responsibility for improving teaching in higher education: academic developers (ADs).

In this chapter, we study how an AD plans and leads a seminar in university pedagogy
on constructive alignment through the means of deliberative communication (see
Chapter 3). By deliberative communication we mean how he lets all voices be heard, and
demonstrate respect and tolerance for different perspectives, yet also how academics in
the context of contemporary public universities become aware of the necessity to reach
legitimate compromises in a web of possible contesting commitments.[1] He is particularly
concerned with engaging the participants in a critical investigation of constructive alignment, while also demonstrating how new governance and higher education quality
assurance systems, make the use of constructive alignment more problematic.

The seminar is part of the mandatory basic academic development course at Uppsala
University that all newly appointed academics are required to complete. "Constructive
alignment" is a pedagogical approach for planning student-centred teaching in higher
education with the aim of creating more structure by aligning learning outcomes, assessment and learning activities (Biggs, 1996). In recent decades, constructive alignment has
been highly influential globally; in fact, it has become so dominant that it has, indirectly,
also become the answer to what good higher education teaching actually is (Damşa & de
Lange, 2019; Fransson & Friberg, 2015; Magnússon & Rytzler, 2018).

The AD whose practice we study is wary of the strengths of constructive alignment in the design of study programmes and to facilitate students' learning (Damşa & de Lange, 2019; Larkin & Richardson, 2013; Liaqat, 2018). However, despite its strengths, the AD sees constructive alignment as a pedagogical paradox, since it is not possible to plan for the unpredictable learning outcomes that all teaching and learning activities entail. During his research on higher education, the AD engaged critically with the concept of constructive alignment and recently published an article in which he discusses this thoroughly (Wickström, 2015). The AD's knowledge and insights on constructive alignment offered a good starting point for a discussion between the three authors of this chapter (one of whom is the AD), of what can be learnt about leading a process that intends to problematise this broadly established means for (supposedly good) university teaching. From this discussion, we decided to follow the process by which the AD planned a seminar about constructive alignment, to observe how he carried it through, and afterwards, to reflect on it. More specifically, our design enabled a process in which two of the authors of this chapter, taking the roles of critical friends, could reflect with, and challenge, the AD before and after the seminar.

The overriding purpose of this chapter is two-fold. First, we intend to deepen our understanding of the promises and challenges of deliberative communication as a means for leading and teaching as, and for, public good. Second, we explore our own experiences by using deliberative communication as a research approach, examining if and how it opens up and stimulates collective learning between the AD and the two critical friends. From what we learn, we discuss the promise of, and challenges with, deliberative communication as an approach to developing collaborative professionalism among academics (Hargreaves & O'Connor, 2018).

Before describing the case and the research process in detail, we present the pedagogical idea of constructive alignment and how this approach in recent years has become a governance tool aligned with the "accountability logic" (see Chapter 4) that higher education policy is currently influenced by. We then situate the case in relation to the context of the study. After this, we present elements of the AD's planning, teaching and reflections on how he leads the teaching. Throughout, the process is challenged by and discussed with the two critical friends. Finally, we provide some concluding reflections on the pedagogical challenges posed by dominant teaching models, and consider the promise of deliberative communication to promote the public good.

Constructive alignment: pedagogical approach *and* political governance tool

Constructive alignment is an approach or, as it is sometimes described, a model for designing courses in higher education. Since it was introduced by Biggs (1996) and further developed in *Teaching for Quality Learning: What the Student Does* (Biggs and Tang, 2007, 2011), it has gained global influence (Liaqat, 2018). Although it is well accepted that teaching is a situated activity, the principles of constructive alignment have been espoused as quality criteria for 'good teaching' at both international and national political levels. In the European context this can be exemplified by its use in the Bologna process and how it is treated in handbooks for academic teaching (Elmgren & Henriksson, 2018; Schyberg, 2009), and in curricula for pedagogical programmes for academics (Ruge et al., 2019).

The underlying theory of learning in constructive alignment is constructivism, which posits that learning is an active, constructive process: that people actively construct or create their own subjective representations of reality. The alignment aspect refers to the establishment of a teaching environment in which teaching activities support and lead to the achievement of the desired learning outcomes – developed and determined by academics – and demonstrated by students when they have learnt what was intended (Biggs & Tang, 2007). A pedagogical design built on the principles of constructive alignment thus promotes transparency and predictability and ensures internal coherence between learning activities, anticipated outcomes and forms of assessment (Ashwin, 2014). This implies that all teaching and learning activities should be "constructively aligned" with the intended learning objectives and outcomes, while the required assignments and assessments should ensure that the course elements support each other and work in the same direction (Biggs & Tang, 2011). Descriptions of learning outcomes and assessment criteria need to be clear, to give students sufficient information to enhance their engagement and to predict the knowledge and skills they are expected to demonstrate after completing their education.

As already indicated, constructive alignment was first developed as a pedagogical tool to transform university teaching so as to pay attention to students' learning, rather than merely "delivering knowledge", and to better align content, learning activities and assessment forms (Biggs, 1996). However, today it is no longer simply a pedagogical tool for academics; it has been adopted in higher education policy as an instrument in the governance of higher education (Ruge et al., 2019). This movement from a pedagogical to a policy and governance discourse implies that constructive alignment has become a powerful means of governance.

Today, constructive alignment is embedded within societal changes, trends and discourses, including a drift towards outcome-based governance, increasingly influential market forces, and the impacts of what international research refers to as New Public Management (NPM), Total Quality Management and 'accountability' (Ball, Maguire & Braun, 2012; Dahler-Larsen, 2012; Wahlström, 2009). Specifically, the principles of constructive alignment fit well with the requirement for transparency and predefined learning outcomes[2] and have thus become important in most quality assurance systems developed for higher education (Wickström, 2015). Such orientations challenge the logic of academics' professional responsibility (see Chapter 4) and their autonomy to make professional judgements on what is important learning, their freedom to design teaching which opens up space for unpredictable learning. There is a risk that such predefined teaching designs limits the possibility of grabbing "golden" teaching moments, and spending time on that which is not measurable (Osberg & Biesta, 2010; Solbrekke, 2008). From a public good perspective, it might be problematic if students become even more concerned with learning what is to be tested at exams, than for example collaboration with other students. As presented in Chapter 8, studies indicate that societal and social engagement among students tend to diminish during their higher education trajectories.

The local context

The AD we study holds a doctorate and has more than ten years of experience in his role as a course leader. He is also deputy head of the Unit for Academic Development at his university. According to the AD, designing a curriculum, learning situations and assessment forms for students with diverse backgrounds and capabilities requires a critical view of how and when the principles underlying constructive alignment support (or hinder) personal formation, critical thinking and deliberative communication, and helping students see themselves as epistemic contributors to the public good (Walker, 2018). In previous research he has problematised the hegemonical position of constructive alignment in higher education and educational development (Wickström, 2015). In line with other scholars, he emphasises that learning must also be understood as an unpredictable and unstable process and that the concept of constructive alignment risks marginalising both the teacher and the learner as subjects and actors (Osberg & Biesta, 2010). He also questioned the educational implications of working too unilaterally with it, thus making an instrumental use of constructive alignment (Friberg, 2015; Magnússon & Rytzler, 2018).

In addition to the AD's own professional background it is important to acknowledge the local context for this case: Uppsala University, founded in 1477, is the oldest university in Scandinavia with a long academic tradition. Within the university administration there is a special Unit for Academic Development with academic staff from all disciplines. The ADs employed at this unit come from different disciplines and most hold doctoral degrees. All have extensive educational experience. Organisationally, the Unit for Academic Development is situated in "a third space" between administration and teaching/research. This third space position connects the unit closely with the administrative leadership and an accountability logic. In such circumstances, the AD is expected to enact leadership on behalf of the university management and loyally follow the commitments implied in a quality assurance system, while also leading teaching and learning processes for academic colleagues engaged in teaching and research. An important consequence of being located within administration is that ADs are administrative rather than academic employees, and are thus precluded from university research funding.

The specific seminar chosen for this study is part of a mandatory course that introduces new academics to teaching in higher education. There is some variation of content and focus in the seminars included in the course, and the seminar reported on here is the only one in which constructive alignment is the primary focus. The AD intends to introduce constructive alignment for university teachers in a way that encourages them to think critically about its strengths *and* limitations as a pedagogical tool. The plan is to introduce constructive alignment and then arrange for an interactive workshop, through the means of deliberative communication, in which the participants use it as a tool for analysing their own courses.

Thus, the AD himself may be characterised as placed within a web of commitments (see Chapter 4) implying that he has to find legitimate compromises between somewhat contesting interests and values. He is committed to the national policy for academic development that his university follows, and to the curriculum of the actual course which emphasises the commitment to teach constructive alignment. At the same time, he must live up to his own professional values that aspire to providing higher education as, and for, public good. The combination of this AD's professional background with his expert knowledge about constructive alignment, situated within the context of Uppsala University, provides an interesting case that may enable us to develop new insights and knowledge of the possibilities and challenges of leading academic development as, and for, public good.

Method

Consistent with the methodology of all the cases in this book, we have applied an abductive and reflexive insider–outsider approach inspired by the principles of deliberative communication. This implied an active collaboration between critical friends/researchers and the AD, both in the development of the case and reflections on practice (see Chapter 5 for elaboration on the method). In this case, we also prioritised spending two days together in the AD's home institution, Uppsala, for post-seminar reflections. This, in our view, helped us create an atmosphere of trust and relational respect and tolerance characteristic of deliberative communication, and encouraged the AD's self-reflections on his experiences with the seminar and to take them beyond a 'comfort zone'.

Table 6.1 presents the chronology of the research process and aims to demonstrate one way of studying how leading higher education as, and for, public good may be enacted.

Deliberative communication as a means of critically investigating "constructive alignment"

In the presentation that follows, the analytical focus is, first, the pre-seminar planning conversation and the AD's *intentions*; second, on how the process was led in *practice*; and third, on the post-seminar *reflections*.

Intentions: pre-seminar conversation

According to the AD's plan, the purpose of the seminar was three-fold. First, he wanted the critical friends to observe how he interpreted constructive alignment and introduced it to the academics, both as a general pedagogical idea and structure for designing university teaching and learning, and as a national policy and means of quality assurance to structure and measure 'good teaching'. Second, the AD

TABLE 7.1 Methods and data source

Event	Activities	Who participated	Data sources generated	How data sources were used
Early September 2017	Writing a plan for the seminar	AD	First draft of the plan	The draft was sent to the critical friends
Mid- September 2017	Preparation for pre-seminar conversation	Critical friends, first individually and then together	Written reflections on the draft	Questions, comments, etc. were formulated
Late September 2017	Pre-seminar planning conversation on the draft	AD and critical friends	Notes and video recording (1) of the discussion	The AD's intentions were identified and pedagogical choices discussed
Early October 2017	Revision of the plan for the seminar	AD	Revised plan	The revised plan was used for the seminar and sent to the critical friends
Mid-October 2017	Seminar	AD	Video recording (2) of the seminar	The video was sent to the critical friends
Early January 2018	Preparation for the post-seminar conversation	Critical friends/ researchers first individually and then together	Written reflections and video (2) analysis of seminar	Preparations were made for the debrief with AD, including identifying themes and selecting (video) examples for discussion
Mid-January 2018	Two-day post-seminar reflections based on pre-teaching planning, and on the observation of the seminar	AD and critical friends/ researchers	Notes and video (1, 2) + new video (3) recording of the post-seminar reflections	All data produced were summarised for analysis and report
Ultimo January 2018	Individual memos on the process	AD and Critical friends/ researchers	Memos of the research process	Collective reflection on the learning experiences

wanted feedback on how he enacted the academic values he embraced, such as higher education as, and for, public good, nurturing democracy, and critical thinking. Last, but not least, he requested feedback on the manner in which he deployed deliberative communication as a means of eliciting different perspectives on constructive alignment and its relevance across different university disciplines.

Following the AD's requests, the critical friends first, individually and then together, developed questions for the pre-seminar conversation. Based on the AD's plan, their aim was to encourage the AD to think through how he would introduce the concept of constructive alignment and facilitate discussions, building on his own expressed ideals of openness, public good and academic integrity. During the conversation, the AD emphasised the importance of using deliberative communication in a way that encouraged course participants to engage, individually and collectively, in a critical reflection on the strengths and limitations of constructive alignment as a pedagogical tool, as well as the possible consequences of using it as a tool of political governance. He explained that he was concerned about the risk that constructive alignment, as a pedagogical tool, may restrict higher education as, and for, public good, as it could limit the focus of learning to pre-determined and measurable outcomes. To him, this risked neglecting important learning for students, in particular regarding their formation as persons, professionals and active citizens – values and capacities that may be more difficult to measure within the accountability logic. His intention was thus to present and alter between different perspectives, through deliberative communication, in order to open up a reflective awareness of the underlying pedagogical principles of constructive alignment while remaining loyal to the commitment to introduce it as a pedagogic means for planning teaching in higher education.

Although the written plan was very clear on the tensions embedded in constructive alignment, it was not clear how these tensions could be communicated in the seminar and thus transformed and led in pedagogical practice. For example, in the plan, the AD describes how constructive alignment:

> could be labelled as a part of an NPM ideology designed to standardise and harmonise higher education, and in the following – to reduce the agency of academic scholars. Still it is a very efficient and instrumental tool for designing courses.

For the critical friends, it was thus important to challenge the AD on the demands this intention would put on him, as leader of the process. The following questions exemplify some of the questions asked by the critical friends.

"Would you say that there is an 'original' idea about constructive alignment that later has been 'kidnapped' by NPM?" This question facilitated discussion of how, more than 20 years after constructive alignment was introduced, it could be understood as embedded in a complex web of commitments. One of the outcomes of that conversation was that, due to a dominant focus on quality, assessment, etc. (Bergh 2015), we anticipate new value conflicts and tensions emerging, conflicts that are not necessarily "within" the model itself, but will occur as a consequence of the way it is interpreted and enacted under the influence of dominant con-temporary discourses.

One of the critical friends asked the AD: "When it concerns value conflicts, have you reflected on what kinds of value conflicts that you think might come to the fore?" This discussion opened up new questions on how to lead the seminar and how to use deliberative communication as a pedagogical means. For example, one of the critical friends asked: "Once some value conflicts have been identified, how can you lead the process to enable a deliberative discussion among the participants?"

After the pre-seminar conversation with critical friends, the AD adjusted the plan in advance of the seminar. In his notes written after the conversation he wrote that:

> [The two] critical friends challenged me both to describe – in detail – my objectives and ideas carefully, and they challenged my thoughts on how these were going to be realised, limitations I certainly had.

Practice: leading the seminar using deliberative communication

While the seminar was a full-day activity, the total time recorded on video was slightly over 90 minutes. As the structure of the day alternated between discussions led by the AD and autonomous work by smaller groups, it was decided to record only those sessions where the AD actively led the process. Although this limited the amount of data gathered, it provided full access to situations in which the AD acted as a leader.

At the start of the seminar, the AD explained how the day was going to be structured: it would start with a focus on the concept of constructive alignment, followed by work in smaller subject-based groups based on course plans with a focus on goals, learning outcomes and assessment. After around 15 minutes, the AD formulated a question on the institutionalised process by which students learn, that is the teaching situation: "What do students need to do to achieve the goals?" While this question had the potential to prompt discussion about goals, the process of teaching and learning, and pedagogical questions such as the relation between the content to be taught and the roles of teachers and students, it did not do so. Instead, the central term that the AD followed up from his question was the verb "do": that is, following the insights from constructive alignment that teaching and learning activities should be constructively aligned with the intended learning objectives and outcomes. A little bit later, the AD formulated a similar question to exemplify assessment: "What do students need to do to show that they have achieved the goals?"

The way in which the seminar was introduced indicates that the AD's dominant focus was on students "doing" and to "show what they have learned for others". Consequently, attention was not directed towards how academics, through their pedagogical choices, can enable dynamic educational processes or how certain interpretations of constructive alignment may condition learning and teaching in specific ways. This means, for example, that issues or tensions that might arise in relation to different kinds of goals were neither mentioned nor problematised.

Following his introduction, the AD continued with a more elaborate presentation on what he termed the "model" (referring to constructive alignment), describing its background and how it was initially formulated by Biggs (1996). After approximately 20 minutes, the AD opened up for questions and comments from the participants. One participant raised a question about the relation between constructive alignment as an ideal and what teaching looks like in practice, in "real life". When the participant further elaborated on his question it became clear that he meant that the two are rooted in different logics: one in an administrative ideal and the other in a complex reality. Another participant commented that she recognised the idea from the way course plans are constructed nowadays. The AD responded by referring to the Bologna process, saying that constructive alignment has grown in dominance over the last ten years, and that it cannot be taken for granted that it fits for all kinds of knowledge. He then summarised some of the criticism formulated by himself and other researchers.

During the AD's summary of the criticism, some new questions were raised by the participants. However, rather than availing of these opportunities to open up a deliberative conversation, he responded as an "expert". One question, for example, concerned whether there are other competing models for structuring teaching in higher education. Another participant asked: "How is it possible to find a balance between goals that are either too abstract or too concrete?" When the latter elaborated on the question, it became clear that she meant that more abstract goals can give room for different interpretations but there is also a risk that they will become vague. On the other hand, while goals that are more concrete can fulfil demands on clarity, they might also lead to a narrower learning process. When the critical friends subsequently reviewed the video, they agreed that those questions had great potential to be discussed through deliberative communication, but that the AD's apparent primary concern had been to say what he had planned. Nevertheless, there was no doubt that he welcomed questions from the participants, and that they were comfortable to do that. The way the AD led the process thus created a welcoming and encouraging atmosphere. Before dividing up the participants to work in groups of four to five each, the AD explained the work to be done and invited questions and requests for clarification.

After the lunch break, when the participants returned from the group work, the AD initially concluded that he had been around in the different groups and that he had noticed that questions on assessment and examination already had been touched on. Apart from that, no follow-up was made on the previous discussions. Instead, he used the next 35 minutes to talk about assessment and examination, inviting comments and questions, and introduced theoretical perspectives and concepts such as summative and formative assessment. This part of the seminar ended with a workshop in which participants analysed examinations and assessments from the perspective of constructive alignment.

When the critical friends later analysed the video, they agreed that the AD had, during the seminar, demonstrated his knowledge of constructive alignment in a typically academic way. His choice to give a 20-minute lecture, and afterwards open up for questions, is a commonly used structure amongst academics. However, the way he lectured did not really help him exploit the possibilities inherent in some of the questions he received during the lecture to initiate deliberative communication. The participants were undoubtedly engaged by what he lectured on, but the AD was so committed to introducing them to constructive alignment as a tool, that he missed some teachable moments (Woods & Jeffrey, 1996) which he could have used to initiate deliberative communication and critical reflections.

Reflections: creating the spirit of deliberative communication

The two critical friends started preparing for the post-seminar reflections before they met in Uppsala. This gave them an initial opportunity to individually reflect upon the AD's actions in light of his intentions, and then to exchange their interpretations and develop a common guide for how to work together with the AD. They first watched the seminar video individually. Based on the notes they prepared on their reflections and observations, they then had a Skype call to prepare a guide for the face-to-face post-seminar conversation with the AD. This was scheduled to take place a week later at Uppsala University, during a 24-hour period in January 2018.

During the Skype conversation, the critical friends revisited the context in which the AD worked and recapitulated the discussion from the pre-seminar conversation. They agreed that the primary aim for the post-seminar was to engage the AD in reflecting on how he had led the seminar in such a way as to engage the participants to reflect critically on constructive alignment by using deliberative communication. Additionally, they would challenge the AD to consider the strengths and weaknesses of deliberative communication in practice.

The post-seminar meeting began with an hour-long lunch which provided the two critical friends with an opportunity to engage in small talk with the AD and to gain a better sense of the context in which he worked. As the meeting was held in one of the rooms in the AD's institution, this location facilitated spontaneous meetings with the AD's colleagues during breaks. These informal conversations laid the ground for the discussion to come.

The post-seminar conversation started with all three – the two critical friends and the AD – recapitulating the process by watching the videos of the pre-seminar conversation and the seminar. It was agreed to review both videos all the way through, taking notes individually. After the shared experience following this activity, the post-seminar reflections continued for 90 minutes. Initially, the AD described what he had uncovered regarding his intentions with using deliberative communication and the extent to which these were fulfilled. He said:

> It's quite challenging to see yourself like this ... Well, I think the tone and the atmosphere is positive, but there is very little dialogue in the first part, which I don't like. In addition, I think I am quite sweeping and unclear, and that it would have been better if I had stopped when the participants asked questions. I could have listened more carefully instead of being so quick to give answers, and it could have been better to encourage and invite them into the discussion.

The AD's reflections paved the way for the critical friends to enter into a dialogue based on the principles of deliberative communication and to encourage him to reflect further upon the way he had led the process. The AD explained that he approached constructive alignment in the context of a basic university pedagogy course, which clearly differed "from what I would have chosen if it had been arranged as a research seminar, where there would have been much more space for theoretical reasoning" (AD). Within the confines of the seminar, however, he averred that there was an explicit expectation from the participants, as well as from the university management, that the academics would learn tools to help them develop "good teaching" approaches. By way of response, one of the critical friends asked the AD why he chose to term constructive alignment as a "model", and the AD replied.

> As I use it here, it kind of becomes a model. I don't go theoretically deep. Even if the intention from Biggs was pedagogical it was later shown to fit very well into the governing of higher education, and thus to effectively hook onto other contemporary trends.

In the conversation that followed, the two critical friends and the AD discussed the implications of his answer. To what extent is it possible to combine different expectations? Is there a risk that some will dominate and others be marginalised? What are the consequences of making different choices? What do academics need to know about university teaching? How could the AD have acted differently in relation to his own intentions as expressed in the plan and the pre-seminar conversation? What autonomy or agency does the AD have?

During the discussion, the AD commented that the way he was challenged by the two critical friends was quite demanding, but also very constructive for his own formation and competence building, as he formulated it:

> I have really appreciated how you have asked me questions. They have been sharp and critical, but also very constructive. When I have listened to you, I have got a sense of the underlying critique, at the same time as you have approached it in a way that has triggered me to further elaborate on it. (AD)

One of the critical friends responded to this comment by saying that being honest in a respectful yet challenging way is both an ethical responsibility and a collegial and professional challenge. In the following discussion, the AD and the two critical friends concluded that the process in itself, guided by the principles of deliberative communication, in particular the ones emphasising respect and tolerance for the concrete other, and letting all perspectives be negotiated, had been valuable for developing both individual and collective will-formation. We see the contours of the relationship between intellectual virtues such as courage, open-mindedness and honesty and the principles in deliberative communication.[3]

According to the AD, to reflect on how he led, and his own agency in relation to expectations from others, made him much more aware of his position as a leader in higher education, within a complex web of multiple and often conflicting commitments. He indicated that, despite his own critical view, his practice may have overshadowed his intention to encourage critical reflection on the role of constructive alignment in higher education as, and for, public good.

The two critical friends invested the time to stay in Uppsala for two days, which enabled them to remain on site with the AD in his home institution. Organising the post-seminar reflections in this way undoubtedly gave them time to dig deep into his intentions, concrete actions and reflections on how to lead and teach by means of deliberative communication, as well as to prepare the ground for enacting deliberative communication as a research method.

When the post-seminar reflections resumed the following morning, the critical friends took the opportunity to adjust their approach for the conversation. In that way, the questions prepared for the AD, became more focused on what he achieved and what he did not achieve during the seminar, in relation to his intentions. In particular, the questions challenged the AD to further qualify his reflection on the way he led the seminar in relation to his own academic values.

Concluding reflections on the potential of deliberative communication

The case presented here reproduces snapshots of a much longer process in which the three authors engaged in reflective conversation, trying to understand and make sense of the challenges and potentialities of the role of ADs in the contemporary higher education landscape. Notwithstanding the limits of this approach, our experience is that the case provided valuable knowledge in line with the purpose of the study. While the purpose was revised and refined several times during the process, it helped us to keep focus and lend direction to the case. We return to it now and provide some concluding reflections about the ways in which the process of teaching and learning about constructive alignment, when led by an AD who seeks also to deploy deliberative communication, may enable or hinder the potential of higher education as, and for, public good.

To conclude this case, we begin with an ethical observation. We acknowledge that, for the AD, it was quite challenging to see himself in action and to take the risk of being transparent and open with colleagues. This experience was very important for all three participants: the AD and the two critical friends. To set up a case like this puts great demands on trust, respect and openness to ensure ethical responsibility towards – and for – each other. Our experience is that such values are primarily relational, but we also want to emphasise the importance of advance planning and structure. A joint exploration of pedagogical practice requires the courage to invite colleagues to critically investigate one's own practice, the will to listen carefully to and respect each other, and, importantly, to ensure that the process has direction.

In relation to this case, we also reflect upon the complex relationship between theoretical ideals and practice. The case exemplifies the tensions and conflicts embedded in contemporary higher education institutions and activities that can challenge us to discuss what higher education is for as well as the means used to achieve this. What becomes evident through the analysis is how challenging, complex and unpredictable leading academic development processes can be. Teaching is, by its very nature, unpredictable. This uncertainty increases with attempts to lead in a web of commitments. Even though the AD problematises and defines constructive alignment as a political governance tool, his commitment to follow the university policy of introducing it as a model for planning teaching appears to supersede the responsibility to approach it much more critically.

Another concern that emerges from the case is about the role of ADs and the opportunities at their disposal to use their agency, even though the space for possible actions is framed and conditioned very differently (Fremstad et al., 2019). In the seminar, there were several situations where the AD could have acted differently, which he acknowledged in subsequent conversation. For example, he could have problematised the difference between talking about constructive alignment as a "model" and all the different expectations that might reduce our understanding by making it more instrumental than it necessarily needs to be. As he commented in reflective mode: "I could have been a better listener and I could more actively had invited the participants to a common exploration through deliberative communication about different tensions that appear in and around constructive alignment". However, it is important to remember that a pedagogical practice can never mirror a theoretical ideal, which is not a disavowal of the necessity for having visions and ideals.

Throughout the process for this study, our appreciation of just how fruitful it is to reflect and collaborate among colleagues in a structured way was considerably enhanced. Raising awareness of the limitation of all models, tools or approaches, like constructive alignment, may help academics to acknowledge that the improvement of leadership and teaching should be far more of a collective endeavour than at present. A shared commitment to develop higher education for the public good thus requires collaborative professionalism (Hargreaves & O'Connor, 2018). An important issue for further exploration is, therefore, how creative meetings between individual professional and inter-professional skills can contribute to raising awareness of what teaching as, and for, public good might mean, and how it can be enacted.

Notes

1 See Chapter 4 for a more thorough elaboration of the concept web of commitments.
2 See Chapter 4 for further explanation and characterisation of an accountability logic.
3 See Chapter 6 for a further elaboration on the relationship between deliberative communication and intellectual virtues.

References

Ashwin, P. (2014). Knowledge, curriculum and student understanding. *Higher Education, 67,* 123–126.

Ball, S. J., Maguire, M. & Braun, A. (2012). *How Schools do Policy: Policy Enactments in Secondary Schools.* London: Routledge.

Bergh, A. (2015). Local educational actors doing of education – a study of how local autonomy meets international and national quality policy rhetoric. *NordSTEP, Nordic Journal of Studies in Educational Policy, 1*(2), 42–50.

Biggs, J. (1996). Enhancing teaching through constructive alignment. *Higher Education, 32,* 347–364.

Biggs, J. & Tang, C. (2007). *Teaching for Quality Learning at University: What the Student Does.* 3rd edn. Glasgow: Society into Research in Higher Education.

Biggs, J. & Tang, C. (2011). *Teaching for Quality Learning at University: What the Student Does.* 4th edn. Glasgow: Society into Research in Higher Education.

Dahler-Larsen, P. (2012). *The Evaluation Society.* Stanford: Stanford University Press.

Damşa, C. & de Lange, T. (2019). Student-centred learning environments in higher education – from conceptualization to design. *UNIPED, 42*(1), 9–26. doi:10.18261/i.

Elmgren, M. & Henriksson, A. S. (2018). *Academic Teaching.* Lund: Studentlitteratur.

Fransson, O. & Friberg, T. (2015) Constructive alignment: from professional teaching technique to governnance of profession. *European Journal of Higher Education, 5*(2), 141–156.

Fremstad, E., Bergh, A., Solbrekke, T. D. & Fossland, T. (2019). Deliberative academic development: the potential and challenge of agency. *International Journal for Academic Development.* doi:10.1080/1360144X.2019.1631169.

Friberg, T. (2015). A holistic, self-reflective perspective on victimization within higher education in Sweden. *Critical Studies in Education, 56*(3), 384–394.

Hargreaves, A. & O'Connor, M. T. (2018). Leading collaborative professionalism. Centre for Strategic Education, Victoria. http://www.andyhargreaves.com/uploads/5/2/9/2/5292616/seminar_series_274-april2018.pdf (downloaded 26 April 2019).

Larkin, H. & Richardson, B. (2013). Creating high challenge/high support academic environments through constructive alignment: student outcomes. *Teaching in Higher Education, 18*(2). http://dx.doi.org/10.1080/13562517.2012.696541.

Liaqat, A. (2018). The design of curriculum, assessment and evaluation in higher education with constructive alignment. *Journal of Education and e-learning Research, 5*(1), 72–78, doi:10.20448/journal.509.2018.51.72.78.

Little, D. & Green, D. A. (2012). Betwixt and between: academic developers in the margins. *International Journal for Academic Development, 17*(3), 203–215. doi:10.1080/1360144X.2012.700895.

Magnússon, G. & Rytzler, J. (2018). Approaching higher education with Didaktik: University teaching for intellectual emancipation. *European Journal of Higher Education.* doi:10.1080/21568235.2018.1515030.

Osberg, D. & Biesta, G. (eds). (2010). *Complexity Theory and the Politics of Education.* Rotterdam: Sense Publishers.

Roxå, T. & Mårtensson, K. (2009). Significant conversations and significant networks – exploring the backstage of the teaching arena. *Studies in Higher Education, 34*(5), 547–559.

Ruge, G., Tokede, O. & Tivendale, L. (2019). Implementing constructive alignment in higher education: cross-institutional perspectives from Australia. *Higher Education Research & Development.* doi:10.1080/07294360.2019.1586842.

Schyberg, S. (2009). Studentcentrering – en förutsättning för studentens lärande. In M. Stigmar (ed.), *Högskolepedagogik: Att vara professionell som lärare i högskolan,* pp. 45–58. Stockholm: Liber.

Solbrekke, T. D. (2008). Educating for professional responsibility: a normative dimension of higher education. *Utbildning & Demokrati/Education & Democracy, 17*(2), 73–96.

Wahlström, N. (2009). *Mellan leverans och utbildning: Om lärande i en mål- och resultatstyrd skola.* Göteborg: Daidalos.

Walker, M. (2018). Dimensions of higher education and the public good in South Africa. *Higher Education, 76*(3), 555–569.

Wickström, J. (2015). Dekonstruerad länkning: en kritisk läsning av Constructive Alignment inom svensk högskolepedagogik och pedagogisk utveckling. *Utbildning och Demokrati, 24*(3), 25–47.

Woods, P. & Jeffrey, B. (1996). *Teachable Moments: The Art of Teaching in Primary Schools.* Maidenhead: Open University Press.

8

DELIBERATIVE LEADERSHIP

Moving beyond dialogue

*Kristin Ewins, Ester Fremstad, Trine Fossland and
Ragnhild Sandvoll*

How do you enact your professional responsibility as an academic? Imagine what a mandate you have. Just stop and contemplate: "I'm engaging with a whole generation of young people, and I've got a social mandate to contribute to forming them as citizens". Teaching is about forming capable citizens who may contribute to democracy, to professional life, and, not least in relation to the mission of the Arctic University at Tromsø, to sustaining the Arctic areas. It's frightening in a way, but also a reason to be proud: as part of our professional responsibility we can contribute to something that has significance in a larger context. It's easy to forget what teaching at university is really about when working with the concrete bits, such as learning outcomes or constructive alignment. Lift the gaze!

Introduction

The opening quote is taken from the very end of the course session under study in this chapter. It illustrates how leadership in higher education – here enacted by academic developers (ADs) – can and should raise larger questions about academics' professional responsibility. With passionate conviction, the ADs convey the public purpose of higher education and academics' responsibility to contribute to the formation of democratically minded, professionally shrewd citizens. We call this normative mode of leadership for public good *deliberative leadership*. In this chapter, we explore potentials and challenges for ADs in their roles as deliberative leaders, in particular when attempting to strengthen fellow academics' capacity for professional responsibility.[1] Our notion of deliberative leadership draws on three theoretical strands: first, the concept of deliberative communication elaborated in Chapter 3; second, Kandlbinder's notion of deliberative academic development (2007); and third, observations of ADs as (potential) educational leaders in a web of commitments (see Chapter 4), positioned as both horizontal and vertical brokers of educational ideas and practices (Sugrue et al., 2017). Deliberative leadership involves contributing to academics' reflection on, understanding of and enactment of teaching and learning as, and for, public good. Furthermore, it implies performing educational leadership by means of deliberative communication.

To deepen our understanding of the approaches ADs need to take in order to enact deliberative leadership, we study two ADs as they prepare, conduct and reflect on a course session. The aim of the session is to nurture academics' professional responsibility through a discussion about learning outcomes and constructive alignment in relation to professional responsibility. The case illustrates in concrete ways central topics in the current literature on academic development: in particular, how ADs are positioned between designated institutional leaders and fellow academics in a complex web of commitments in which the potential to enact deliberative leadership may be hampered by internal or external expectations, such as managerial policy to put into practice, governmental goals to be fulfilled or engrained in pedagogical practices (Fremstad et al., 2019).

In this chapter, we are especially interested in what makes deliberative leadership possible. To this end, we begin by situating the case within current research on academic development as well as within the implementation of the National Qualifications Framework (NQF) in Norwegian higher education during the last ten years. We then introduce the case and its specifics before turning to our analysis. As the analysis progresses, we make a number of observations and suggestions about the potentials and challenges of deliberative leadership in higher education.

The National Qualifications Framework: learning outcomes and legitimate compromises

ADs are increasingly expected to support institutional leaders in adapting educational practices to meet expectations from government. Previous research has emphasised such top-down pressures on ADs as crucial to understanding academic development today (Land, 2004; Gibbs, 2013; Debowski, 2014; Stensaker et al., 2017; Sugrue et al., 2017), and as central to envisioning and forming roles and practices for ADs that capture their key responsibilities (Fremstad et al., 2019). The implementation of the NQF across Norwegian universities provides an illustrative example of expectations from government that ADs are required to put into practice (Handal et al., 2014). The NQF is a politically determined, regulatory framework for the formulation of learning outcomes, developed and implemented in the Norwegian context as part of the Bologna process. It includes developing a shared scheme for descriptors of students' qualifications based on the European Qualifications Framework (EQF; Bologna Working Group, 2005).[2]

The NQF was established in 2009 as Norway's implementation of the EQF, with general descriptors for each degree level (Norwegian Ministry of Education and Research, 2011). The descriptors have standardised the ways in which institutions and academics are expected to formulate learning outcomes, categorising them under knowledge, skills and general competencies. Departing from a previous autonomy in how institutions and academics had worked, often with a focus on content and teaching rather than on students' learning (Handal et al., 2014), the framework embodied a mode of external and technocratic steering by "soft governance" (Karseth & Solbrekke, 2010; Bento, 2013). We know from previous research that academics tend to view the process of implementing the NQF, not as academic-professional work but as administrative work (Sørskår, 2015). Since its implementation, the NQF has been perceived as a steering tool associated with an "accountability logic" as opposed to a "responsibility logic" (see Chapter 4), where the emphasis on external and top-down directives grates against traditional values of collegial leadership.[3] On the other hand, studies also suggest that educational leaders who engage in developing learning outcomes through encouraging a sense of shared responsibility for educational programmes may stimulate a stronger commitment and engagement among academics, by, for instance, establishing a shared vision for the programme and a sense of a disciplinary or professional community centred around education (Gibbs, Knapper & Piccini, 2009; Karseth & Solbrekke, 2016; Solbrekke & Karseth, 2016; Solbrekke & Stensaker, 2016).

Notwithstanding such positive results, several researchers warn that the increased orientation towards employability and transferable skills may lead higher education to "produce" students with skills primarily useful for the immediate needs of the labour market, while failing to educate students for an unknown future; that is, to enable the formation of active, critical and democratically engaged citizens (Bergan, Harkavy & Van't Land, 2013, p. i; Solbrekke & Karseth, 2016, p. 77; Tight, 2013; Biesta, 2006). Teaching for public good is crucial to the educational mission of public universities (see Chapter 3). It is our contention in this book that helping to form graduates who are motivated and capable of contributing to democratic societal development in an increasingly complex and globalised society is essential to our professional responsibility as academics. We need to "ensure that we do not find ourselves locked into more regressive structures and limited representations of learning, and social and professional practices that weaken our potential commitment to 'the' common good" (McEwen & Trede, 2016, p. 225). If we take McEwen and Trede's call seriously, academics also need to create room for learning beyond the specifications set by formulated learning outcomes; that is, learning that cannot be measured or unpredictable learning that takes place through educational activities and human interaction. As the tip of an iceberg, the NQF is a visible sign of a larger process of market orientation, commodification and modularisation which has pushed higher education in an instrumental direction (see Chapter 2), and which excludes the unforeseen as well as modes of learning and human growth which are difficult to predefine and assess.

To understand ADs' professional role in this ambiguous context of increased political steering, on the one hand, and more traditional autonomous and collegial work, on the other, it may be helpful to conceive of it as placed precisely within the tensions, first, between domesticating and liberating purposes, and, second, between individual and institutional purposes (Land, 2004). Multiple expectations have made this role more ambiguous over the last couple of decades. Today, ADs are often expected to operate on an institutional level as well as working directly with departments or individual academics. This means that academic development takes place within a political geography that imposes its own strain on the sensitive work of making legitimate compromises amid often conflicting horizontal and vertical responsibilities, and liberating and domesticating purposes.[4] For both good and ill, ADs are entangled in the power dynamics of their institutions (Peseta, 2014; Roxå & Mårtensson, 2016). Acknowledging the institutional power afforded to ADs (Cousin, 2013) is necessary for understanding ADs' professional responsibility and how they may enact deliberative leadership within the complex web of commitments in which they operate.

The complexity of pressures and expectations, notwithstanding, there is still room for action. While required to adhere to the NQF, ADs and fellow academics can decide – based on their professional discretion – precisely how and for what purposes they work with learning outcomes (Solbrekke & Karseth, 2016). It is crucial that the ownership of the educational process remains with the academics. They need to have a strong mandate over their practice in order to operate as professionally responsible agents in an increasingly complex landscape of external and internal leadership structures. Such mandate enables academics to form a critical-constructive approach, for which collegial discussions are essential (Solbrekke & Karseth, 2016). Collegial discussions are also examples of contexts in which ADs can lead fellow academics for public good. In their day-to-day practice, ADs lead by brokering, critically and constructively negotiating the tension between politically defined structures (such as the NQF) and professional and critical judgement, discretion and autonomy (see Chapters 1 and 4). As brokers, they have the potential to become agents of change for public good. The case studied in this chapter illustrates some of the potentials and challenges open to ADs while attempting to practise deliberative leadership in this complex context.

The case

The case consists of a session in which two experienced ADs aim to lead a deliberative discussion on learning outcomes. Our material also includes planning documentation and reflections by the ADs on the aims of the session, on how to lead it and on experiences from the session. Table 8.1 provides a summary of our empirical material and how we have used it.

In line with the methodology common to all the cases in this book, we have made use of an abductive and reflexive insider–outsider approach. Insights into how deliberative leadership for public good may be enacted in the context of academic development have been developed by moving between empirical data and theory in collaboration between ADs and critical friends/researchers when planning the course session and reflecting on what took place.

The session studied is part of a three-day course for experienced academics on developing a teaching portfolio. The course is open to academics with more than five years' experience of teaching in higher education. The topic of the session is learning outcomes and their impact on professional responsibility. The session

TABLE 8.1 Methods and data sources

Time	What took place	Who participated	How used for analytical purposes
August 2017	Planning document	ADs	To identify aims for the session and prepare for the first conversation between ADs and two critical friends.
August 2017	Pre-session conversation about the amis of the session and how to conduct it.	ADs and critical friends	To identify aims for the session and potential challenges for practice.
October 2017	Course session of one hour and 20 minutes: Learning outcomes as a mutual commitment or a baseline for developing professional responsibility?	ADs and 12 course participants	To identify possibilities for and challenges to deliberative leadership by means of concrete examples.
May 2018	Post-session conversation about what the researchers observed in the session and the ADs' experiences of and reflections on the planning document, the pre-session conversation with critical friends and the session itself.	ADs and critical friends/researchers	To explore AD's reflections on their deliberative leadership for public good when faced with video recordings and researchers' observations, reflections and questions. To identify and further explore potentials and challenges of deliberative leadership.
February 2019	Reflection document	ADs and critical friends/researchers	To identify what we (ADs, critical friends and researchers) learned from the process.

studied lasts for one hour and 20 minutes, and follows immediately after sessions on constructive alignment and professional responsibility. It is led by two ADs with another 12 academics participating, representing a range of disciplines including health sciences, teacher education, economics and mathematics. In preparation for the session, participants have been asked to watch a video lecture on the theoretical and political basis of learning outcomes and the NQF. They all have experience working with learning outcomes in different teaching or leading capacities at the university.

The ADs open the session by drawing on discussions from the earlier session on professional responsibility. They raise questions about academics' professional responsibility in relation to the prescribed use of learning outcomes and constructive alignment in teaching practice at the university. In the planning document, shared with the critical friends before the session, the ADs state that "the overall purpose [of the seminar] is to raise questions about professional responsibility related to learning outcomes, and increase the course participants' awareness of whether/how this responsibility is/can be enacted in their teaching practice". This statement was elaborated in the pre-session conversation with the critical friends, in which the ADs described how they wanted to use deliberative communication during the session to "facilitate good discussions among academics, discussions ... that open up and facilitate reflections about their practice and responsibilities in their teaching". Later in the conversation, they described their intention of "raising the awareness among academics about their professional responsibilities" as a means of working for "the values, beliefs and moral responsibilities required to uphold public good".

Early on in the session, the ADs present four questions which they want the participants to discuss (Box 8.1). As part of their instructions, the ADs tell the participants that "we want all voices to be heard". They choose not to mention deliberative communication as such. In the post-session conversation with critical friends, the ADs clarify that they "did not want the participants to be too focused on the method, but to concentrate on the questions". Also, as part of the instructions, the ADs encourage the participants to relate their discussions closely to their own experiences of working with learning outcomes. The discussion is organised as a think, pair, square, share sequence, in which participants start by reflecting individually on the set questions, and then discuss their reflections first in pairs and then in fours, before sharing their reflections with the whole group.

BOX 8.1 QUESTIONS GIVEN TO COURSE PARTICIPANTS FOR A THINK, PAIR, SHARE, SQUARE EXERCISE

1. How do you understand the concept of learning outcomes?
2. What significance do they have for your teaching practice?
3. What views on learning outcomes do you meet among your colleagues?
4. How do you work collegially with learning outcomes?

The think, pair, square part of the exercise takes around 25 minutes and is followed by the share element in the form of a plenary discussion. In this part of the session, the ADs field the participants' different viewpoints and perspectives. They move from group to group to allow for all voices to be heard. With nods and encouraging comments or questions they affirm what the participants say and open up for elaborations and clarifications. The participants share their experiences of working with learning outcomes, with examples representing contrasting perspectives on the use of learning outcomes and the NQF. For instance, one participant describes the introduction of the NQF as a move towards administrative steering:

> No one disagreed that it was a good idea to have a good description of what we want the students to learn, but when it came to the NQF and we needed to rewrite and reclassify, that felt completely pointless [...] It wasn't well

communicated what the purpose with this was. We were just told that this is what it's supposed to look like now.

By contrast, another group maintains that "the categories [knowledge, skills, general competencies] have contributed to a better discussion about what we should teach".

The primary interaction in the room is between the ADs and the individual groups. There is minimal interaction between the different groups. Throughout the plenary discussion, the ADs are standing at the front of the room and the attention of the participants is uniformly directed towards them. The plenary discussion is broken off after about 20 minutes, once all the groups have reported from their discussions. One of the ADs then gives a report of an article that takes a critical stance towards constructive alignment. The participants are encouraged to consider this critical perspective in the continued discussion. The plenary discussion then continues. There is now more interaction between the different groups. The ADs also ask more probing questions that challenge the views presented.

Deliberative leadership: potentials and challenges

What we are interested in when analysing the case just described is the potential for ADs to enact deliberative leadership in their interactions with fellow academics, but also the challenges they face when doing so. As we suggested briefly in the introduction, deliberative leadership is a mode of leading that may enhance academics' awareness of and ability to teach for public good. It means putting deliberative communication into practice and giving it a direction.

In the case, we observe three phases characterised by different modes of interaction between the participants and the ADs. The introduction of the session is marked by familiarity, warmth and confidence as one of the ADs talks to the participants in a grounded, authoritative voice and with a steady gaze. The mode of interaction, however, is very different when the ADs initiate the first part of the plenary discussion. Their voices are more tentative, the gaze scanning the room, lacking the previous calm. The ADs seem to have their main focus on letting all voices be heard, to the point where some of the poignancy of what is being said is lost to the discussion; for instance, disciplinary differences in the implementation of learning outcomes are left without comment. The questions become leading, seemingly eliciting a particular reply, as in "Does it make you focus more on what you're teaching?" or "Do you think learning outcomes have made you conscious of students' learning?" Opportunities to be critical or problematise what the participants have said are mostly lost. The ADs focus instead on affirming what the participants say with nods and encouraging words. The ADs move from group to group sequentially. Again, the focus seems to be on ensuring that all voices are heard, rather than on pulling out potential contrasts between the groups. As a consequence, interaction only takes place between the ADs and the groups, rather than between the groups themselves. We sense an unease in the ADs' leadership in this phase of the session that was not there at the beginning.

In the second part of the plenary discussion, however, we identify a third phase that, like the first, is characterised by presence and confidence. The ADs have moved from a preoccupation with affirmation to a deeper engagement with the ideas in the room. The questions from the ADs now pick up on contrasting perspectives or syntheses, and push the participants' comments further: "How can we change from a top-down-perspective – with learning outcomes as designed for teaching – to a more student-centred perspective?" By contrast with the values implicit in the more leading questions, the ADs now dare to inhabit their values, as here, clearly bringing the student perspective to the fore, a perspective that has been strikingly absent in the participants' discussions. The ADs go on to ask more open questions that engage the different perspectives in the room and also link to the previous session on professional responsibility: "What do learning outcomes do with our roles as academics?" They pull out the challenges of the perceived problems of political steering of teaching in higher education – "we have got so many restrictions, in terms of administration and how you can design your teaching" – to clarify points that have been made about the importance of pedagogical competence to be able to enact professional responsibility and adopt a critical stance to expectations from the outside: "the less pedagogical competence you have, the more you are steered from outside, unable to protest". As a consequence of enacting deliberative leadership, through posing open yet critical questions, and foregrounding critical perspectives on political steering, the discussion in the room deepens and becomes more critical; for instance, the perspective is lifted from the immediacy of the participants' local contexts to comparing the conditions for different subjects. The map of interactions also changes: participants from different groups respond directly to one another, rather than directing their comments at the ADs. In the following we explore further the opportunities and challenges to deliberative leadership that we have discerned in these three phases of interaction.

Deliberative leadership: conflicting expectations – legitimate compromises

As suggested earlier in this chapter, working with learning outcomes in accordance with the NQF constitutes a current example of how a top-down policy may, at once, stimulate fruitful pedagogical reasoning *and* challenge critical autonomy for academics. In addition, the framework as such – by virtue of its schematic structure – may adversely steer academics to adopt an instrumental approach to education at the cost of educational purposes associated with public good, such as the formation of creative, critical, engaged and responsible human beings, professionals and citizens. How we as educators approach learning outcomes is crucial to how well we can practise professional responsibility for public good. The position that ADs often find themselves in, somewhere at the intersection of critical autonomy and a requirement to meet national and institutional expectations, can (as elaborated in Chapter 4) be usefully described as a web of commitments that requires legitimate compromises. The present case illustrates how ADs' enactment of professional responsibility not only requires a good sense of what is at stake, continuously dealing with this tension and showing an openness to negotiate and reach legitimate compromises, but that the key factor in forming their practice for public good is the capacity to *combine* sound reasoning around directives from above or outside *with* critical deliberation based on research, humanistic values and a normative democratic stance. In this is also demonstrated the potential for ADs to become role models for their fellow academics.

Our case suggests that this is a demanding task. Enacting deliberative leadership challenges elements of the bottom-up approach that ADs often take, an approach that uses participants' experiences as points of departure. In the post-session conversation, the ADs locate their starting point precisely in their fellow academics' everyday experience: "We could have started the discussion with professional responsibility, but I think that could have been left hanging. So we began with learning outcomes which is very concrete, where everyone is". In the session itself, we observe that the ADs stay largely within the comfort zone of the bottom-up approach when interacting with the group. While the focus here on the perspectives and experiences of the participants are fruitful for connecting with their daily work, the discussion struggles to reach the helicopter perspective essential for a deliberation on professional responsibility and public good. Despite the shift towards the end of the session, when the ADs start asking more critical questions, the discussions among the participants remain close to their everyday experience; for instance, the participants refer to their work "in the health department", "in mathematics" or "within teacher training" as a prefix to an example they are bringing to the discussion.

The inter-disciplinary composition of the groups of colleagues with whom ADs often work attaches a further dimension to ADs' webs of commitments: all participants, regardless of disciplinary loyalties, need to be challenged to look beyond their own horizons, often within a limited timeframe. Under these pressures, there may be an inherent risk for compliance rather than legitimate compromise; however, disciplinary differences also provide plenty of low-hanging fruit in the form of contrast and potential conflict so central to deliberative communication. In the case, the bottom-up approach ultimately falls short of getting the participants to "lift the gaze" in order to see their professional responsibility from the overarching perspective that was pinpointed in the quote at the beginning of this chapter. We conclude from this example that enacting deliberative leadership requires some form of authority that serves to provide the deliberative discussions with direction.

Deliberative leadership: authority, voice and passion

In the post-session conversations, the ADs critically reflected on how eager they had been to affirm participants' views: "When you're there, you're so focused on getting everyone's view represented. We really lost the critical perspective. I can see now that we lost several opportunities to pick up on tensions and potential conflicting perspectives in what the participants said".

It is precisely bringing out such contrasts which is at the core of deliberative communication:

> the dimension of conflict and confrontation (of different views) is substantially central to, and constitutive of, deliberative communication as a procedural phenomenon. This dimension implies both openly conflicting views and a search for and attempt to expose relatively minor differences, which are seen in deliberative communication as crucial to investigate and possibly to resolve.
>
> (Englund, 2006, pp. 513–14)

But, as expressed in the post-session conversation, the ADs also see problems with deliberative communication as a mode of practice:

> We need to be critical of the concepts that we ourselves use, critical of ourselves. Deliberative communication is an ideal, but we need to think more practice-oriented. We need to contextualise it. Kandlbinder's concept of deliberative academic development is useful here. We all want to do it, but it is demanding and difficult. And it is not necessarily the role that is expected of us to take by course participants or the university leadership. But the deliberative approach is necessary for us to enact our professional responsibility.

Enacting deliberative leadership in active contact with fellow academics is highly demanding, requiring ADs to grab hold of what the participants are bringing to the room and putting the different perspectives in critical relation to one another. The major challenge in the case is to put the different views presented by the participants in dialogue in a way that helps them "lift the gaze" in the discussions. Based on our observations, it seems that for this to be achieved, ADs need to bring a clear voice of authority to the room. This conclusion resonates with Biesta (2007) who suggests that beyond the nuts and bolts of what works in the classroom, academics are role models, which in turn means that beyond ensuring that their students fulfil the learning outcomes for the course, they are contributing to the formation of students as persons and citizens. Through a parallel process, ADs are contributing not only with tools that may make fellow academics better at teaching, but with the formation of these academics into colleagues with an aptitude for professional responsibility, who find room for action within a complex web of commitments, in which legitimate compromises are not always easy to find.

In order to uphold a democratic and open dialogue, and not closing and repressing collective reflections, this authority needs to take the form of a sophisticated pedagogy that seizes "teachable moments" – moments where unresolved tensions can be used as sites of possibilities for collective exploration, rather than a pedagogy of the kind of authority that offers predefined answers.[5] Authoritative voices run the risk of silencing other voices; however, authority in deliberative leadership embeds the attentiveness to respect and respond to other voices. Indeed, ADs have a professional responsibility to provide collegial discussions with direction, and to bring about deliberative dialogue that moves participants towards some form of collective will-formation, by contrast with a cacophony of voices and viewpoints. Not least, ADs have a professional responsibility of moving their fellow academics beyond words, so that deliberative discussion can influence educational practices, individual as well as institutional. Enacting the normative stance and authority required for deliberative leadership carries the potential to impact on institutional webs of commitments and what may count as legitimate compromise.

For a good example of deliberative leadership in action, we would like to return to the opening quote. The voice is strong, engaged, authoritative; the body language signals presence and strength. In this mode, the AD conveys normative values about the public purpose of higher education. Here, the purpose not only of the session but of higher education as such is clearly, if generally, articulated. Moreover, it is done with passion, engagement and courage, engaging not only with the cognitive aspect of professional responsibility, but even more so with the affective aspect of being an educator within higher education in general and at this specific university in particular. This mode of speaking not only to the minds but also to the hearts of academics is an aspect sorely neglected by educational research (see also Chapter 5). In this particular case, we may ask ourselves what might have happened within the course session if the authoritative and passionate closing remarks had been the introduction to the session. Would this have enabled a different way of enacting leadership?

In the collegial context in which ADs work, (potential) authority does not necessarily come with the status of a specific position, but rather from research-based knowledge and experience of higher education. When the ADs in our case break off the discussion to present a research article, we interpret this as an attempt to establish legitimacy for their work by anchoring it in research. The ADs confirm this interpretation in the post-session conversation by emphasising the importance of "showing that what we do as ADs is research-based". There is, however, an important contrast here between the mode of authority enacted by the normative stance adopted by the ADs at the end of the session, on the one hand, and the detached report on the article on constructive alignment, on the other. The report is done in the third person, which means that while participants are gaining a critical, research-based perspective on constructive alignment, it stays detached from a grounded sense of authority on behalf of the ADs themselves. The perspective offered by the article is relevant, but lacks the affective element of being embodied in the voice of the AD. The authority inherent in deliberative leadership would require the critical perspectives to be owned by the voice that conveyed them. For this to happen, ADs need to feel confident – through their own research and through research-based study – in their knowledge and insights about policies; past, current and possible future practices; and a conviction about the purposes of higher education and its implications for practice. But even when authority and deliberative leadership is maintained, one of the greatest challenges for academic development work remains: to make a difference in practice.

Deliberative leadership: moving beyond words

> In the last few years, there has been less and less resistance to and more and more positive feedback on the work we do as ADs, but I still feel that it's a lot of talking, an awful lot of talking. Does it make a difference? If you're thinking that professional responsibility for an academic is just about reflecting, then you're wrong. It's about action. It's about how you meet the students and how you design your teaching, and how you work with quality of education.

The quote is taken from the post-session conversation between ADs and critical friends. It looks with some frustration at the potential for ADs of making a difference in practice. Loosely steered collegial discussion is a common mode of practice among ADs. While acknowledging that "the academics who attend our courses really appreciate the opportunity to meet and discuss their development as teachers, and not least to have time for reflection for once", the ADs identify a massive challenge in how such discussions may be translated into actual change in academics' teaching practice: "Does it become more than words? How do we ensure that discussions about professional responsibility and public good have implications for academics in their teaching practice?" While the ADs maintain that "through facilitating such discussion, through talking about learning outcomes, through getting academics to reflect on their own professional responsibility, they articulate any room for action", in the session itself, we observed that the participants were struggling to express notions of professional responsibility and articulate a room for action. Again, we conclude that some of these difficulties resulted from the approach of focusing on the participants' viewpoints and the absence of a clear normative steer from the ADs. In the post-session conversation, it becomes evident that the ADs' own conception of academics' professional responsibility is also vague:

> it is strange how hard it is to put your finger on what professional responsibility for academics consists of, but it's about humanistic values and democracy. I can see now that it would have been good to have had a clearer idea of what professional responsibility for academics means, for doing more with the discussion.

This uncertainty around the concept of professional responsibility may in part explain what we observed as tentativeness and a reluctance to embody an authoritative voice in phase two of the session. Again, our observations illustrate that in order for ADs to engage academics in deliberations on professional responsibility, ADs need to "own" the notion of professional responsibility. A comparison may be made with a notion such as that of student-centredness, a concept ADs standardly address with confidence, knowledge base, engagement and authority, elements that were wanting in our observations of ADs leading a discussion on professional responsibility and public good. Expanding the role of academic development to include the broader responsibilities of academics means expanding ADs' repertoire of questions and practices, which in turn requires widening their knowledge base.

The ADs' self-critical reflections alongside our observations provide further evidence of how difficult it can be to practise deliberative leadership within a complex web of commitments. As Nerland (2016) has argued, professionals need to understand the rationale, knowledge, values and implications that lie behind what is expected of them in order to combine directives from above or outside with critical deliberations based on research, values and a normative stance when forming their practices. It is precisely on the basis of such knowledge that ADs can build the authority and voice necessary to practise deliberative leadership. Part of such leadership is ADs' abilities to convey this knowledge to fellow academics and help them translate it into practice. In the present case, it would involve initiating academics in the thinking (pedagogical as well as social and economic) behind the NQF, the values and practices it implies and, equally important, the values and practices that the NQF leaves out. What we observe in the session studied, however, is that it is in the very final comments of the session that the possibility for such translation work is first suggested. The session itself stops short of venturing into the potentially important moment of empowering the participants.

A key component of deliberative leadership when enacted by ADs is the ability to challenge fellow academics' thinking and – through dialogue – play a concrete role in finding ways of combining professional judgement with national and institutional directives. Ultimately, deliberative leadership requires the ability to both see and use existing room for individual and collective action, or the ability of finding creative ways of carving out such space. In the case of ADs, deliberate leadership requires a conceptual research-based understanding combined with practical pedagogical knowledge.

Conclusion

Lifting the gaze is a prerequisite for deliberative leadership for public good within higher education. Indeed, the purpose of deliberative leadership is to engage professional responsibility by "moving beyond dialogue to include actions informed by moral reasoning", thus redressing "the imbalance between technical know-how, moral stance and collective action" (McEwen & Trede, 2016, p. 224; Solbrekke et al., 2016). Confirming previous research (Solbrekke & Fremstad, 2018), the case suggests that ADs cannot tackle the responsibility of deliberative leadership individually. Collective discussions about the conditions of higher education and collegial responsibility need to form the foundations of practice. Furthermore, collegial responsibility needs to be research-based as well as based on normative deliberations about the values we, as a profession, want to promote. While, as claimed by Kandlbinder (2007, p. 57), it may be that "discussions change not only the arguments but also the people themselves", ADs have a responsibility to aid fellow academics by translating educational research, norms and values into practice. This responsibility includes conveying the practical implications of institutional demands and structures.

The present case illustrates, in concrete and practical ways, first, how deliberative leadership involves the challenge of *combining* top-down directives with critical autonomy; second, how this form of leadership requires an authoritative voice, whose authority is accepted as legitimate by fellow academics; and, third, how critical reflection, awareness and deliberative discussions ought not to be ends in themselves, but need to make a difference for academics' practices. Moreover, deliberative leadership must be grounded and alert. Being inclusive of all voices may be laudable from a pedagogical perspective, but from the perspective of deliberative leadership it is necessary to move beyond straightforward inclusiveness to building on diverse contributions with a view to challenge perspectives, thus potentially also unsettling established webs of commitments. This means that it is not enough to see and affirm the participants in the room, the discussion needs to be led in a way that ensures that voices are heard and respected through a process of being challenged and potentially changed. Deliberative leadership requires inhabiting the confidence and courage to pitting potentially conflicting perspectives and ideas against each other, all the while embodying the passion and authority to lead the process with legitimacy. In studying the challenges faced by the ADs in their attempt to enact deliberative leadership, we see a risk in emphasising too strongly the "consensus" part of deliberative communication. We want to emphasise, instead, the need for a polyphonic democracy, to be realised – positively – through negotiating and reaching legitimate compromises (see also Chapter 4).

As brokers between external polices, institutional leaders and fellow academics, ADs are continuously faced with the considerable political and pedagogical challenge of creating space for imaginative and creative engagement between policy and practice. Deliberative leadership is a means of seeking out legitimate compromises – consistent with professional responsibility – within these complex webs of commitments. However, the case demonstrates repeatedly just how challenging deliberative leadership is in practice. Still, we can at least begin to imagine how the higher education landscape might shift if institutional leaders were to practice deliberative leadership on a larger scale. The pace of change might be reduced to more manageable timeframes, thus extending the opportunity for considering public good and reconfiguring webs of commitments in ways that would enable legitimate compromise over unreflective compliance, paving the way for a more sustainable future.

Notes

1 Chapter 4 in this book usefully elaborates on the concept of "professional responsibility". For previous discussions of ADs' contributions to educational leadership, see, for instance, Kandlbinder (2007), Solbrekke & Fremstad (2018) and Fremstad et al. (2019).
2 The founding idea behind the European Qualifications Framework (EQF) had been to contribute to quality assurance through a threefold focus on 1) progression and constructive alignment in pedagogical design and assessment; 2) documentation of students' qualifications in a way that would support mobility; and 3) transparency for students as well as employers with regards to the aims and outcomes of higher education (Bologna Working Group, 2005).
3 See Chapter 4 for an elaboration of the distinction between the two concepts. Also Stensaker & Harvey (2011) give an account of the "accountability logic" in relation to the work of ADs. For empirical studies on the implementation of the National

Qualifications Framework (NQF), see, for instance, Bento (2013), Irving (2015), Solbrekke & Karseth (2016, p. 68) and Solbrekke & Fremstad (2018).

4 Based on an empirical study of ADs' orientations, Land (2004) proposed a model that included the dimensions individual–institutional and domesticating–liberating to map out the different orientations. The tensions between different orientations and expectations has since been addressed by, for example, Kandlbinder (2007), Holmes & Manathunga (2012), Di Napoli (2014) and Fremstad et al. (2019).

5 Woods and Jeffrey (1996) usefully describe "teachable moments" in the context of primary education; however, the model is equally applicable for tertiary education.

References

Bento, F. C. (2013). *Organizational complexity: Leadership and change in research-intensive academic departments*. Unpublished doctoral dissertation. Norwegian University of Science and Technology, Trondheim, Norway.

Bergan, S., Harkavy, I., & Van't Land, H. (eds). (2013). *Higher Education Series: Vol. 18. Reimagining democratic societies: A new era of personal and social responsibility*. Strasbourg: Council of Europe.

Biesta, G. (2006). *Beyond learning: Democratic education for a human future*. New York: Routledge.

Biesta, G. (2007). Why "what works" won't work: Evidence-based practice and the democratic deficit in educational research. *Educational Theory, 57*(1), 1–22. doi:10.1111/j.1741-5446.2006.00241.x

Bologna Working Group. (2005). *A framework for qualifications of the European Higher Education Area: Bologna Working Group report on qualifications frameworks*. Copenhagen: Danish Ministry of Science, Technology and Innovation. Retrieved from: http://ecahe.eu/w/index.php/Framework_for_Qualifications_of_the_European_Higher_Education_Area

Cousin, G. (2013). Evidencing the value of educational development by asking awkward questions. In V. Bamber (ed.), *Evidencing the value of educational development* (pp. 19–22). London: Staff and Educational Development Association.

Debowski, S. (2014). From agents of change to partners in arms: The emerging academic developer role. *International Journal for Academic Development, 19*(1), 50–56. doi:10.1080/1360144X.2013.862621

Di Napoli, R. (2014). Value gaming and political ontology: Between resistance and compliance in academic development. *International Journal for Academic Development, 19*(1), 4–11.doi:10. 1080/1360144X.2013. 848358

Englund, T. (2006). Deliberative communication: A pragmatist proposal. *Journal of Curriculum Studies, 38*(5), 503–520.

Fremstad, E., Bergh, A., Solbrekke, T. D., & Fossland, T. (2019). Deliberative academic development: The potential and challenge of agency. *International Journal for Academic Development*. doi:10.1080/1360144X.2019.1631169

Gibbs, G. (2013). Reflections on the changing nature of educational development. *International Journal for Academic Development, 18*(1), 4–14. doi:10.1080/1360144X.2013.751691

Gibbs, G., Knapper, C., & Piccini, S. (eds). (2009). *Departmental leadership of teaching in research-intensive universities*. London: The Leadership Foundation for Higher Education.

Handal, G., Lycke, K. H., Mårtensson, K., Roxå, T., Skodvin, A., & Solbrekke, T. D. (2014). The role of academic developers in transforming Bologna regulations to a national and institutional context. *International Journal for Academic Development, 19*(1), 12–25. doi:10.1080/1360144X.2013.849254

Holmes, T., & Manathunga, C. (2012). Of passports, maps, and suitcases: Geopolitical metaphors in academic development. *International Journal for Academic Development, 17*(3), 193–195. doi:10.1080/1360144X.2012.701086

Irving, K. (2015). Leading learning and teaching: An exploration of "local" leadership in academic departments in the UK. *Tertiary Education and Management, 21*(3), 186–199.

Kandlbinder, P. (2007). The challenge of deliberation for academic development. *International Journal for Academic Development, 12*(1), 55–59. doi:10.1080/13601440701217345

Karseth, B., & Solbrekke, T. D. (2010). Qualifications frameworks: The avenue towards convergence in European higher education? *European Journal of Education, 45*(4), 563–577.

Karseth, B., & Solbrekke, T. D. (2016). Curriculum trends in European higher education: The pursuit of the Humboldtian University Ideas. In S. Slaughter & J. T. Barrett (eds), *Higher education, stratification, and workforce development: Competitive advantage in Europe, the US, and Canada* (pp. 215–233). Cham: Springer.

Land, R. (2004). *Educational development: Discourse, identity and practice.* Maidenhead: Open University Press.

McEwen, C., & Trede, F. (2016). Educating deliberate professionals: Beyond reflective and deliberative practitioners. In F. Trede & C. McEwen (eds), *Educating the deliberate professional: Professional and practice-based learning* (pp. 223–229). Cham: Springer.

Nerland, M. (2016). Learning to master profession-specific knowledge practices: A prerequisite for the deliberate practitioner? In F. Trede & C. McEwen (eds), *Educating the deliberate professional: Professional and practice-based learning* (pp. 127–139). Cham: Springer.

Norwegian Ministry of Education and Research. (2011). *National qualifications framework for lifelong learning.* Oslo: Kunnskapsdepartementet. Retrieved from: https://www.regjerin gen.no/globalassets/upload/kd/vedlegg/kompetanse/nkr2011mvedlegg.pdf

Peseta, T. L. (2014). Agency and stewardship in academic development: The problem of speaking truth to power. *International Journal for Academic Development, 19*(1), 65–69. doi:10.1080/1360144X.2013.868809

Roxå, T., & Mårtensson, K. (2016). Agency and structure in academic development practices: Are we liberating academic teachers or are we part of a machinery suppressing them? *International Journal for Academic Development, 22*(2), 95–105. doi:10.1080/ 1360144X.2016.1218883

Solbrekke, T. D., & Fremstad, E. (2018). Universitets- og høgskolepedagogers profesjonelle ansvar [Academic developers' professional responsibility]. *UNIPED, 41*(3). doi:10.18261/ ISSN.1893-8981-2018-03-05.

Solbrekke, T. D., & Karseth, B. (2016). Kvalifikasjonsrammeverk og læringsutbytte: Til besvær eller nytte? [Qualifications framework and learning outcomes: For better or worse?]. In H. Strømsø, K. H. Lycke & P. Lauvås (eds), *Når læring er det viktigste: Undervisning i høyere utdanning [When learning is what is most important: Teaching in higher education]* (pp. 57–82). Oslo: Cappelen Akademisk Forlag.

Solbrekke, T. D., & Stensaker, B. (2016). Utdanningsledelse: Stimulering av et felles engasjement for studieprogrammene? [Educational leadership: Does it stimulate a common engagement with study programmes?]. *UNIPED, 39*(2), 144–157. doi:10.18261/ issn.1893-8981-2016-02-05

Solbrekke, T. D., Englund, T., Karseth, B., & Beck, E. E. (2016). Educating for professional responsibility: From critical thinking to deliberative communication, or why critical thinking is not enough. In F. Trede & C. McEwen (eds), *Educating the deliberate professional: Professional and practice-based learning* (pp. 29–44).Cham:Springer.

Sørskår, A. K. (2015). Survey of learning outcome descriptors. Oslo: Norwegian Agency for Quality Assurance in Education. Retrieved from :https://www.nokut.no/contentassets/

40568ec86aab411ba43c5a880ae339b5/kartlegging-av-laringsutbyttebeskrivelser_sluttrapp ort_2015-7.pdf

Stensaker, B., & Harvey, L. (eds). (2011). *Accountability in higher education: Global perspectives on trust and power.* New York: Routledge.

Stensaker, B., Van der Vaart, R., Solbrekke, T. D. & Wittek, A. L. (2017). The expansion of academic development: The challenges of organizational coordination and collaboration. In B. Stensaker, G. Bilbow, L. Breslow & R. Van der Vaart (eds), *Strengthening teaching and learning in research universities: Strategies and initiatives for institutional change* (pp. 19–42). New York: Palgrave Macmillan.

Sugrue, C., Englund, T., Solbrekke, T. D., & Fossland, T. (2017). Trends in the practices of academic developers: Trajectories of higher education? *Studies in Higher Education, 43*(12), 2336–2353. doi:10.1080/03075079.2017.1326026

Tight, M. (2013). Students: Customers, clients or pawns? *Higher Education Policy*, 26(3), 292–307.

Woods, P., & Jeffrey, B. (1996). *Teachable moments: The art of teaching in primary schools.* Maidenhead: Open University Press.

9

DELIBERATIVE COMMUNICATION AS PEDAGOGICAL LEADERSHIP

Promoting public good?

Tone Dyrdal Solbrekke and Ester Fremstad

> The high days of the concept of the public or common good in relation to higher education and research seem to be over. How to bend this trend? ... Universities do not exist for themselves or for members of their academic communities in the first place. Their role and use is a societal one ... If society is to benefit, how can this best be done?
>
> *(http://bolognaprocess2019.it/)*

Introduction

The citation above is from the call for papers to the Bologna seminar on 24–25 June 2019, Bologna Process Beyond 2020: Fundamental Values of the European Higher Education Area, and sets the tone for this chapter. Twenty years after the Bologna process was initiated there is rising concern with the orientation(s) of contemporary universities[1] which suggests the necessity to include academics in higher education policy-making. The invitation announced a call to critically investigate notions of public good and the extent to which the values higher education promotes enable students and staff to serve society. From the perspective of serving society the case in this chapter is explored. Concerned with the current trends that move the academy away from important societal contributions, the academic developer (AD) in this case feels compelled to critically deliberate on the contributions and purpose of higher education in society and to explore their practical implications for educational practices.

The AD believes in the dual potential of deliberative communication (see Chapter 3) as a pedagogical approach to leading as well as teaching. In her view, deliberative communication may be used to encourage academics to critically articulate and deliberate on the societal role of higher education and in turn they may see how to deploy this form of communication in their own teaching when the purpose is to nurture students' sense of societal responsibility. Kandlbinder (2007) has labelled this approach "deliberative academic development" and argued its importance in the current political context of academic development. Our research interest here is thus to explore and critically analyse this AD's intentions, practice and reflections on using deliberative communication in her own academic development course. We are particularly interested in her reflections on the ethical and moral aspects of teaching combined with her knowledge and experience, collectively interwoven to constitute her praxis.[2] While the case is primarily about the AD's intentions, actions and reflexive experiences, it also provides an account of more generative promises and challenges of deliberative communication as pedagogical approach in teaching and leading.

Before we describe the method and the case and its specific context in more detail, we briefly situate the case within the current context of academic development and the roles and responsibilities the current situation implies as the AD's motivation is strongly linked to this context. The case is structured in three thematic sections, the themes emerging through the analysis. The first section portrays how the AD aims to broaden the scope of academic development to include the notion of higher education as, and for, public good. The second section describes how she initiates deliberative communication to open up varied perspectives on the purpose of higher education amongst the participants in a basic university pedagogy course. The third section identifies some missed opportunities for fully realising the potential of deliberative communication. In the concluding section we identify some capacities required to develop deliberative communication as pedagogy for leading and teaching.

ADs' responsibility to promote higher education as and for public good

The main professional responsibility of ADs has always been to improve higher education teaching (Gibbs, 2013). However, intensified efforts to qualify all newly appointed academics for teaching, in tandem with expectations from institutional leaders to take a leading role in the implementation of national and institutional educational policies and strategies, have expanded ADs' responsibilities (Gaebel et al., 2018; Sugrue et al., 2017; Sutherland, 2018). For some ADs, such increased pressure to unquestioningly meet new, and externally defined, expectations contradicts their understanding of professional responsibility, and they strive to reach legitimate compromises in a web of commitments,[3] including a mix of expectations defined by institutional leaders as well as academic colleagues, and the ADs' own knowledge base and values.

For example, pedagogical models such as "constructive alignment" and its emphasis on aligning content, teaching and assessment activities with prescribed learning outcomes have gained prominence as a means of improving teaching in higher education (see Chapter 7). According to this AD's conception of how to lead educational processes as a public good, it is questionable whether such a model sufficiently includes this overall purpose. At a time when universities are under pressure to deliver employable candidates to businesses and promote "values" such as being "mobile and flexible", many academics, including ADs, regard the prioritisation of instrumental and economic goals as endangering a broader conception of the societal benefit or public good that accrues from higher education (Fremstad, 2016, Fremstad et al., 2019). From this perspective and recognising that ADs are increasingly involved in designing educational leadership programmes (Stensaker et al., 2017), it is vital to address how ADs lead, and for what purpose. It is timely, then, to critically investigate how ADs can encourage academics to deliberate on the purpose of higher education, what societal responsibility may imply and the implications for teaching in different disciplines. Doing so involves becoming more aware of one's own praxis and the formative impact of teaching. From this perspective we explore the ADs' efforts to contribute to increased awareness of the implications of teaching as, and for, public good to in courses in university pedagogy.

Methods and data sources

Consistent with the common methodology of all the cases in this book, we have applied an abductive and reflexive insider–outsider approach inspired by the principles of deliberative communication for the study of the case. This implied active collaboration between critical friends/researchers and the AD both in planning the teaching session and when the AD reflected on the experiences in order to become more aware of her praxis.[4] In this case we also draw on data from the sequence the AD had with her fellow course leader when planning the session, and previous conversations she had with academics across the university about teaching students about their future societal responsibility. Collectively, the analysis of the AD's intentions, practice and self-reflections on her practice helped gain more insight into the AD's praxis and the potential and challenges of deliberative communication as a pedagogy to lead academic development processes. The methods, data sources and analysis process are summarised in the table below.

Case and context

The AD in this case has held a temporary post as an academic developer for five years. The history of the academic development unit in which she works stretches back more than 50 years, and the ADs have academic positions within the Department of Education at the University of Oslo. The ADs' academic status combined with the unit's extensive experience have positioned them as peers vis-à-vis other academics in their institution. Over the years, the unit has gained relatively high credibility among most university leaders, other academics and administrative staff across the university (Fremstad et al., 2019; Lycke & Handal, 2018). In 2015, an external evaluation of the unit's work concluded that the university pedagogy courses were generally considered to be of high quality (Engelsrud, Kristensen, & Søfteland, 2015). This was confirmed in 2016 by the pro-rector for

TABLE 9.1 Methods and data sources

Time	What took place	Participants	Analytical purpose
August 2017	Presentation of the purpose of and plan for the session (video-recorded)	AD and research partners in formation team	To identify aims of the session in conjunction with the first conversation between ADs and critical friends
January 2018	Conversations with academics who aim to teach societal responsibility (audio-recorded)	AD and four academics from three different disciplines	To identify motivations for and experiences with teaching societal responsibilities
January 2018	Conversation about aims and plans for session (audio-recorded)	AD and two critical friends	To identify potential ways of leading higher education for public good
May 2018	Planning of course and session (Notes and video recording)	AD and AD colleague	To identify the AD's intention for the session and potential challenges of leading by means of deliberative communication
May 2018	Conversation about edited plan for the session (audio-recorded)	AD and critical friends	To identify revised approaches to leading the session, and the reasoning behind the revisions
September 2018	Course session on the purpose of higher education (video-recorded)	AD and course participants	To explore AD's leadership actions in practice in light of the principles of deliberative communication
February 2019	Individual reflections/notes on the process Individual logs	AD and critical friends	As a meta-reflection on the method and what was learned from it
March 2019	Preparation of semi-structured conversation about leading the session by means of deliberative communication Document for AD	Critical friends/researchers	Preparation for reflection on the experience of the session in light of purpose and aims
March 2019	Conversation about what the researchers observed in the session and the AD's experiences of and reflections on intentions and experiences in leading the session amidst a web of commitments, promises and challenges of deliberative communication as a pedagogy (video-recorded and individual reflection document)	AD and critical friends/researchers	Identifying the AD's web of commitments and her reflections on the experience of leading by means of deliberative communication for the public good. To identify and further explore potential and challenges of leadership in universities. To identify what we (ADs, critical friends and researchers) learned from the process

education, who also underlined the ADs' research: "It is important for the credibility of the unit, and the university needs the knowledge from their research".[5]

Against this backdrop, the AD could have been at ease with how she and her AD colleagues performed their work and simply continued business as usual. There was no apparent need to change the way they ran the university pedagogy courses. However, her own research on academics' societal responsibility, university teaching for public good, and the role and responsibility of academic developers within the current context of higher education[6] initiated and nurtured awareness of and reflections on the need to strengthen the focus on higher education as and for public good. This research, combined with the experience and confidence gained through five years of academic development work, contributed to the AD's agency and courage to argue for the need to address the purpose of higher education and academics' societal responsibilities to contribute to the public good more explicitly in the university's pedagogy courses. In the post-seminar conversation with her critical friends, she reflected on her own development as a leader of academic development processes and said that until she started to include such issues in her courses she had "not lived up to the commitment to strengthen the focus on higher education as, and for, public good".

> much like Roxå and Mårtensson (2017) describe – rather than forming my practices based on critical examination of values, ideas of higher education and potential contributions of academic development, I have simply more or less adopted course designs and pedagogical approaches from senior colleagues without questioning them.

Beginning to realise her role in contributing to educational leadership positioned to potentially influence conceptions of the purpose of higher education, she sees it as her "responsibility to inspire academics to develop a stronger awareness about their professional responsibility and the formative aspect of university teaching". In her view this implies "addressing the question of the overall purpose of higher education and ask how we may reconceptualise and develop teaching approaches that contribute to education as and for public good".

The practice under scrutiny in this case is a 40-minute session, part of the basic university pedagogy course, which takes place at the beginning of the second two-day course seminar. The 30 participants, from across most of the disciplines at the university, are (mainly) relatively newly appointed academics in temporary positions. As indicated above, the main intention of the AD in this session is to facilitate deliberative communication about the purpose of higher education with a specific focus on societal responsibility and its implications for educational practice. As she explained to the AD colleague with whom she planned and led the course, "I want to discuss what kind of societal responsibility we have. Higher education as a societal responsibility, and what kind of candidates do we educate? What kind of citizens and professionals do we wish to educate?"

The quote above suggests that a core commitment for this AD stems from her view that it is crucial to develop and maintain teaching approaches which encourage students' holistic formation, in the sense that they contribute to their capacities to be active citizens as part of their personal and professional development. This conviction is also a result of her conversations with academics from different disciplines about teaching for societal responsibility, which she arranged a few months earlier. In pre-seminar conversations with her critical friends she described how these academics acknowledged their societal responsibility as academics and their commitment to teach their students about the societal responsibilities implied in academic professional work. The fact that "they saw it as important to more explicitly integrate societal responsibilities in university teaching, yet struggled to find ways of managing it", as she recalled it, encouraged her to include the topic in the basic university pedagogy course.

Further, in the recording of the meeting in which she and her colleague planned the course, we observe the importance of support from her AD colleague in order to make the theme an integral part of the course. They shared reflection on how they could frame the topic. Her colleague said, "I think this is about the kind of attitudes academics promote, and how they relate to knowledge. It is not only about critical thinking which is very cognitive … it is more about attitudes". The AD confirmed: "This is what we want to encourage and make more articulate". Simultaneously she expressed a concern about the multiple commitments new academics have to deal with and said: "It is of course a matter of how much time we can spend on this". She is wary the fact that young academics in public universities live under constant pressure to deliver high-quality research, while they are also increasingly expected to improve their teaching (Levecque et al., 2017). In a pre-seminar conversation with her critical friends, the AD underlined this by saying, "I am a bit reluctant to require too much of them in an already stressed work- day". While acknowledging the course participants' multiple commitments she is also wary her own responsibility and commitment to cover the main course topics her AD unit had agreed upon. The AD maintains that she is "conscious of the tension between providing academics with more immediately 'useful' teaching tools, and initiating pedagogical reflection that captures both the purpose of higher education *and* the complexities of educational activities". A central aim is thus to make the session "meaningful to the course participants", even though reflections on the societal responsibility of higher education may be experienced as "abstract by some of the course participants", as she phrased it. Thus, when planning the session, she argues that:

there is no point simply lecturing about the purpose of higher education. Rather, the course participants need to engage with the question. A first step could be inspiring them to talk about the generic normative mandate embedded in university education. A second step could be to initiate reflections on how this [normative mandate] may be included when planning teaching in their specific discipline or professional programme. I think it is important to give them enough time to reflect and to encourage them to reflect upon what this might look like in their own teaching practice.

The AD wants to facilitate meaningful deliberations for all course participants and to connect educational ideals and practices. Her intention is to start with the societal responsibility of higher education and ask all participants to articulate their conceptions so that all voices can be heard and different views are given equal consideration, all important principles of deliberative communication.

Broadening the scope of teaching and learning

A profound commitment for this AD is to "broaden the scope of teaching and learning", as she frames it in a pre-seminar conversation with her critical friends. By using deliberative communication she wants to bring awareness to societal responsibility and to the political and formative influences of education, and thus "stimulate the participants to move beyond ideals and reflections, to see what they may imply for their teaching, and by this contribute to the participants' increased awareness of their praxis".

A challenge she points out as crucial in this regard is the lack of vocabulary for discussion of praxis. On this point she is in line with Barnett (2004) and Biesta (2006), among others, who point out that we need to develop a language which connects teaching and learning with the values and purposes of education, in order to be able to make deliberate choices for leading education. Aiming to connect these two "languages", the AD starts the session with a slide introducing some pedagogical concepts and tools for planning teaching:

With the slide on the screen, she argues that academics tend to be most concerned with *what* to teach and *how* to teach when they plan their teaching. She then says:

What I want us to do here and now is to attend to the "why dimension". Disciplinary content and pedagogical research and reasoning are essential when planning our teaching. Equally important, though more seldom attended to, are the purpose, normative mandate and values of higher education.

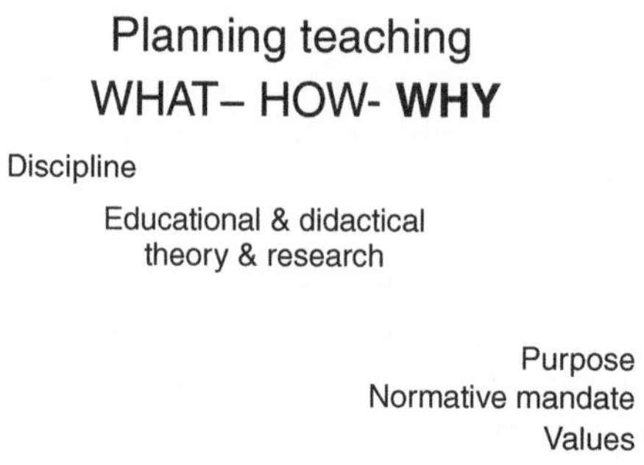

Planning teaching
WHAT– HOW– **WHY**

Discipline

Educational & didactical
theory & research

Purpose
Normative mandate
Values

FIGURE 9.1 The first slide of the session.

Next, she proceeds to a model called "didactic relational thinking",[7] which she introduced in the first seminar of the course a month earlier.

She reminds the participants of how this "thinking model" captures dimensions and complexities which are excluded from the more dominant "constructive alignment" model. While acknowledging the strengths of aligning prescribed learning goals, teaching and learning activities, and assessment forms, she argues that "'didactic relational thinking' also reminds us that teaching is always a relational and complex endeavour involving multiple participants with varied interests, but also that we must relate our local teaching to the societal responsibility of higher education". While she is in line with those who argue that there is a risk embedded in all models to foreclose non-predictable learning, she demonstrates how didactic relational thinking may broaden the scope of teaching and learning, not least because it includes – and thereby reminds us to articulate – the purpose of higher education as an important framing of all teaching. She says:

> It is important to articulate the overall normative mandate of higher education, as this is based in values which we do not very often talk about … Moreover, in addition to including didactical categories beyond aims, activities and assessment, didactic relational thinking includes more of the complex relational aspects of teaching. It more explicitly includes the participants [teachers and students] in the teaching and learning process, the physical conditions and other resources available, and also emphasises the overall *purpose* of all university teaching.

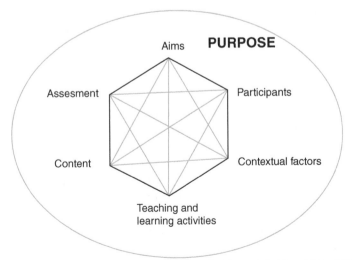

Didactic relational thinking

Aims   **PURPOSE**

Assesment   Participants

Content   Contextual factors

Teaching and
learning activities

(Adapted and translated from Bjørndal & Lieberg 1978)

FIGURE 9.2 Slide showing the model "didactic relational thinking".

In this quotation, the AD flags a normative stance and by that points out a direction for further reflections on university teaching. After this introduction, her intention was, as she articulated it in post-seminar conversations, "to engage the participants in deliberative communication about the purpose of higher education and implications for educational practice".

Initiating deliberative communication

Before initiating deliberative communication, the AD wanted to evoke the participants' moral engagement with teaching and the purposes of higher education. She refers to studies indicating that activities and values related to public good seem to diminish during university studies. One study concludes that medical students leave medical school less empathetic than when they entered. Another portrays how biology students' engagement in the community of students and in voluntary work for environmental organisations is superseded by a focus on individual exam results. A study from psychology indicates that, because of the increased pressure to publish, academics do not have time, either in research or teaching, to critically reflect and discuss the influence of their discipline on our self-understanding as human beings and society.[8] Finally, she includes a story of a student who had been advised to leave the university and theology studies, since, due to disabilities related to speech and movement, they claim she could never practice as a priest.

In the post-seminar reflection, the AD told her critical friends that this introduction was intended to serve a dual aim: "to draw on research to qualify my arguments and in turn make a moral rationale for the need to bring back issues of public good more explicitly in higher education". Furthermore, the studies were

> meant to illustrate relevance for different disciplines … to present a research-based critique and a wish to pursue a specific direction. In addition, there is something affective in the examples. They may evoke emotions, and by that create an interest and sense of relevance.

The quote underlines how this AD sought to emphasise both the intellectual and emotional formative influence of addressing the question of purpose. Choosing the studies she did demonstrates how she uses research to confirm her own stance, yet also, as she summarised in the course session: "They illustrate that something is at stake in higher education. Now I wish to hear what you see as the main purpose of higher education". By this she clearly indicated a direction for the further deliberation, yet without imposing on them a definition of the overall purpose of higher education. Rather, she leaves the participants to discuss in groups of two.

This way of leading the session, with only a relatively brief introduction, and without defining the societal responsibility and contribution of higher education, indicates a strong commitment to let the participants reflect and articulate their own conceptions. In this way she encourages them to try out a language while also facilitating a first step towards deliberative communication by encouraging all to present their views. Arranging the participants in groups of two without her presence also allowed another core principle in deliberative communication to be enacted, namely to let the participants communicate and deliberate without the AD's control and to stimulate argumentative discussions among the participants with the aim of shedding light on them from different points of view. The activity in the room at this point suggested that the participants were very much engaged in the question.

After a few minutes, the AD stops the group discussions and initiates a plenary discussion, asking them to share what they "see as the purpose of higher education". Leading the session in a dialogical and inclusive manner, she uses the course participants' names to invite them to present their meanings and, asking for their views, listens and uses her body language by nodding and smiling to indicate that all participants' perspectives are important. The way she leads the session reflects respect and tolerance, and she provides room for all voices. Her approach creates an atmosphere which makes the participants comfortable enough to share their understandings, and, by writing down all the input on an iPad which is projected onto a screen, she ensures that all perspectives are acknowledged and that everybody can see the various understandings which emerged in the discussion. This section lasts for 30 minutes, and similar to the group discussions revealed high energy and activity.

An important principle of leading deliberative communication is to encourage the participants to articulate and elaborate their perspectives and arguments. During the session, this was done several times by the AD, who asked probing questions, either directed to the person who articulated the specific viewpoint or more widely to everyone in the room, as the examples below illustrate:

PARTICIPANT 1: The individual receives higher education from society. Thus, we have a responsibility to give back to society.

AD: How do we give back to society?

PARTICIPANT 1: Providing society with knowledge.

PARTICIPANT 2: Within each discipline, the individual must create their own sense of how to give back to society. And the teacher should nurture students' engagement.

PARTICIPANT 3: The most important way of providing society with knowledge is through the candidates we educate.

AD: What do they [the candidates] need to bring with them, then?

PARTICIPANT 4: Updated knowledge.

AD: Anything else?

PARTICIPANT 5: Curiosity.

This example demonstrates how probing questions directed to everyone in the room can develop a more collective elaboration of a perspective. In this situation the AD acts as moderator, passing the discussion around to those who raise their hands. In the following example, similar probing is performed, but in this case directed to the person posing the perspective:

PARTICIPANT: Critical thinking, within academia it has a specific meaning. It is a specific way of relating to information and knowledge. It is not value-neutral (…)

AD: That is interesting. You said it is not value-neutral. What do you mean by that?

PARTICIPANT: No, of course not.

AD: Tell us more …

Following this exchange, a discussion about values emerges between some of the participants, and different views are expressed. The AD maintains her role as moderator, passing the discussion around to those raising their hands, with no interruption, until she considers it necessary to lead the discussion back to the theme of the session. Her summary and question initiate more deliberations among the participants:

AD: Okay, what I hear is that there are some values, ideals, that we wish to nurture, related to democracy and scientific reasoning. So: What does this look like in teaching? Do you explicitly relate to such values when you teach?

PARTICIPANT 1: Yes … but it is quite difficult!

AD: What is difficult?

PARTICIPANT 1: You very soon become occupied with teaching the disciplinary content, and the overall purpose of higher education is lost from view.

PARTICIPANT 2: We need to make values more explicit when we teach. We tend to overvalue students' capacities to see these.

PARTICIPANT 3: I think we need to teach the students about the values that underlie the theories we teach them.

This sequence indicates how the AD lead by being a moderator of the plenary conversation, using probing questions rather than responding to individual accounts seemingly stimulates a collective [public] engagement in what we may define as issues related to praxis. However, whether this initiative develops further deliberative communication thus enabling the participants see how to promote values of public good is contingent on how it is followed up. As the session is approaching its end, the AD summarises by saying: "I got a lot to think about, and I hope that you have got something to think about also. And now it is time for lunch". There is no information on how the deliberation may continue over the lunch – or after – and we are left with unanswered questions on how – or whether – more informal ongoing deliberation on how to teach societal responsibility in and across different disciplines was encouraged. It is reasonable, therefore, to argue that while the leading approach the AD chose opened the discussion to different perspectives and stimulated awareness about significant dimensions of higher education and societal responsibilities, the potential to move from a cacophony of different views to setting them against each other, and to move from ideals to the concrete praxis of teaching, remained underexploited in the session. Likewise, while a basis for deliberative communication was evident, the AD missed several "teachable moments" (Woods & Jeffrey, 1996) with potential for more extended deliberative communication.

Missed opportunities

During the session, the course participants provided several arguments and statements about the purpose of higher education which seemed to contradict each other. These created moments in which the AD could have encouraged explorations of the varied perspectives and stimulated deliberations on pedagogy and purpose. For different reasons, however, these situations remained unexploited. Insights into the reasons may tell us more about what is required to take advantage of these teachable moments to facilitate deliberative communication as a way of leading academic development. The AD's reflections on why she missed these opportunities to encourage more in-depth deliberative communication provide essential insight into what it takes to support deliberative communication in the context of academic development. The post-seminar conversations with critical friends were essential to bring out these reflections. In the following section we present some selected "missed opportunities", chosen because they elicited a range of reflections on what it takes to lead a deliberative communication process which encourages reflections on praxis.

In one example, a participant responds to the overall question about the purpose of higher education and argues that "critical thinking – it is a prerequisite for democracy, and an important aim for education". Here, the AD has the opportunity to respond and ask for more elaboration on implications for education. However, by choosing to merely add the participant's input to her notes on the iPad and move on to other participants, she missed the opportunity to open up the discussion for a deliberation on his stance.

Another situation directly invites a deliberation on the purpose of higher education and everyday teaching, when a participant states:

> Some of the purpose of higher education is that we shall spread knowledge and create debates in the public. And then it is a highly problematic situation now, where in many disciplines we create a language and a field of knowledge that is inaccessible for those we are actually doing it for. (…) We have to bring knowledge out to society, not stay within our offices.

While this situation actually invites elaboration on the AD's concern with the lack of language to connect purpose and teaching, rather than addressing this she merely invites another participant to contribute. Thus she lost a moment in which deliberations on, for example, what "bringing knowledge out to society" entails rather than hiding in your office and what it may imply in terms of teaching for public good.

A third opportunity was missed when one of the course participants, well into the plenary discussion, seemingly challenges the AD's stances as indicated through the way she presented the study on empathy in medical education in the introduction to the session. The participant argues that a professional physician needs to develop "distance" rather than "empathy" in order to perform their work in a professionally responsible manner. The AD chooses to respond to this utterance merely by acknowledging the physician's view and by hinting at disciplinary variations. However, in the post-session conversation with her critical friends, she says:

> It could have been an opportunity to problematise ... and nuance ... I could have raised questions like, why is it so? Why does it look like that? And I could have engaged the other participants' perspectives and I could have asked what kind of medical doctors do we want to educate? Don't we want empathetic doctors? And what does that imply for how we teach?

In all the situations described above, probing questions could have stimulated a more collective deliberation, producing different views and arguments on how to bring public good to the fore in higher education. However, the AD did not manage to exploit all opportunities to encourage different views and perspectives and further deliberative communication. While it is, from a pedagogical point of view, important also to acknowledge that teachable moments arise in almost all teaching episodes and that it is not either desirable or appropriate to exploit them all, it is reasonable to argue that the situations above represent golden moments the AD could have benefitted from to bring deliberation forward.

In the post-seminar conversations with her critical friends, the AD reflects on her chosen strategies for leading the session and admits that, in these situations, she felt a bit "stuck" in her web of commitments and how to reach legitimate compromises between individuals' interests and the commitment to lead the conversation in the direction she wanted for the whole group. For example, she says, "Sometimes, you have a specific direction in mind for the conversations, and a comment simply disrupts the direction and flow". Participant responses which unexpectedly lead the conversation "astray" from the envisioned path cause the AD to try to find ways of stopping what at the time is experienced as side-tracking the discussion. However, in hindsight she sees that such opportunities could have engaged the participants in deliberative exchanges of perspectives and arguments, which might be more meaningful than just keeping the conversation on track. While this reflective conversation provides further evidence of just how complex these teaching episodes are, it also demonstrates potential for making better use of teachable moments in the future.

Another tension arises between what she describes as "practical and immediate usefulness on the one hand and the critical reflection and discussion about the educational mission on the other hand". She knows that many course participants expect to learn "tips and tricks" which they may directly apply to daily teaching. Many also expect to learn "best practices" – what, according to evidence, works best. However, from a pedagogical perspective, the AD, as indicated above, sees it as more important to support academics' agency to define and pursue educational aims by building "awareness about higher education and public good, and implications for teaching". Still, she describes how her fear of not creating meaningful situations which the participants experience as useful and relevant influenced her choice of responses. For example, the comment about medical students and empathy is one example, she reflected in a post-seminar conversation. Being preoccupied with making meaningful learning situations for all participants causes uncertainty about the entire session and in particular regarding unexpected responses. Handling the unforeseen is essential in leading deliberative communication, while, in this case, pursuing a planned direction of the conversation was also seen as essential. The fact that the participants are from a range of disciplines adds to this tension:

> To handle this interdisciplinarity is demanding. I was concerned with making the discussion relevant for everyone and not becoming too profession-specific. Meanwhile, the intention was to become concrete ... So, it's a weighing of concerns ... and it has to happen so fast when you stand there. I think the biggest challenge is to be confident enough about spending time on this and not give in for the direct "usefulness" and trust that they experience deliberations on the purpose as meaningful. And also, it is about having a repertoire of responses to handle the unpredictable, and the courage to raise these issues.

Even when having the courage to spend time on deliberations which may not be seen as directly applicable to teaching, the AD continues to struggle between the need for immediate usefulness and the capability to reflect and deliberate. That the participants in this course are academics at an early stage of their university careers creates a new commitment for the AD to cater for colleagues in a situation of extreme pressure. She says:

> They hold temporary positions and are thus under pressure to perform high-quality research to qualify for permanent positions. Additionally, they tend to have a more short-term timeframe for their teaching activities, as well as limited degree of influence on courses and programmes.

In this contexts, what the participants may be asked to absorb and engage with in terms of moral and critical reasoning is restrained by more short-term needs in terms of coping with their teaching load as merely one of several expectations. However, the AD has experiences from earlier courses that confirm that investing time in reflection processes which may stand out as less immediately "useful" for their daily teaching was also appreciated and that "the participants find the question of purpose highly relevant". The AD comes back to this in post-seminar conversations as she ponders on the influence from deliberative communication. In hindsight she argues that "the value of the deliberations may have remained limited as I did not have a follow-up plan". Nevertheless, the belief in deliberative communication remains, but she acknowledges that it requires more time, and a pedagogical and didactic language that integrates societal responsibility in teaching:

> I wanted to start small and not spend the whole morning on it but try to relate the other topics of the day to the topic of this session. This showed to be difficult, though. I believe we need to find some concepts which better

connect "teaching and learning" to formation and the normative mandate. They need language tools to work with. We need to spend more time on this so they have time to actually work with "what does this look like in my field". There are limits to how concrete you can become and still be relevant in a cross-disciplinary forum.

She underlines that "the point of the reflections is to help the participants become more aware their own praxes". This brings us to some final reflections on what is required to develop deliberate communication as a praxis while also promoting public good in higher education.

The quest for courage, repertoire and a community of practice to promote public good

This chapter's focus has been on the exploration of an AD's praxis when trying to fulfil her commitment to bring issues of public good more explicitly into university pedagogy by using deliberative communication. In this last section, we will share some of what we learned from the case as we believe it has relevance for all academics engaged in leading and teaching.

First, in the context of contemporary public universities, multiple forces are challenging more time-consuming pedagogical processes such as deliberative communication to address academics' professional responsibility and the purpose of higher education. The *why* question tends to be marginalised in university teaching (Fremstad et al., 2019; Karseth & Solbrekke, 2016). Such ideas may, therefore, encounter resistance from academics who are more concerned with learning tips and tricks on how to go about demonstrating high-quality teaching defined as, for example, blended learning and more student centredness. Thus, spending time on the moral and societal aspects of teaching in higher education requires not only courage to act but also the capacity to reach legitimate compromise within a web of commitments created by multiple expectations and needs. This case reveals how difficult it might be to teach what you preach but nevertheless how necessary it is to be true to your professional commitments.

Some of the challenges the AD experienced may be understood as inevitable because of the immediacy of classroom engagement in a university pedagogy course and other teaching in higher education. Lortie (1975) reminds us of the degrees of "presentism" due to the immediacy of exchanges, as, for example, when the AD just moved on to finish off the session rather than making provision for participants to continue their deliberations. She also experienced how difficult it was to connect (more directly) the purposes of higher education with teaching and learning. Reflecting on this, she also returns to her view that both she (as an AD) and her academic colleagues "lack an appropriate vocabulary that can address the normative dimensions of education and relate it to the language of teaching and learning". She emphasises the importance of such language and a broader repertoire of strategies in order to lead processes of deliberative communication. From her own experience in this case, she also underlines the necessity of "maintaining the conviction that this is important and relevant, and that it is our role to do it – yet hard to do on your own". She emphasises the need to develop a community of practice among ADs in which questions about the normative mandate and public good are part of their deliberations on the purpose of academic development in the context of twenty-first-century public universities. As she sees it, it is an AD's responsibility to invest in the question of "how to integrate the issue of purpose and public good and academic development". And, reflecting on how to move this forward, she admits, "I guess I have a responsibility to try to include my colleagues in such deliberations", a responsibility we believe all academics share, not least those in formal educational leadership positions.

The courage to act by means of deliberative communication also indicates the vulnerable position leaders of a deliberative communicative process are in, as the process demands the capacity to expose your own normative stances and also to risk losing control, prepare for and include the unexpected. It requires the commitment and capacity to listen and tolerate perspectives which may challenge your personal or professional convictions and values. It requires the capacity to seize the golden moments in which deliberative communication may become teachable moments, as well as planning for emergent opportunities. Moreover, it requires both confidence and a repertoire of responses to meet the unforeseen articulations and perspectives which come to the fore in an open-ended, deliberative discussion. Last, but not least, we must all respect the multiplicity of values and interests in higher education and accept that leading and teaching involve negotiating legitimate compromises in the tensions between different commitments and conceptions of public good. A first step towards developing praxes for public good is by acknowledging the complexity of leading and teaching, and the value of shared reflections and deliberations on public good. For that purpose we need to develop conceptual thinking tools and a language that incorporates moral and societal responsibilities with discipline knowledge and skills, in everyday teaching practices.

Acknowledgment

We gratefully acknowledge the contribution of Johan Wickström's engagement with the initial analysis and deliberations on data.

Notes

1 See Chapter 2 for how we, inspired by Barnett (2011), conceptualise four different university orientations, and their underlying values, and how contemporary public universities tend to have more than one orientation yet are increasingly dominated by an entrepreneurial orientation.
2 We use praxis as it is elaborated in Chapter 1; the notion of praxis combines critical and ethical reflection with disciplinary knowledge, expertise, humanity and finesse.
3 See Chapter 4 for elaboration of what we mean when we assert that the tensions between the logics of "responsibility" and "accountability" must be negotiated in order

to behave in a professionally responsible manner amidst a web of commitments in which legitimate compromises must be reached (May, 1996; Solbrekke & Fremstad, 2018).
4 See introduction to Part II of the book for elaboration on the method.
5 As part of the Formation project (see introduction to Part II of the book), all institutional leaders, pro-rectors for education, were interviewed about the mission of public universities, their aspirations to fulfil this mission and the role of the ADs in fulfilling the purpose of higher education.
6 The AD has done research in recent years on questions related to the purpose of higher education in different ways (Beck et al., 2015; Fremstad, 2016; Fremstad et al., 2019; Solbrekke & Fremstad, 2018). The AD has been inspired in her approach by other scholars' argumentation on the need for ADs to contribute to more active questioning on what kind of organisation, leadership, teaching and learning supports the purpose of higher education (Kandlbinder, 2007; Manathunga, 2011; Sutherland, 2018).
7 This model was developed by the two Norwegian curriculum theorists Bjørndal and Lieberg in the 1970s.
8 In this sequence, the AD draws on research in different university programmes referred to in Fremstad (2016) and in Karseth & Solbrekke (2006).

References

Barnett, R. (2004). Foreword. In B. Macfarlane, *Teaching with Integrity: The Ethics of Higher Education Practice*. Abingdon: Routledge.

Barnett, R. (2011). The idea of the university in the twenty-first century: where's the Imagination? *The Journal of Higher Education*, *1*(2), 88–94.

Beck, E. E., Solbrekke, T. D., Sutphen, M., & Fremstad, E. (2015). When mere knowledge is not enough: the potential of bildung as self-determination, co-determination and solidarity. *Higher Education Research & Development*, *34*(3) 445–457. doi:10.1080/07294360.2014.973373

Biesta, G. J. J. (2006) *Beyond Learning: Democratic Education for a Human Future*. New York: Routledge.

Bjørndal, B., & Lieberg, S. (1978). Nye veier i didaktikken? en innføring i didaktiske emner og begreper. (New didactic approaches? an introduction to didactic themes and concepts) Oslo: Aschehoug.

Bologna Process Beyond 2020: Fundamental values of the EHEA. Invitation to academic seminar Bologna, 24–25 June 2019. http://bolognaprocess2019.it/abstract-submission/ (downloaded 10 May 2019).

Dwyer, S. C., & Buckle, J. L. (2009). The space between: on being an insider–outsider in qualitative research. *International Journal of Qualitative Methods*, *8*(1), 54–63.

Engelsrud, G., Kristensen, S., & Søfteland, Å. (2015) *Programevaluering av kurs i pedagogisk basiskompetanse ved Universitetet i Oslo*. Rapport fra evalueringskomiteen.

Fremstad, E. (2016). Taking responsibility toward the public: university academics' imaginaries and experiences. PhD thesis. University of Oslo, Norway. http://urn.nb.no/URN: NBN:no-54526.

Fremstad, E., Bergh, A., Solbrekke, T. D., & Fossland, T. (2019). Deliberative academic development: the potential and challenge of agency. *International Journal for Academic Development*. doi:10.1080/1360144X.2019.1631169.

Gaebel, M., Zhang, T., Bunescu, L., & Stoeber, H. (2018). *Trends 2018: Learning and Teaching in the European Higher Education Area*, European University Association. Retrieved 26 June 2019, from https://eua.eu/resources/publications/757:trends-2018-learning-and-teaching-in-the-european-higher-education-area.html

Gibbs, G. (2013). Reflections on the changing nature of academic development. *International Journal for Academic Development*, *18*(1), 4–14.

Kandlbinder, P. (2007). The challenge of deliberation for academic development. *International Journal for Academic Development, 12*(1), 55–59.

Karseth, B., & Solbrekke, T. D. (2006). Characteristics of graduate professional education: expectations and experiences in psychology and law. *London Review of Education, 4*(2), 149–167.

Karseth, B., & Solbrekke, T. D. (2016). Curriculum trends in European higher education: the pursuit of the Humboldtian University Ideas.In S. Slaughter & J. T. Barrett (eds), *Higher Education, Stratification, and Workforce Development: Competitive Advantage in Europe, the US, and Canada* (pp. 215–233). Cham: Springer.

Levecque, K., Anseel, F., De Beuckelaer, A., Van der Heyden, J., & Gisle, L. (2017). Work organization and mental health problems in PhD students. *Research Policy, 46*(4), 868–879.

Lortie, D. (1975). *Schoolteacher: A Sociological Study*. Chicago: University of Chicago Press.

Manathunga, C. (2011). The field of educational development: histories and critical questions. *Studies in Continuing Education, 33*(3), 347–362. doi:10.1080/0158037X.2011.613375

Marginson, S. (2007) The public/private divide in higher education: a global revision. *Higher Education, 53*(3), 307–333.

May, L. (1996). *The Socially Responsive Self: Social Theory and Professional Ethics*. Chicago: Chicago University Press.

Pusser, B. (2006) *Reconsidering Higher Education and the Public Good: The Role of Public Spaces, in Governance and the Public Good State*. Albany: State University of New York Press.

Robinson, S., & Katulushi, C. (eds). (2004). *Values in Higher Education*. Leeds: Aureus Publishing.

Roxå, T., & Mårtensson, K. (2017). Agency and structure in academic development practices: are we liberating academic teachers or are we part of a machinery suppressing them? *International Journal for Academic Development, 22*(2), 95–105. doi:10.1080/1360144X.2016.1218883

Solbrekke, T. D., & Fremstad, E. (2018). *Universitets- og høgskolepedagogers profesjonelle ansvar. [Academic developers' professional responsibility]*. Oslo: Tidsskrift for universitets og høgskolepedagogikk.

Stensaker, B., Bilbow, G. T., Breslow, L., & Van Der Vaart, R. (eds). (2017). *Strengthening Teaching and Learning in Research Universities: Strategies and Initiatives for Institutional Change*. London: Palgrave Macmillan.

Sugrue, C., Englund, T., Solbrekke, T. D., & Fossland, T. (2017). Trends in the practices of academic developers: trajectories of higher education?*Studies in Higher Education, 43*(12), 2336–2353.

Sutherland, K. A. (2018). Holistic academic development: Is it time to think more broadly about the academic development project? *International Journal for Academic Development, 23*(4), 261–273.

Sutphen, M., Solbrekke, T. D., & Sugrue, C. (2018). Toward articulating an academic praxis by interrogating university strategic plans. *Studies in Higher Education, 44*(8), 1–13. doi:10.1080/03075079.2018.1440384

Woods, P., & Jeffrey, B. (1996). *Teachable Moments: The Art of Teaching in Primary Schools*. Milton Keynes: Open University Press.

10

NURTURING PEDAGOGICAL PRAXIS THROUGH DELIBERATIVE COMMUNICATION

Ragnhild Sandvoll, Andreas Bergh and Tone Dyrdal Solbrekke

Introduction

> I believe in deliberative communication as a public good. It involves some values and principles that I really want to stimulate among academics. But how do I go about it?

While indicating a degree of uncertainty regarding how to practise deliberative communication, the above statement from an experienced academic developer (AD) denotes a genuine commitment to introduce deliberative communication to her repertoire (see Chapter 3) as a pedagogical means for leading higher education as, and for, public good. Such ambition, resonates with the many researchers who have pointed out the need to critically investigate the formative aspects of different teaching and assessment practices (Sullivan & Rosin, 2008) in light of the purpose of higher education to educate students with a capacity to act in a professionally responsible manner in future work practice (Beck et al., 2015; Colby et al., 2011; Walker, 2018). Against this backdrop, this chapter analyses how the AD quoted above uses deliberative communication in practice as an approach to leading higher education as, and for, public good.

The specific case we explore is part of the AD's consultation work at the University of Oslo, and a consequence of an initiative taken by the deans of study at the Faculty of Dentistry who approached the AD for assistance in their ongoing work with academic development and transforming (improving) clinical supervision practices. The overall aim of the initiative is to develop more transparent supervision and assessment practices that support students' formation in becoming professionally responsible dentists. The expression "professionally responsible" emphasises the normative mandate that entrusts higher education institutions with the responsibility to provide society with highly skilled professionals, citizens and leaders who will work for both individual and public good (Solbrekke, 2007). The goal for the case studied here was to lead the process of developing formative assessment procedures communicating *what* to be evaluated, *how* and *why*. The intention, announced by the dean of study, was that more transparent procedures would contribute to the learning environment in which the students could grow personally and help them become professionally responsible dentists. However, creating learning situations that support such formation in clinical situations is challenging, and the Faculty turned to the AD for pedagogical support. The AD has expertise in the field of educational leadership and professional education, with a specific interest in how university teaching may cultivate students' sense of professional responsibility (Solbrekke, 2007, 2008; Solbrekke & Sugrue, 2014). As the AD has been a consultant to the Faculty since 2012, and she had worked closely with both formal and informal educational leaders at several levels at the Faculty, they knew her quite well. Thus, the case represents an AD who is practising what Debowski (2014) defines as an equal partner rather than a centralist expert. The initiative taken to develop new assessment rubrics is a result of close collaboration between the AD and the faculty staff over time.

While such a role indicates trust in the AD and her expertise as a university pedagogue, it may also be indicative of how university leaders at different levels increasingly tend to delegate to ADs the leadership responsibility for transforming teaching practices (Stensaker et al., 2017; Taylor, 2005). Very rarely are new leadership initiatives from senior leaders applauded by all (Handal et al., 2014; Youngs, 2017). Rather they are often met with resistance or at least scepticism and must be negotiated to reach legitimate compromises in the tension between different interests (see Chapter 4). Such delegated responsibility implies brokering responsibilities to cope with possible tensions that may emerge in the web of commitments that leading educational processes embed (Fremstad et al., 2019; Handal et al., 2014). Finally, the different commitments must be negotiated with the AD's values and aspirations in order to reach legitimate compromises on how to lead the process. In this case it concerns how to reach a level of agreement needed to develop a more common assessment practice while also contributing to the knowledge and expertise of colleagues (Debowski, 2014).[1]

Against this backdrop, our intention is to gain more insight into the potential of and challenges with using deliberative communication as a pedagogical approach in leading academic development processes as, and for, public good.

The research questions are:

1.   How does the AD, through deliberative communication, lead the process of academic development when developing formative assessment procedures to enhance professional responsibility?
2.   What possibilities and challenges emerge in the process of leading?

The presentation of the case is structured as follows. We begin by situating the case within the ongoing work at the Faculty of Dentistry, and this is followed by a description of the method deployed to study the case. Thereafter, we provide an analysis of the findings structured by first describing the AD's stated commitments and ambitions. Guided by the first research question we then present some substantive findings under three subheadings. The final section identifies some implications of the case study for leading higher education as, and for, public good, which thus answers the second research question.

Contextualising the case

Being a professional programme, the dental education is regulated by a jurisdiction common to all professional education programmes in health, social work and education in Norway. This regulation defines the criteria for "suitability assessment" (*skikkethetsvurdering*) of students in eight bullet points (Norwegian Government, 2006).[2] "Suitability" is a concept used to describe whether a professional is behaving in a responsible way. In the context of professional education, it is used to indicate how educational leaders must determine whether or not a student is "suitable" as a student and will be "suitable" to work in a professionally responsible manner in the future. The regulation defines irresponsible behaviour in professional work and clarifies that, if a student performs unacceptably in light of one or more of the criteria (Norwegian Government, 2006), he or she runs the risk of being excluded from the programme, thus diminishing or losing the opportunity to be certified as a dentist. "Suitability" in professional education therefore bears the same meaning as being professionally responsible (Solbrekke, 2007) and, as such, guides students on their trajectories towards becoming professionally responsible dentists. The focus on educating professionally responsible dentists entails "making educated professionals humans and socially responsible through its moral and cultural training towards a moral individualism" (Chapter 3, p. 3), thus a contribution as and for both private and public good.

As part of their efforts to develop more common assessment rubrics that support their students' holistic formation, the staff at the faculty had worked for more than three years with developing a shared template for clinical assessment, but struggled to reach legitimate compromise on what to include and how to use such a template. This is the stage of the process in which the AD got involved.

Based on the request to support them in the development of the template, the AD and the Faculty of Dentistry agreed on a "development project". While this "project" is an ongoing process at the time of writing this chapter the case study is restricted to activities that took place between May 2017 and March 2018. The context of the case is an annual introductory course in clinical supervision for professional dentists who are part-time *instructors* to supervise student dentists in clinical work at the Faculty.[3] We concentrate on the AD and her collaboration with one of the educational leaders hereafter described as the *supervisor*. This individual's responsibility was to supervise one group of five instructors, a group assigned the task of developing and testing a template for assessing students' knowledge, skills and attitudes in clinical work.

This template is a development of a previous one used by some instructors, but without any commitments that it be used by all instructors across the clinics. Thus, the faculty wanted to develop a new template that would guide all instructors on how to do formative assessment of students while also making the evaluation process more transparent and predictable for their students. This was a challenge, and also important in order to enhance the continuous suitability assessment (*løpende skikkethetsvurdering*) process. In order to find a common base for the template, the AD introduced the "suitability regulation" to the leaders at the Faculty as a reference for the assessment template, and also to all participants and supervisors in the course in clinical supervision.

Methods

Consistent with the methodology of all the cases in this book we have applied an abductive and reflexive insider–outsider approach inspired by the principles of deliberative communication for the study of the case (see introduction to Part II for elaboration on the method). This implied active reflections among the critical friends/researchers and the AD on the complex dynamics between the AD, supervisor and instructors, and how to reach a legitimate compromise between the commitment of the AD to lead the process and the commitment to support the supervisor while not taking over her responsibility to lead the group meetings.

Table 10.1 summarises the empirical material for the study and how it is used for the case analysis.

Informed consent was obtained from the supervisor and the instructors, and they were advised that they could withdraw at any time.

The AD and the supervisor met before and after every group meeting with the instructors, to discuss and reflect on the strategies the supervisor sought to use to encourage clinical supervision practices that nurture a sense of professional responsibility. In addition, the AD participated in the group meetings together with the instructors and the supervisor, mainly to support the supervisor in her endeavour of leading the group work.

Due to the many layers of the case (meetings between the AD and the supervisor in addition to four group meetings, all video recorded), the data are very rich and the analysis was conducted by the two researchers in several iterative steps (reading the log, watching the videos, categorising, reading relevant literature and returning to the material), followed by ongoing deliberations to reach agreement on the parts of the case that would be subject to more in-depth analysis. We decided to focus on group meetings where we identified situations illustrative of some of the tensions arising between the AD's different commitments.

In the next step of the analysis, we searched for sequences in which we identified dilemmas and challenges emerging when the AD used or attempted to use deliberative communication in her interactions with the supervisor and the instructors. The abductive analysis, inspired by Alvesson and Sköldberg (2000), created a dynamic process of data- and theory-driven modifications, while the iterative deliberations on interpretations between the two researchers, and the revisiting of the data material, prevented us from jumping to premature conclusions, a risk compounded by theory-laden expectations (Tjora, 2010).

TABLE 10.1 Methods and data sources

Time	What took place	Types of data sources	Who participated	Use for analytical purposes
Spring 2017	Planning	Planning document	AD	As preparation for the first conversation between the AD and the two critical friends
August 2017	Conversation about the purpose of the project and reflections on the AD's values and aspirations and how to enact deliberative communication	Video	AD and critical friends	To get an overview of the AD's intentions and plans on how to carry them through
Fall 2017 Four meetings	Discussion of the concept of "professional responsibility" and introduction of deliberative communication as a pedagogical approach Clarification of the roles and responsibilities of the AD and the supervisor in the upcoming group meetings with the instructors	Video	AD and supervisor	To identify possibilities and challenges by using deliberative communication as a means to explore the role of the AD in relation to the role of the supervisor
Fall 2017: Four group meetings	Work with and discussions about assessment templates in relation to the guidance of dental students in clinics. Both the AD and the supervisor intend to use deliberative communication as a means	AD's log and video	AD, supervisor and instructors	To identify possibilities and challenges using deliberative communication To explore the AD's leadership in practice
April 2018: A meeting following the completion of all group meetings	Reflection on what has been learnt concerning the development of an assessment template for professional responsibility and the use of deliberative communication	Video	AD and supervisor	To identify possibilities and challenges using deliberative communication To explore the role of the AD in relation to the role of the supervisor
May 2018	Conversation about what the researchers observed in the empirical material and the AD's experiences from the case, including the meetings with the supervisor, the group of instructors and the critical friends	Notes and video	AD and critical friends/researchers	To explore the AD's reflections on her enactment of deliberative communication when faced with videos and researchers' observations and questions To explore the possibilities and challenges inherent in deliberative leadership

Guided by the research questions, below we present and analyse illustrations from the case with the support of concepts and theories applied through the abductive process.

Leading through deliberative communication in a web of commitments

In the earliest conversation with her critical friends, the AD articulated a two-fold motivation for using deliberative communication. She said:

> First, I want to use deliberative communication to reach a legitimate compromise on a template to encourage formative assessment that nurtures students' holistic formation personally, professionally and as active citizens, and second, to gain experience and develop expertise in using deliberative communication in supervision and teaching generally to foster deliberative academic development as Kandlbinder defines it.[4]
>
> *(AD, August 2017)*

The AD maintained that she wanted to use deliberative communication to encourage the academics to challenge each other's perspectives on what professional responsibility implies. She stated:

> Using deliberative communication might help the instructors to open up for different perspectives on how to enact formative assessment. It is important to allow all voices equal space and respect in order to reach a legitimate compromise for a common assessment practices.
>
> *(AD, August 2017)*

This double ambition was a driving force for the AD in a case which represents several layers of commitments. She knew that the Faculty leaders trusted her to lead the process and pedagogically "qualify" the work with the assessment template, and to enact brokering if competing and conflicting values arose during the process. From an academic development perspective, she was committed to encourage the supervisor to find her own way of leading and supervising the instructors when they worked with the assessment template. This included a commitment to support the leaders in a discipline in which the AD was not expert, while also sharing her professional expertise as a pedagogue and leader within the field of academic development.

Her commitment to using deliberative communication as a pedagogy is revealed in the first planning meeting with the supervisor where she elaborated the principles of deliberative communication and argued that "deliberative communication is, in my view, a good way of promoting professional responsibility and in turn serve as a public good" (AD, August 2017). In the same meeting she encouraged the supervisor to try to use deliberative communication as a means of leading the group meetings with the instructors. Such ambition required that she endeavour to both supervise and role model how to make the group meetings a learning environment for both the supervisor and the instructors in which the principles of deliberative communication were followed. These principles stand for the idea of how to lead communication in a procedural way where different opinions and values are set against each other, to be discussed in a respectful way with a view to research consensus (see Chapter 3). This meant encouraging all instructors to speak out during the group meetings, respect and tolerate different perspectives, while also reaching a legitimate compromise on the template. She was also very conscious of the commitment to the overall purpose of dental education. To her, this meant contributing to the development of an assessment template representing a legitimate compromise between promoting the formation of student dentists and professional responsibility, and the more instrumental needs to measure and evaluate students according to the regulatory requirements of "suitability assessment".[5]

The commitment to using deliberative communication was apparent in this case and was clearly articulated in the planning of the process, but what impact did it have on the AD's actual contribution to the interaction with the supervisor and instructors?

Deliberative communication as praxis: challenging the use of everyday language

In the group meetings, when the instructors, under supervision from the supervisor supported by the AD, worked to develop the template, a frequently raised topic was how language was used in both the template and the actual supervision of students. By asking critical questions, the AD encouraged the instructors to reflect on their understanding of concepts used in the draft, some of which were based on everyday language used to describe professional settings and, thus, could be imprecise. As an example, the AD pointed to the assessment template and said:

> Look at these conceptions for assessing students' professionalism: "being kind", "being relaxed" and "look like you are feeling confident". These concepts characterise students, but is it given that they are understood similarly among you instructors? And how may "being kind" be considered as a sign of professional responsibility? What is the meaning of the concept "being confident", which is written in the format, compared with the concepts "evenly good" and "excellent"?

One of the instructors answered: "Well, I am not sure about the concept 'evenly good'. Then, is 'being confident' better?" Another instructor continued:

> "Being confident" – I have to admit that I think it is a very good concept. It shows that it is something beyond the assessment of the individual student, and it shows that there is a judgement based on several considerations. A dentist who is feeling confident is a dentist that can step up in the middle of a treatment and ask: "What am I really doing now?" And that, as I see it, is a

professionally responsible dentist who is able to take a step backwards, stop and reflect on the clinical situation.

The AD challenged the instructors to reflect on their use of language, and in doing so, the instructors realised that they understood concepts used in the draft of the assessment template very differently. Aspiring to reach a shared understanding, the AD aimed at encouraging awareness of how concepts can be interpreted differently, yet may be open for change of meaning (Breivik, Fosse & Rødnes, 2014) through interactions with others (Wertsch, 1991). She did not point to other, more concise conceptions; rather, she invited all the instructors to question and develop the concepts in the assessment template. Based on these discussions, they also changed some of the conceptions used in the assessment format. These deliberations also demonstrate that, apart from questioning the meaning of everyday terminology, it is necessary also to revisit such important language regularly. Otherwise, the routines of practice, the busyness of everyday interactions may ignore the more cerebral, reflective dimension inherent in praxis (see Chapters 1 and 11), thus reducing professional responsibility of instructors and supervisors to mere practical routines, ritual performance.

Among the instructors, a shared language can be considered important for discussions of how to assess students' professional skills and attitudes at clinics. It may also help the instructors to develop their own sense of professional responsibility.

While differences in interpretation of key terms may be due to the absence of reflective deliberation with colleagues, it may also be a result of differences in values, orientations and aspirations among the instructors. When enacting deliberative communication, different opinions and values should be set against each other and challenged (Englund, 2006). Among the instructors, supported by the AD, there was more elaboration than confrontation about the language use. Affirming different voices is important from a pedagogical and a deliberative perspective, conflicts or confrontations of different views and values are substantial and central to deliberative communication. However, in Chapter 3 Englund and Bergh argue that situations with small differences in perspectives and values also have potential for deliberative communication when there is a possibility for learning and developing from what these differences imply. Situations of conflicts and confrontations form a continuum ranging from small differences to more obvious disagreements or conflicts. The differences in language use among the instructors were relatively small, while, nevertheless, implying potential to learn from and develop an understanding of the differences.

Deliberative communication praxis: the (possible) contribution of teachable moments

During the group meetings, there were times when the AD asked the instructors critical questions regarding the use of language while simultaneously demonstrating the importance of being inclusive and supportive of different voices; another important dimension of deliberative communication. While this seemed to work well, it is legitimate to ask: was there potential for stronger controversies, confrontations and conflicts that the AD could have used to challenge the academics' perspectives, values and aspirations related to the assessment of students' professional responsibility in clinical situations? For example, at one of the group meetings, an instructor asked another more experienced colleague about what to do with students who insist on behaving in a certain way and who ignore instructors' advice. The experienced instructor answered:

> Well, I think differently here. I don't know what the pedagogue says about it, but I, well, of course, I understand that there is one supervisor and one to be supervised, and I understand that there is a resistance to be supervised. But it depends on how you, as a supervisor, cope with it. There is a need to use different approaches in the supervision of different students.

When the instructor addressed the AD this way, it may be interpreted in a dual way. One interpretation is that he wanted to mark a certain professional distance by calling her "the pedagogue". This might suggests a kind of scepticism to whether the pedagogue fully understand the clinical settings in which they supervise. Another interpretation may be that he actually challenged the pedagogue to be more concrete on her opinion. However, it is less interesting what the instructor actually meant. What *is* evident is that the AD did not respond directly to this statement.

The role of AD often implies being a pedagogical expert in a context in which disciplinary knowledge reigns supreme; thus, an AD's situation is contingent (Sugrue et al., 2017). There was a potential in this situation to solicit different opinions, conflicting views and values to engage in a deliberative discussion of subject positions, authority, legitimacy, power and relations. In other words, this situation can be described as a teachable moment (Woods & Jeffrey, 1996): a moment in which a teacher has a fleeting, unplanned opportunity to offer insight to the students. However, by not acting in this situation the AD did not make use of a teachable moment that could have been exploited for opening up for deliberative communication.

Enacting deliberative communication is challenging. When the AD in the post-conversation, with the critical friends, reflected on this situation she explained that she was careful not to intrude into the role of the supervisor who was in charge of leading the meetings. She wanted to be a partner in the collaboration, not simply the expert in developing formative assessment procedures to nurture students' development as professionally responsible dentists. For this reason, she refrained from intervening too much in the participants' discussions in the group meetings.

These considerations exemplify the web of commitments ADs navigate: in this case, justifying their own legitimacy while focusing on the development of a formative assessment template of students' professional responsibilities; and the possibility of discussing subject positions, authority, legitimacy, power and relations. This shows that such normative theoretical ideals as deliberative communication are not fully reflected in practice; rather, they are goals for which to strive in order to reach legitimate comprises in the work of academic development. However, as Rowland (2007, p. 9) argued, the uncertainties in the work of an AD should be celebrated "in an environment that needs to give more space for doubt, contestation and deliberation".

Deliberative communication: legitimate compromise between the roles of expert and equal partner

In this case, the AD and the supervisor worked closely together in leading the process of instructors developing a formative assessment template. The AD had encouraged the supervisor to use deliberative communication as a pedagogy but did not challenge or push her to deploy it in the group meetings with the instructors. Their relationship was friendly and relaxed, and the two appeared to be friends, another benefit that had accrued over time, strengthening relationships, mutuality and trust. Before the first group meeting with the instructors, they discussed their roles and responsibilities and agreed that the supervisor, together with the instructors, should lead the work on the development of the template. However, the supervisor made clear that she wanted the AD to take an active part in the discussions at the group meetings, as the AD had competences they needed for their work. The videos from the group meetings clearly showed that the supervisor took the lead at the group meetings, while the AD sat back and listened. In some discussions, however, the AD took a more active role by framing the discussions and raising critical questions. On a few occasions, the supervisor approached the AD directly. For example, in one meeting, the supervisor asked the instructors about the usefulness of a draft of the assessment template that had been used with students during their clinics. When nobody answered, the supervisor looked at the AD and said: "Now you have to say something". It seemed she needed support to engage the instructors in the discussion and she reached for the safety net of calling on the expert. Significantly, the AD responded by first commenting on her own role (i.e. the more active role she and the supervisor had discussed), then pointed at one instructor and asked her about her experiences with using the template. This launched the group conversation. It also demonstrated the possibility that the presence of the pedagogical expert inhibited the supervisor, thus the AD was being careful, while cast in the role of expert, not to undermine the position of the supervisor as group leader – another subtlety of praxis.

The AD has a background as a pedagogue, and she has worked as a leader in different settings for many years. Within the Faculty of Dentistry, the field of science has very different epistemologies and ontologies in comparison with the social science. The AD has very limited disciplinary knowledge in dentistry, but she has expert competence in developing the instructors' understanding of professional responsibility, and she seemed to contribute to the interpretation of the "suitability regulations" to practice and their reconstruction into praxis in clinical situations. In the final meeting between the supervisor and the AD in April 2018, the supervisor emphasised that she saw the AD as the expert:

> You are contributing with another language, with another subject to have you together with me at the meetings made me feel safer in the work with the instructors. The whole process has been very good. Your contribution has been connected to a subject – to science. It's not only talking and feeling; it is more substantial.

The expertise of the AD provided a safety net for the supervisor, but without the AD reflexively staying "out of the way", it is possible that the supervisor becomes dependent on the expertise rather than moving towards building her own deliberative communication competence. Nevertheless, these teachable moments serve as timely reminders that sophisticated praxis takes time, effort and expertise to become accomplished, and it is a never-ending process, far removed from a "tricks for teachers" mindset.

The supervisor underlined the importance for the process of the AD's contributions as a representative from another scientific science. She acknowledged the AD's authority and legitimacy based on the AD's professional role and expert knowledge. However, these acknowledgements seemed more related to the AD's leadership role and her expertise in professional responsibility than to her contributions to attempts at deliberative communication in the meetings. In their final meeting after the last group meeting, the AD asked the supervisor what she thought about deliberative communication and how she had experienced it. The supervisor answered:

> It is sometimes so many words when you read about the idea of deliberative communication and the five principles, but at the same time, it looks very logical. But I had not heard about it before. I mean, it is not part of my disciplinary background. Still, I had a clear idea how to do it, but ... Well, in the group meetings, there are so many things to remember and to be aware of when you are there. This deliberative communication is a new approach for me. I like to have control here. I have to admit that sometimes I felt that I had no control.

The above quote suggests that, in the work of developing the assessment template together with the instructors, the supervisor did not focus primarily on deliberative communication. Instead, she sought to manage and address the many other processes involved. It may also be the case that for more expert users of deliberative communication, it becomes an invisible element of the pedagogical fabric, while for novice users more immediate aspects of the teaching–learning situation make it difficult to reach the principles of deliberative communication with an appropriate degree of fluency. Deliberative praxis, while a work in progress that may be assisted by the active contribution of a pedagogical expert, is also a delicate flower in the web of commitments such relationships inhabit, where finding legitimate compromise between expert and partner is uncertain, altering from moment to moment, yet crucially significant for the cultivation and enhancement of praxis.

Concluding remarks

In this chapter, we have reported on a case study of one AD who collaborated with an educational leader at the Faculty of Dentistry to improve the clinical supervision and assessment of dental students. The AD articulated a clear aspiration to lead the process by using deliberative communication as a pedagogical approach to academic development. Deliberative communication was used as an endeavour for intellectual work: to build a mutual understanding of how to assess students' professional responsibility in clinical work. Sutherland (2018) argues that academic development must relate to a broader perspective than simply enhancing individual academics in their teaching, implying a focus on the purposes of teaching and a broadened discussion about higher education in relation to public good. The AD exemplified this perspective throughout the case by asking the supervisor and the instructors questions about how to define a professionally responsible dentist and by encouraging discussions about how to assess professional responsibility.

In this case, three different topics describe the different possibilities and challenges the AD faced when using deliberative communication as, and for, public good. First, one potential that arose with the use of deliberative communication seemed to be an increased awareness among the instructors of the use of language and the development of a more professional language regarding the supervision and assessment of students. A shared language can help build a community of practice related to teaching and supervising in clinics, which might, in turn, provide a gateway to a deeper professional understanding, thereby strengthening instructors' professional role as supervisors for students in clinical settings.

Second, it can be challenging to use deliberative communication when conflicts are evident. This is a paradox, as conflicts and confrontation are "substantially central to, and constitutive of, deliberative communication as a procedural phenomenon" (Englund, 2006, p. 513). ADs operate in a web of commitment and must take into consideration different disciplines and professions when searching for a legitimate compromise. How to enact deliberative communication will depend on the context. The AD observed in this case study had legitimacy at the Faculty of Dentistry after several years of collaboration, but still she can be challenged to develop her own repertoire to exploit the possibilities in conflicts and confrontations when working with academics.

The third topic that arose in the case concerned the AD's leadership role. She continuously had to negotiate with herself how to navigate between providing the academics with expertise about professional responsibility, teaching and learning with being an equal partner working together with them to develop more professional assessment and supervision. Being an AD implies being an expert on processes that enhance teaching and learning. Nevertheless, being an expert does not mean that ADs tell people what to do; instead, being a professional AD seems to be about facilitating processes in which the participants (here, the supervisor and the instructors) take ownership of the development and define what is important for them. The AD in the case engaged in an adaptive, collaborative partnership with the supervisor and, to a certain extent, the instructors, to influence and develop educational practice. The supervisor underlined that the initiative at the Faculty of Dentistry would not have had the same quality without the AD's contribution.

This leads us to a final and summarising question: namely, what different qualities the AD, in this studied case, has contributed with? Here, we agree with Kandlbinder (2007) who has argued that academic development practices might be rethought in terms of the processes of deliberation. By following this experienced AD, who clearly stated that she believes in deliberative communication as, and for, public good, we have contributed empirical knowledge by putting the light on possibilities as well as challenges that emerged as the AD sought to lead the process by supporting the supervisor in her leadership of the group of instructors. Aspiring to use deliberative communication means being aware of the relationships and communications among those with whom you are working. It is about listening, deliberating, seeking arguments and valuing openness when different opinions and values are set against one another. In this case, this has been tried out in the process of reaching a legitimate compromise on a common template for assessing student dentists, suitability for becoming responsible dentists. Enabling the participants and supervisors to make nuances judgements and decisions consistent with this suitable assessment regulation can be seen as an encouragement of public good in the process of challenging, recalibrating and seeking legitimate compromises between competing perspectives, values and aspirations in higher education. Based on the analysis, we conclude that the commitment to try out the principles of deliberative communication enabled both the AD and the supervisor contribute to making the process a public good for the instructors, while also becoming more aware of their own praxis. However, to what extent the template as a pedagogical tool actually will encourage a more coherent and predictable practice, in the work with students, is an empirical questions that needs to be further studied.

Notes

1 See Chapter 4 for more examples on how ADs may cope and lead within webs of commitments.
2 The criteria to be used when assessing the suitability of a student for the study programmes in health education are:

   a) the student shows a lack of willingness or ability for care, understanding and respect for patients, clients or users;
   b) the student shows a lack of willingness or ability to cooperate and to establish relationships of trust and communicate with patients, clients, relatives and collaboration partners;
   c) the student shows threatening or offensive behaviour in the context of their studies;
   d) the student abuses substances or acquires medicines illegally;
   e) the student has problems of a nature that seriously compromises his/her functions towards his/her surroundings;

f) the student shows too little self-insight regarding tasks in his/her studies and his/her future professional role;

g) the student shows negligence and commits irresponsible actions that may entail risks for patients, clients or user;

h) the student shows a lack of willingness or ability to change unacceptable behaviour in accordance with guidance.

https://www.regjeringen.no/globalassets/upload/kd/vedlegg/uh/forskrifter/regulation_ suitability_higher_education.pdf

3 This course has been led and developed by the AD and another AD in close collaboration with two educational leaders at the Faculty of Dentistry since 2012. The main aim of this course is to qualify newly appointed instructors in supervising and evaluating students in clinical work. The group working with developing a template for use in evaluation of students in clinical work is part of the obligatory course assignments. The course ran over three days: a two-day seminar in September 2017 and one-day seminar in January 2018. There are 25 participants and they are divided into five groups to do development work on different themes between the two seminars. In this case we focus on the group working with developing a new evaluation template.

4 In Kandlbinder's definition (2007) this means that academic developers should facilitate processes that critically discuss how university teaching may encourage critical thinking and consciousness of academics' responsibilities.

5 See Chapter 4 for an elaboration of "responsibility" and "accountability" logics and the embedded tensions between these.

References

Alvesson, M., & Sköldberg, K. (2000). *Reflexive Methodology*. London: Sage Publications.

Beck, E. E., Solbrekke, T. D., Sutphen, M. & Fremstad, E. (2015). When mere knowledge is not enough: the potential of bildung as self-determination, co-determination and solidarity. *Higher Education Research & Development, 34*(3), 445–457. doi:10.1080/07294360.2014.973373

Brevik, L. M., Fosse, B. O., & Rødnes, K. A. (2014). Language, learning, and teacher professionalism: an investigation of specialized language use among pupils, teachers, and student teachers. *International Journal of Educational Research, 68*, 46–55.

Colby, A., Ehrlich, T., Sullivan, W. M., & Dolle, J. R. (2011). *Rethinking Undergraduate Business Education: Liberal Learning for the Profession*. San Francisco: Jossey-Bass.

Debowski, S. (2014). From agents of change to partners in arms: the emerging academic developer role. *International Journal for Academic Development, 19*(1), 50–56.

Englund, T. (2006). Deliberative communication: a pragmatist proposal. *Journal of Curriculum Studies, 38*(5), 503–520.

Fremstad, E., Bergh, A., Solbrekke, T. D., & Fossland, T. (2019). Deliberative academic development: the potential and challenge of agency. *International Journal for Academic Development.* doi:10.1080/1360144X.2019.1631169

Handal, G., Lycke, K. H., Mårtensson, K., Roxå, T., Skodvin, A., & Solbrekke, T. D. (2014). The role of academic developers in transforming Bologna regulations to a national and institutional context. *International Journal for Academic Development, 19*(19), 12–25.

Kandlbinder, P. (2007). The challenge of deliberation for academic developers. *International Journal of Academic Development, 12*(1), 55–59.

Norwegian Government (2006). *Forskrift om skikkethetsvurdering i høyere utdanning* [*Regulation on suitability assessment in higher education*]. https://lovdata.no/dokument/SF/forskrift/ 2006-06-30-859 (downloaded 8 August 2019).

May, L. (1996). *The Socially Responsive Self: Social Theory and Professional Ethic*. Chicago: Chicago University Press.

Rowland, S. (2007). Academic development: a site of creative doubt and contestation, *International Journal for Academic Development, 12*(1), 9–14.

Schon, D. (1983). *The Reflective Practitioner.* New York: Sage Publications.

Solbrekke, T. D. (2007). *Understanding conceptions of professional responsibility* (unpublished doctoral dissertation). University of Oslo, Oslo.

Solbrekke, T. D. (2008). Professional responsibility as legitimate compromises—from communities of education to communities of work. *Studies in Higher Education, 33*(4), 485–500.

Solbrekke, T. D., & Englund, T. (2011). Bringing professional responsibility back in. *Studies in Higher Education, 36*(7), 847–861.

Solbrekke, T. D., & Fremstad, E. (2018). Universitets—og høgskolepedagogers profesjonelle ansvar [Academic developers' professional responsibility]. *Uniped, 3*(41), 229–245.

Solbrekke, T. D., & Sugrue, C. (2014). Professional accreditation of initial teacher education programmes: teacher educators' strategies—between 'accountability' and 'professional responsibility'? *Teaching and Teacher Education, 37,* 11–20.

Stensaker, B. (2018). Academic development as cultural work: responding to the organizational complexity of modern higher education institutions. *International Journal for Academic Development, 23*(4), 274–285.

Stensaker, B., van der Vaart, R., Solbrekk, T. D., & Wittek, L. (2017). The expansion of academic development: the challenges of organizational coordination and collaboration. InB. Stensaker, G. Bilbow, L. Breslow & R. Van der Vaart (eds), *Strengthening Teaching and Learning in Research Universities: Strategies and Initiatives for Institutional Change* (19–42). New York: Palgrave Macmillan.

Sugrue, C., Englund, T.; Solbrekke, T. D. & Fossland, T. (2017). Trends in the practices of academic developers: trajectories of higher education? *Studies in Higher Education, 43*(12), 2336–2353.

Sullivan, W. M., & Rosin, M. S. (2008). *A New Agenda for Higher Education. Shaping a Life of the Mind for Practice.* San Francisco: Jossey-Bass.

Sutherland, K. A. (2018). Holistic academic development: is it time to think more broadly about academic development project? *International Journal for Academic Development, 23*(4), 261–273.

Taylor, K. L. (2005). Academic development as institutional leadership: an interplay of person, role, strategy, and institution. *International Journal for Academic Development, 10*(1), 31–46.

Tjora, A. (2010). *Kvalitative forskningsmetoder i praksis [Quality research methods in practice].* Oslo: Gyldendal akademisk.

Walker, M. (2018). Dimensions of higher education and the public good in South Africa. *Higher Education, 76*(3), 555–569. doi:10.1007/s10734-017-0225-y

Wertsch, J. (1991). *Voices of the Mind: A Sociocultural Approach to Mediated Action.* Cambridge, MA: Cambridge University Press.

Woods, P. and Jeffrey, B. (1996). *Teachable Moments: The Art of Teaching in Primary Schools.* Buckingham: Open University Press.

Youngs, H. (2017). A critical exploration of distributed leadership in higher education: developing an alternative ontology through leadership-as-practice. *Journal of Higher Education Policy and Management, 39*(2), 140–154.

PART III

11

RE-KINDLING EDUCATION AS PRAXIS

The promise of deliberative leadership

Ciaran Sugrue and Tone Dyrdal Solbrekke

Introduction

In this concluding chapter, deliberation between us (editors) continues apace with the voices in the foregoing chapters reverberating in our conversation, and with you, as reader, being a silent but active participant. By continuing to deploy an abductive and reflexive approach in combination with deliberative communication[1] between us as the authors of this text,[2] we have developed a common argument in this chapter, an argument we hope you find convincing – or at least worth considering. If you have engaged with some of the previous chapters, it will not be surprise that we argue: leading higher education as and for public good calls for proactive leadership that is mindful of the super-complexity that characterises twenty-first-century public universities (Barnett, 2003). Additionally, we argue that leading higher education as, and for, public good necessitates the re-kindling of education as praxis,[3] and that what we define as deliberative leadership,[4] has much to offer. By moving between the concepts and arguments articulated in Chapters 1–4 and the insights and understandings gleaned from five case studies of academic developers (ADs) presented in Chapters 6–10, we revisit prominent aspects of leading higher education as and for public good while simultaneously recasting them as an elaboration of deliberative leadership and its potential to be both a public good as well as a contribution to it. The ADs' experiences of using deliberative communication in different leading and teaching practices and their reflections with critical friends on their own practices and praxis, moral and epistemic assumptions have enabled us to identify and describe the features of *deliberative leadership practice*, while also indicating the promise of *deliberative leadership praxis* as a public good in itself, and with potential to uphold and maintain values that promote sustainable leadership praxes.

In setting out this agenda we are self-consciously aware that the warrants provided by the case studies are restricted since numerically they are confined to four

Scandinavian universities and to the work of ADs who labour in those public institutions. Nevertheless, despite the work of ADs being prescribed and circumscribed in different ways depending on institutional context, we are confident that there are lessons about leading and teaching with more general application. In the tradition of case study work, we take comfort from the assertion that: "a case study researcher can assist readers to generalize for themselves, to use gleanings from that reporting to appreciate other cases of personal or professional interest" (Stake & Mabry, 1998, p. 170)

The work of ADs differs from other academics' leading and teaching responsibilities[5] since they teach academic colleagues rather than students, and they work across all "tribes and territories" in their institution (Becher & Trowler 2001). Some are holders of academic appointments and others occupy administrative positions. Despite these differences, we consider that the ADs' experiences with leading teaching illuminate situations and challenges recognisable to other academics with responsibility for education. The brokering work ADs are obliged to do, between senior leaders and other academics who may – or may not – agree with their university leaders' priorities, illuminate in high relief the complexity and relational tensions embedded in leading education.[6] The cases also demonstrates how educational leadership is not the sole prerogative of formal leaders only. Rather, to borrow an important phrase from "distributed" leadership literature, it needs to be "stretched over" the entire organisation (Spillane, 2006). We have some confidence therefore that the perspectives we present will reverberate among all academics with responsibility for higher education, either as formal or informal leaders, despite institutional, national and international policy variation. Additionally, we anticipate that you will find ready resonance with our articulation of deliberative leadership as praxis, not merely a practice. We invite you to join with us to critically investigate and advocate for a leadership approach that encourages staff and students to deliberate on how the purpose of higher education as a public good may be fulfilled – whatever it entails – within the culture of your respective institutions.

The chapter is structured in four sections. First, we revisit *why* we consider it necessary to articulate deliberative leadership as timely and apposite for twenty-first-century public universities. Second, we describe the different elements we have found as crucial in order to understand and practise deliberative leadership to lead teaching and learning as and for public good, while also indicating that such leadership is as relevant for formal leaders as well as those occupying informal leadership roles within the university as an organisation. Third, we discuss deliberative leadership as praxis and its potential as a sustainable leadership. In doing so, we suggest a mode of working with leadership that may be more democratic and in turn more sustainable than what is indicated within the current practices of New Public Management (NPM) in higher education. In conclusion, while commending deliberative leadership praxis as harbouring considerable possibilities for leading and teaching, we recognise also that it needs to be imbued with imagination and creativity in crafting a sustainable future for all.

Why deliberative leadership?

There is accumulating evidence that managerialism and leadership practices applied since the advent of NPM in higher education are changing the structural and cultural conditions in public universities. The ideas of NPM tend to laud efficient decision-making and decisiveness, and to privilege efficiency over efficacy (Gross Stein, 2001). Such a mindset legitimises lack of appropriate consultation with colleagues, as there is urgency about getting "the job done" – an approach that challenges more traditional and more collegial leadership (Pinheiro et al., 2019). In such circumstances, the agency and courage of individuals to speak up and speak out has potential over time to be curtailed where morale declines and degrees of disengagement and disaffection begin to take hold (Lynch, Grummel & Devine, 2012).

Even in social democratic contexts, in the Nordic countries, in which the case studies (Chapters 5–9) are situated, there is evidence that increased managerialism has a demoralising effect on academics. A recent comprehensive comparative study in 54 public universities in Sweden, Denmark, Norway and Finland confirms that the more entrepreneurial mindsets and practices in the strategic leadership of universities, is experienced as alien to many academics (Geschwind et al., 2019). In similar vein, new evaluation practices of both research and teaching infused by an increasing managerial ethos of measurement have emerged to dominate academic standards and supersede a collegial ethos of judgement (Spence, 2019). Moreover, the entrepreneurial drift in contemporary public universities permeated by increasing bureaucracy (Barnett, 2011) tends to silence the more socially minded visions of higher education as and for public good (see Goddard, Hazelkorn, Kempton & Vallance, 2016). As Chapters 1 and 2 indicate, higher education is becoming more a matter of private gain, individual advantage rather than strengthening social solidarity in ways that promote active citizenship and shared values that fortify engagement and participation in public good issues (Walker, 2018). A study on 25 Norwegian academics in 2014 demonstrated how they developed individual strategies to cope in the current management climate. Some respond with open resistance, while other reactions are more covert, but all tend to be more beneficial for personal gain than serving a public good (Ese, 2019). Thus, leadership practices imbued with elements of NPM over time risk eroding trust and openness and be replaced by defensiveness and suspicion. Such indications are supported by much of educational change literature which is critical of top-down managerialism (Bessant, Robinson & Ormerod, 2015; Ekman, Lindgren & Packendorf, 2018; Hargreaves, Boyle & Harris, 2014; Kalfa, Wilkinson & Gollan, 2018; Kolsaker, 2008, 2014). However, there is as much, if not more, criticism also that bottom-up reform is too ponderous, takes too much time and is frequently used to stymie development. Such either–or thinking is an invitation to take sides – to be sympathetic to senior leaders' dilemma, to get on with the job, or to stand in solidarity with peers and colleagues and insist upon having a say and being heard. Such an approach to institutional leadership is akin to a Mexican stand-off; there needs to be legitimate compromise, and, from our perspective, deliberative communication, that privileges neither superiority of position from above or below, but rather builds on respect and tolerance for the concrete other, has the basis and the tools necessary to get the "warring" parties to engage in the interest of putting education centre stage, thus keeping public good to the fore. Deliberative leadership therefore emerges as being reminiscent of Gidden's "third way", beyond left and right (Giddens, 1999), and perhaps more accurately in "The Global Fourth Way" where it states: "Leadership is not about individuals managing the delivery of imposed reforms, but about developing distributed and sustainable responsibility for innovating and changing together. It is about collective responsibility rather than vertical accountability" (Hargreaves & Shirley, 2012, p. 9). Time, then, to indicate the constituent elements of deliberative leadership, its interrelated horizontal and vertical dynamic processes it entails.

Deliberative leadership: relational and dynamic processes

For us, deliberative leadership is dynamic and relational, and it recognises and respects the multiple perspectives and commitments within contemporary public universities. What does it entail?

A search for published material on "deliberative leadership in higher education" yields a number of perspectives congruent with our ideas, and here we report briefly on them. From a political science disciplinary perspective, there is obvious concern for "deliberative democracy", and its promotion among political parties, students and public alike (Zhang & Meng, 2018). For others such agenda are embraced under notions of more generalised "democratic education" (Sardoc, 2018). Somewhat closer to the focus and purpose of this book there is attention also to "deliberative pedagogy" (Drury, et al., 2016; Manosevicth, 2019; Tibbitts, 2019), while others seek to harness the potential of combining distributed leadership with a deliberative disposition, counselling that such synergies are a positive force for improving the quality of teaching and learning (Fusarelli, Kowalski & Petersen, 2011). Depending on the disciplinary backgrounds of the various authors cited above, they tend to view the challenge of deliberation through a particular lens – it is necessary for democracy, or valuable for education, while the tendency is to assume that putting these together serve a public good. What they share in common is a normative stance; deliberation matters, being committed to values/virtues such as openness, tolerance, respect and inclusion.[7]

Beginning from an educational perspective, our ambition here is to create a new synthesis between teaching and leading and between distributed leadership and deliberative communication to create a more holistic, organisational approach to leading higher education, as and for public good: deliberative leadership. This shift is premised on the understanding that, if deliberation is good for pedagogy, democracy, decision-making and so on, then deliberative leadership in a more holistic all-encompassing manner has greater potential to lead higher education as and for public good.

From a formal leadership perspective, deliberative leadership includes trusting staff and students to take responsibility for the activities they are involved in, while not abdicating from one's own leadership responsibilities. Formal leaders do not rely on taken-for-granted traditions, but encourage staff and students to speak out, and collectively investigate different perspectives, before making decisions on how to fulfil the normative mandate of university education. In the following we develop the argument a bit further, and we start with investigating notions of the normative mandates of public universities.

Institutional mandates: public good

We have previously indicated (Chapter 1) that although matters of governance and finance *of* public higher education are critically important, they are not the primary focus of this book. Rather, concentration has been on the possibilities of strengthening leading and teaching *within* universities. However, a broader perspective on leading higher education as and for public good cannot ignore governance and funding concerns since they have a considerable influence on conceptions of institutional mandate and strategies, leadership approaches, staff and student recruitment policy, research and teaching priorities (Geschwind et al., 2019). For example, in a very recent report on accessibility and affordability of higher education in the US, public universities, "flagship" institutions, are castigated due to the exclusionary nature of their various funding models. The report states: "Only 6 out of 50 flagship institutions meet an affordability benchmark for students who are not from high-income backgrounds. All 50 institutions are easily affordable for a typical high-income student" (Mugglestone, Dancy & Voight, 2019, p. 3). While such financial barriers are problematic from an equity and public good perspective, it is at least theoretically possible that those who have the wherewithal to gain individually from such an education, may also (more indirectly) contribute to public good. At least such evidence suggests that the boundaries between public and private good are muddied considerably. Perhaps even more worrying is the assertion in the same report that "the best path to economic mobility is still a college degree" (Mugglestone, Dancy & Voight, 2019, p. 3) strongly suggesting that the purpose of higher education is to enhance an individual's "economic mobility". While that too may be a contribution to public good, it is strongly suggestive that such a focus may downplay being an active and contributing citizen, or that "character is shaped by education; and that one of the goals of higher education is to instill in the student a love of those things" about which the student "should care" (Kronman, 2019, p. 63). Such policies not only make the boundaries between private and public good porous and blurred, they also reveal conflicting views on how best to serve society; exposing tensions between what is good for the individual and what is a contribution to society writ large, a common good (as indicated in Chapter 3). Obviously, a shared understanding of what may be held in common can no longer (if it ever could) be taken for granted. Intensified expectations and engagement from external stakeholders, politicians and the labour market have spawned an increasing prevalence of entrepreneurial and bureaucratic orientations in public universities.[8] While such orientations in some respects serve a public good by creating jobs, there is also considerable risk that they run counter to a mandate to nurture values such as solidarity and democracy (Sardoc, 2018).

The above examples arise in a US context. How might this reality be exemplified in a European context? By way of response, we turn attention to Ireland, where one of us is employed.

In the Universities Act (Ireland, 1997) published by the Irish government, which constitutes the public universities' contract with society, the word "public" appears in this 41-page document three times only. The first of these three uses of the term "public" is to state that the university has "obligations as to public accountability" (Sect. 14(b) iii). The second relates specifically to the chief financial officer's obligations to "the requirements of accountability for the use of moneys" provided by government, while the third refers to membership of a university's governing authority with representation from a "public company" (Sch.3, 8(1)(a)). While such accountabilities are entirely apposite in the interests of a common good to account for public resources, it is hardly a ringing endorsement of the moral and epistemic obligations to serve the public. However, the legislation does indicate 11 "objects" of the university, perhaps more typically identified as aims or objectives including the responsibilities to society by "advancing knowledge through teaching, scholarly research and scientific investigation" … fostering "a capacity for independent and critical thinking", and promoting learning "in society generally" and "promote the cultural and social life of society, while fostering and respecting the diversity of the university's traditions", but with obligation also "to support and contribute to the realisation of national economic and social development". These objectives may suggest that the architects of the Irish legislation might well argue that the intent was to find an appropriate balance whereby a "good" education for the individual would also percolate to the wider society and in this manner become, if not immediately, over time accrue as a benefit to public good, if only partially held in common. This example indicates that public good as a concept tends to be rather opaque, thus enabling individuals and societies to indicate commitment to the idea of public good while it remains poorly defined. Our call therefore is that public good as central to the mandate of higher education be put back on the agenda, not as an addition but as a core consideration. There needs to be continuous renewal, re-articulation of what public good entails as a precursor to ongoing commitment to its promotion in practice. Even in the Western context of mass higher education where such endeavours may appear redundant, there is an urgency in moving towards more focused deliberations both within and beyond the academy about financial systems and governance structures, as well as how to develop a culture for deliberations on the purpose of higher education, and negotiate legitimate compromises to cope with competing interests within and without higher education. How may such a focus be advanced?

Deliberative leadership: negotiating legitimate compromises in and between webs of commitments

As indicated above, deliberative leadership includes the necessity to negotiate and agree legitimate compromises, invoking the sentiment expressed in the phrase attributed to Winston Churchill that "to jaw-jaw is always better than to war, war". It is important to acknowledge that negotiations always take place in and between tangled webs of commitments (May, 1996).[9] Webs of commitments are unique to each person, and while some commitments may be shared, individuals do not configure them in precisely the same ways. Those with whom we connect in the workplace, and how we determine our commitments, are contingent on the extent to which such ties are "loose" or "bind" us closely to others while mindful also of individual values and priorities (see Achinstein, 2002, pp. 136–137). From a deliberative leadership perspective, recognising the existence of such webs of commitments is thus a crucial point of departure in terms of building relationships with colleagues as a foundation for deliberative leadership and collective engagement. However, understanding that individuals have different commitments, thus also different senses of agency due to position, roles and career stage, is a reciprocal responsibility on all concerned, Nevertheless, the modus vivendi that pertains in the workplace rests particularly with those in formal positions of leadership since they have power to define the overall institutional policies, the strategies and distribute resources to fulfil what they define as public good (Sutphen, Solbrekke & Sugrue, 2018).

Enacting deliberative leadership in a professionally responsible way thus requires consideration and understanding of the tensions that webs of commitments entail, and the necessity to negotiate and reach legitimate compromises between competing interests and needs, whether individual or institutional.

The Irish legislation above demonstrates the necessity to be accountable to the state (politicians) and the public, as well as to the labour market, while also being responsible for the moral and epistemic contributions that the academic community, including students, consider a necessity to provide higher education as public good, thus also contributing to public good. Some of its "11 objects" render the universities responsible for promoting "social and cultural life of society" and while respecting "traditions" further "respect for diversity", arguably contributions to public good, but while accountability for use of public resources is clear, it remains rather ambiguous as to how universities meet these criteria. Nevertheless, professionally responsible leadership entails a critical investigation of our rationales (and motives) for our actions, a self-reflexive means of being professionally responsible for having such duties thrust upon us. In order to do this in a systematic and transparent manner, we suggested in Chapter 4 that deploying the logics of accountability and responsibility as an analytical lens is an important means of deconstruction of some of the current tensions in twenty-first-century public universities (see pp. 58–61).

We drew attention to the language of both logics as being distinct and different; the accountability logic harbouring an "audit" mindset (Power, 1999), while the logic of responsibility is to be more than merely accountable, to "trust" those concerned to live up to their professional responsibilities, a collective responsibility in which each contributes and all share (Hargreaves & O'Connor, 2018). From a professional responsibility and deliberative leadership perspective, academics are obliged to answer to both logics, but as these authors suggest "accountability should be the tiny remainder that is left once responsibility has been subtracted" (p. 133). It is legitimate that the state requires public universities to account for use of taxpayers' money, and politicians have the right to articulate their ambitions for higher education. However, it is an academic responsibility of formal as well as informal leaders, to stand up for their professional values proactively and to give substance to them in concrete ways. For example, it implies that academics have the courage to speak out in public (Said, 1994) if they judge that some practices do not support what they consider to be public good.[10] Providing higher education as and for a public good implies a social and moral responsibility broader than merely reporting on pre-determined, transparent and quantifiable quality criteria and learning outcomes. It depends on critical reflection on whether decisions are being made in a reactive and accountable manner only or as a result of being proactive and responsible to reach a legitimate compromise. Such reflection may enable us to become more aware of our decisions for action and enable us to develop a "moral compass" for practice (Taylor, 1989/1992). As suggested in the preceding chapters, deliberative communication is one way of doing this.

However, asserting the potential of the principles of deliberative communication is neither a quick fix nor a silver bullet. Far from it! If you have already engaged with some of the previous chapters, you may have observed that the ADs represented in the five cases all committed to using deliberative communication in their teaching and leading and, in the process, gained first-hand experience of both the promise and challenges of deliberative communication in practice.[11] An emergent issue common to the cases was the realisation that it is necessary to move beyond notions of "the best argument", a disposition commonly shared among academics, to embrace the idea of legitimate compromise as a precursor to action to which there can be widespread commitment. Consequently, we consider that seeking "the best argument" needs considerable refinement since such a disposition may simply play into the hands of those with positional power or are the more articulate, and outspoken, thus in the process silencing and in large measure disenfranchising others. Consequently, listening, being inclusive, while not a watertight guarantee, nevertheless needs to be in evidence if legitimate compromise is to be a negotiated outcome, and a forerunner to responsible action.

These cases also indicate that leading in a deliberative manner is both time consuming and demanding – a luxury we rarely can afford since the pace of change does not permit such indulgence (Berg & Seeber, 2016). Deadlines for research proposals and publications are increasingly intolerant of such time demands for deliberative communication and considerations of public good. While recognising such challenges, we are nevertheless encouraged by the testimony from the case studies indicating that academics appreciate situations in which deliberative communication is initiated. As a participant in the case study reported in Chapter 9 commented: "We need to make values more explicit when we teach. We tend to over-estimate students' capacities to see these". Such feedback encourages us to maintain our argument for deliberative leadership, since academics too, like students, may lack the capacity to "see" the values embedded in their practice. Particularly in a climate dominated by entrepreneurial orientations in combination with increased competition between universities both in research and teaching (Pinheiro et al., 2019), we tend to prioritise what is measurable rather than less tangible but no less important, "softer" skills and values. Thus, we need to re-kindle intellectual virtues and values nurturing teaching and educational leadership approaches that seek legitimate compromises through deliberative communication while fostering greater awareness of, and commitment to, promoting public good.

Deliberative leadership: principles, virtues, values and legitimate compromises

Advocating a leadership approach that promotes inclusion and critical reflection on the values underlying our actions incurs a consequent responsibility to take seriously the intellectual virtues and values that underpin them, and how these may be most advantageously deployed to maximise their contribution to public good.[12] In Table 11.1 we describe the relational aspects of these various elements and indicate how reflection on these may increase the awareness of the virtues and values embedded in our practices.

Through the processes of deliberative communication, it is more likely also that intellectual virtues, identified (in Chapter 6) as "open-mindedness; courage; curiosity, and honesty" to which we might add integrity and capacity for legitimate compromise. Practising such virtues with honesty and integrity increases the possibility of negotiating legitimate compromise. However, such compromises – in and of themselves – are necessary but not sufficient for action. Rather, it is necessary, in order to determine where to go from here, to excavate the values that underpin various intellectual virtues, and to connect these with considerations of orientations, and the purposes of higher education. The case studies indicate that when faced with the complex immediacy of pedagogical engagement, it is a considerable challenge to be adroit in one's moves and decision-making on the (pedagogical) dance floor, while viewing these manoeuvres with the detachment provided by a vista from the balcony that enables the leader to simultaneously have public good in mind while attending to a particular set of pedagogical circumstances in a teachable moment (Heifetz & Linsky, 2002). In Schön's language this is the capacity to combine reflection-in-action and reflection on action – a hallmark of praxis (Schön, 1991). It was with the benefit of deliberative conversation with critical friends that the ADs in our cases became aware of "teachable moments" as possible gateways to encourage and further deliberative communication (Woods & Jeffrey, 1996) and where "difficult conversations can be had and actively

TABLE 11.1 Deliberative communication: virtues, values and legitimate compromises

Deliberative communication	Baehr's intellectual virtues	Value	Legitimate compromise in a web of commitments	Professionally responsible action
Competing perspectives	Open-mindedness, curiosity	Integrity	Work together as a team, be inclusive. Be open and transparent – put everything on the table.	From practice to praxis
Exercise of tolerance, respect	Open-mindedness and curiosity	Respect	Listen, learn, reflect, deliberate	From practice to praxis
Elements of collective will-formation – seek consensus or at least temporarily/ recognising differences	Honesty and courage	Respect	Moving beyond consensus and disagreement, seeking legitimate compromise	From practice to praxis
Authorities and/ or traditional views may be questioned	Courage, open-mindedness and honesty	Respect Open-mindedness	Actively seek common ground, yet maintaining perspective	From practice to praxis
Argumentative discussions aiming to solve problems	Open-mindedness and curiosity	Trustworthiness Fairness	recognition of difference - key to legitimate compromise	From practice to praxis

instigated" and where "feedback is honest" when provided by critical friends (Hargreaves & O'Connor, 2018, p. 114). Based on such premises, deliberative leadership creates the possibility of being participant and observer simultaneously – in the pedagogical and leadership moment to be immediately attentive while mindful of the bigger picture of public good. Here too the cases indicate that developing deliberative leadership is labour intensive and is built incrementally over time. In order to do this in a sustainable manner, deliberative communication is simultaneously a pedagogy of leading, whereby leading and teaching proceed hand in glove and, in doing so, deliberative leadership holds centre stage, a collective responsibility rather than a delegated or distributed task. This is what deliberative leadership entails, while it needs also to move from practice – a preoccupation with doing leadership – to cultivating and valuing synergies between dance floor and balcony – creating deliberative leadership praxis. The next section turns attention to an elaboration on the promise of deliberative leadership as a sustainable praxis.

Deliberative leadership: sustainable praxis

Deliberative communication is a means of doing leadership while simultaneously it may be used as a set of analytical tools for interrogating one's leadership praxis. The case studies in the preceding chapters reveal that opening up one's praxis to the scrutinising gaze of even a small number of critical friends and fellow researchers may have a significant impact on the formation of individual's leadership capacities. However, it requires the courage to expose professional vulnerabilities whilst engaging with peers with curiosity and profound respect, potentially rewards the professional risks involved with enhancement of one's leading practice as and for public good. Deployment of the principles of deliberative communication commits one to inclusion, to listen to and respect all voices in a university community where collective will formation is a stage in a process that seeks legitimate compromise as a means of determining: where do we go from here? More fundamentally, such questioning is seeking to arrive at decisions that propel towards action, however tentatively. We say tentatively, since it is necessary to recognise that such steps are uncertain, but as the cases indicate, it is necessary to have the "courage" to act, even in conditions of uncertainty, while also recognising that courage too is tempered by expertise.

Chapter 6 in particular demonstrates that deliberative leadership requires the courage to stand by your values, articulate them, while also being willing to change practice through engaging in a deliberative communication process. Negotiating legitimate compromises therefore requires a more critical investigation of individual praxis; the integration of values, knowledge and action, and a willingness to change through a deliberative conversation with others. However, in the context of twenty-first-century public universities, it is necessary to be alert the diversity of academic capital accumulated by both students and academics. Some come to university with intimate familiarity with the academic tradition of communication and argumentation while others have considerably less experience with such capacities. From a public good perspective, it is not sufficient merely to promote "critical thinking" as an end in itself, but to foster and promote deliberative communication (Walker, 2018). Consequently, higher education institutions need to be places where deliberative leadership as a praxis is a characteristic feature, readily evident. As Kronman (2019, p. 109) asserts, "the process of reflection, criticism and sharpened self-awareness ... is at the heart of the enterprise of teaching and learning", capacities that require cultivation (teaching and learning) that are central also to deliberative leadership praxis.

Deliberative leadership as everyone's responsibility carries the collective obligation to move beyond its practice, to combining, dance floor and balcony, doing and reflecting, becoming both participant and observer in a community of praxis that is sustainable. In a socio-cultural context where "sustainable development goals" (SDGs) trip off the tongue with ease, grappling with the enormity of the challenge and the sustainability of current trajectories is daunting to say the least. In such circumstances, how may higher education for example live out its commitment to pursue the UN's Sustainable Development Goals that are to be attained by 2030 (Bologna Process/EHEA, 2018)?

The United Nations' website declares:

> The Sustainable Development Goals are the blueprint to achieve a better and
> more sustainable future for all. They address the global challenges we face,
> including those related to poverty, inequality, climate, environmental degra-
> dation, prosperity, and peace and justice.
>
> *(https://www.un.org/sustainabledevelopment/sustainable-development-goals/)*

There are 17 goals in all, to be achieved by 2030, a mere decade away. While
public good is not mentioned, it is reasonable to assume that achieving these goals
would be an enormous contribution to it. While all have an educative function,
and all "interconnect" thus it is rather invidious to select some as more important
than others. In the context of the present focus on deliberative leadership praxis,
we select three with particular significance for our advocacy of this approach to
leading: quality of education (SDG 4), peace, justice and strong institutions (SDG
16), and partnerships (SDG17). Some may legitimately suggest, however, that
without urgent attention to "climate action" (SDG13), the opportunity to address
all others will be entirely redundant as the inhabitants of planet earth continue on a
path of self-destruction. It may be suggested therefore that SDG13 is the ultimate
public good, one in which we all have a vested interest.

Such a pressing call to action, requires leadership, certainly, but a contribution
from everyone, while we also need leaders and leadership, whether formally
appointed or informally playing a part. In this context, we aver that deliberative
leadership has much to offer. With a firm focus on public good, strong leadership
that is shared, inclusive, accountable is more likely to move beyond powerful vested
interest, to reach legitimate compromises with partners, building sustainability as
these networks of deliberative leadership, communities of practice in public universities generating new knowledge to share and disseminate for public good.

When institutional leaders, their orientations and webs of commitments that
have public rather than self-interest in mind are put through the wringer of deliberative communication in a spirit of openness and pursuit of sustainable possibilities,
the emergent legitimate compromises too are more likely to be in everybody's interest
rather than the most powerful and influential. Sustainable deliberative leadership will
vary considerably from institutional context (its orientations and leadership) to policy
influences, national and international. Deliberative leadership is indispensable to strong
institutions, and while pursuing public good, taking professional responsibility seriously
and to avoid becoming self-interested.

Central to this remit is an epistemic commitment whereby the responsibility of
the academic community is to initiate students into their chosen disciplinary
archive(s), while enabling them to become more aware of the formative aspects of
the communities of practice they become part of – and how they themselves may
become moral and epistemic contributors to these various communities. This is
"uniquely challenging" since "it confronts us with the spectacle of men and
women whose values, habits, instincts, and beliefs were wildly different from our

own" while they also share our humanity (Kronman, 2019, p. 180). This is a "fruitful tension" (along with the logics of accountability and responsibility) while bestowing the benefit of "tolerance for ambiguity", particularly important in pursuit of legitimate compromises, while "the longer one lives with the tension ... the more complex the whole picture becomes" (pp. 180–181). However, the pace of change is inimical to the old adage *festina lente* (hasten slowly), creating an apparent necessity to rush to judgement – to act now, when a more deliberate, considered, measured considerations of possible options is both desirable and appropriate, thus allowing for the cultivation of a disposition that learns to live with ambiguity while wrestling with the task of legitimate compromise as a prelude to action.

Earlier in the chapter we indicated the emergence of NPM as a manifestation of technical reason – a means–end mindset of problem solving, more consumed by "outcomes" in contrast to more traditional academic perceptions of how to lead university education. Our argument for deliberative leadership as a more sustainable approach can trace its roots back to Aristotle, a leadership characterised by open-endedness, which he called praxis:

> which is conduct in a public space with others in which a person without ulterior purpose and with a view to no object detachable from himself, acts in such a way as to realise excellences that he has come to appreciate in his community as constitutive of a worthwhile way of life.
>
> *(Dunne, 1993, p. 10)*

Such engagement, requiring considerable investment of the self in more intimate engagement – dance floor and balcony – necessitates "a kind of knowledge that was more personal and experiential, more supple and less formulable"; a practical knowledge or "wisdom" (ibid.). This is at the heart of deliberative leadership.

However, we are cognisant that enacting deliberative leadership is a demanding endeavour. Nevertheless, while not ignoring the formative influence of university senior leaders' formal roles, positioning, power and status, we argue that as members of public university communities we share a collective responsibility to contribute to the creation of an Agora of ideas – a place of assembly, a shared space where deliberative leadership flourishes and all are welcome to participate on an equal basis. As educators, together with students in a public university milieu where each contributes a rich variety of cultural and academic capital, we need to find ways of strengthening relationships across disciplines and professions based on trust as well as respect and being better able to live with difference, disagreement and dissent while creating and being protective of the space and opportunity for deliberation. Such responsibilities, particularly onerous in public universities, invite questioning also regarding the nature of partnerships, their sustainability across space, culture and language. In a context where not only is global warming accelerating but also the pace of change, there is considerable risk that leadership practice becomes addicted to doing, when there is greater need than ever for a wisdom of leadership; a praxis that necessitates collaborative partners committed to a deliberative disposition. We are sufficiently encouraged by the evidence to suggest that deliberative leadership praxis harbours the potential to cultivate sustainable futures in an open-ended manner. For this to become a reality, we want to insist that leadership lessons need to be woven into future leadership fabrics in ways that retain a focus on excellence in the pursuit and promotion of public good. Public universities in particular and higher education in general need to renew and revitalise more traditional mandates, now less visible or more marginalised, so that despite the rise of populism and its demonisation of expert knowledge, pursuit of truth and expertise continue to be valued and valuable contributions to public good (Kronman, 2019; Norris & Inglehart, 2019). Both theoretically and empirically, we indicate the necessity to renew individual and collective commitment to deliberations on issues of public good in the current climate of higher education. We are respectfully insistent that senior leaders who are responsible for defining the strategies of their universities and who are powerful in defining the orientations of their university (Sugrue et al., 2019; Sutphen, Solbrekke & Sugrue, 2018), need to think through what formative impact their leadership practices have, and they need to consider how whether their leadership nurtures common engagement among staff and students as and for public good. However, there is evidence also that formal preparation for such leadership responsibilities have in many instances been notably absent thus giving greater prominence to implicit leadership theories (see Chapter 2). Consequently, we argue that if universities are to re-kindle education as praxis, it is necessary to pay adequate attention to reflection, individual and collective, more conducive to the cultivation of leadership praxis.

Deliberative leadership praxis: new horizons of sustainable possibilities

At a time when populism of all hues is undermining democratic processes, and the fragility of our planet's ecology becomes more apparent with each passing day, it is clear that business as usual in higher education and beyond is singularly incapable of addressing let alone transforming existing challenges into sustainable futures. We suggest deliberative leadership as a means of championing higher education as and for public good in more sustainable ways than the current offerings of NPM. For some readers, deliberative leadership may be perceived as an unattainable ideal. Our retort is that it would be a failure of courage and imagination if it were left untried. Our case studies demonstrated, admittedly on a small and intimate scale working with critical friends and research colleagues, just how difficult it is to be participant and observer in one's own deliberations, in the process of cultivating a deliberative pedagogical leadership praxis. Given its challenges, this is a task that necessitates institutional adoption. Deliberative leadership has as much potential as time, effort, agency and courage harnessed in a concerted manner will allow. The first challenge is to recognise the scale of the task. As the lyric of a nationalistic Irish ballad proclaims, "night is darkest just before the dawn", but it presages the moment when new light arrives on the horizon.[13] Horatio too, in the opening scene of Shakespeare's *Hamlet*, declares: "But look, the morn, in russet mantle clad, Walks o'er the dew of yon high eastward hill". In "the cold light of day" deliberative leadership praxis has potential to shed light on hitherto hidden possibilities, made more urgent by recognition that "education cannot live in darkness" (Bengtsen & Barnett, 2017, p. 127). The second challenge is to recognise that in the absence of certainty of success, it is necessary to have the courage to sally forth in consort with colleagues, to build a sustainable deliberative leadership that does not anticipate sudden flashes of inspiration, "but more an imaginative sensitivity to the smouldering core of collective and joint imaginative spaces within everyday higher education practice" (p. 125). Deliberative leadership praxis too needs imagination and creativity, perhaps not quite the "kindly light" of which Newman wrote (see Foreword). Rather, the wisdom that deliberative leadership praxis harbours will facilitate and render more attainable a "future university … as a more humane place for learning – fallible and rugged, but with possibilities for open-ended learning and growth" (p. 130). We (re-)commend deliberative leadership praxis as a potent conduit for such possible universities for sustainable futures.

Notes

1 In our dialogue we apply the principles of deliberative communication as elaborated in Chapter 3, while also building the argument for deliberative leadership.
2 The research design and methods are thoroughly described in Chapter 5.
3 We use praxis as it is elaborated in Chapter 1, and emphasise that praxis requires the individual and collective will to combine critical and ethical reflection with disciplinary knowledge and expertise to develop educational leadership capacities.
4 While Chapter 8 introduced the idea of "deliberative leadership", here we elaborate deliberative leadership as an alternative to "managerialism" and "leaderism" as developed within the framework of neo-liberalism and New Public Management of public universities (Geschwind et al., 2019).
5 See Chapters 1 and 4 for a more elaborate argument for the relevance of using the cases of ADs in leading higher education as and for public good.
6 The case in Chapter 7 illustrates how an AD has to struggle in the tension between compliance with the policy of the university and what he believes is professionally responsible action.
7 Chapter 6 demonstrates the relationship between the principles of deliberative communication and intellectual virtues.
8 These orientations are elaborated on in Chapter 2.
9 See Chapter 4 where there is an elaboration on how academic leading and teaching are navigated within a web of commitments.
10 In the case study reported in Chapter 6, a female AD leader challenge a well-established authoritative voice in order to live up to what she believes will make her academic development courses a public good.
11 Chapters 6–9 provide examples from shorter university pedagogy courses, while Chapter 10 demonstrates the use in consultation work over a longer period.
12 The significance of intellectual virtues and their enrichment of deliberative communication was a significant focus in Chapter 6.
13 The ballad, hankering after a united Ireland, "we're on the one road", leaves little room for inclusion of those with divergent views, intended to rouse nationalistic fervour, far removed from the intent of deliberative leadership!

References

Achinstein, B. (2002). *Community, Diversity and Conflict among Schoolteachers: The Ties that Blind*. New York: Teachers College Press.

Barnett, R. (2003). *Beyond All Reason Living with Ideology in the University*. Milton Keynes: Open University Press.

Barnett, R. (2011). *Being a University*. London: Routledge.

Becher, T., & Trowler, P. (2001) *Academic Tribes and Territories: Intellectual Enquiry and the Cultures of Disciplines* (2nd edn). Buckingham: Open University Press/SRHE.

Bengtsen, S., & Barnett, R. (2017). Confronting the dark side of higher education. *Journal of Philosophy of Education, 51*(1), 114–131.

Berg, M., & Seeber, B. K. (2016). *The Slow Professor: Challenging the Culture of Speed in the Academy*. Toronto: University of Toronto Press.

Bessant, S., Robinson, Z. P., & Ormerod, R. M. (2015). Neoliberalism, new public management and the sustainable development agenda of higher education: history, contradictions and synergies. *Environmental Education Research, 21*(3), 417–432. doi:10.1080/13504622.2014.993933

Drury, S. A. M., Andre, D., Seton, G., & Wentzel, J. (2016). Assessing deliberative pedagogy: using a learning outcomes rubric to assess tradeoffs and tensions. *Journal of Public Deliberation, 12*(1), 1–29.

Dunne, J. (1993). *Back to the Rough Ground 'Phronesis' and 'Techne' in Modern Philosophy and in Aristotle*. Notre Dame: University of Notre Dame Press.

Ekman, M., Lindgren, M., & Packendorf, J. (2018). Universities need leadership, academics need management: discursive tensions and voids in the deregulation of Swedish higher education legislation. *Higher Education, 75*, 299–321. doi:10.1007/s10734-017-0140-2

Ese, J. (2019) *Defending the University? Academics' Reactions to Managerialism in Norwegian Higher Education*. Faculty of Arts and Social Sciences, Working Life Science. Doctoral thesis, Karlstad University.

Fusarelli, L. D., Kowalski, T. J., & Petersen, G. J. (2011). Distributive leadership, civic engagement, and deliberative democracy as vehicles for school improvement. *Leadership and Policy in School Improvement, 10*(1), 43–62. doi:10.1080/15700760903342392

Geschwind, L., Hansen, H. F., Pinheiro, R. & Pulkkinen, K. (2019). Governing performance in the Nordic universities: where are we heading and what have we learned? In R. Pinheiro, L. Geschwind, H. F. Hansen & K. Pulkkinen (eds), *Reforms, Organizational Change and Performance in Higher Education: A Comparative Account from the Nordic Countries*, pp. 269–298. Cham: Palgrave Macmillan Springer (eBook). https://doi.org/10.1007/978-3-030-11738-2

Giddens, A. (1999). *The Third Way: The Renewal of Social Democracy*. Malden: Blackwell.

Goddard, J., Hazelkorn, E., Kempton, L., & Vallance, P. (2016). *The Civic University: The Policy and Leadership Challenges*. Cheltenham: Edward Elgar Publishing.

Gross Stein, J. (2001). *The Cult of Efficiency*. Toronto: Anansi Press.

Hargreaves, A., Boyle, A., & Harris, A. (2014). *Uplifting Leadership*. San Francisco: Jossey Bass.

Hargreaves, A., & O'Connor, M. T. (2018). *Collaborative Professionalism when Teaching Together Means Learning for All*. Thousand Oaks: Corwin Books.

Hargreaves, A., & Shirley, D. (2012). *The Global Fourth Way: The Quest for Educational Excellence*. Thousand Oaks: Corwin and Ontario Principals' Council.

Heifetz, R. A., & Linsky, M. (2002). *Leadership on the Line: Staying Alive through the Dangers of Leading*. Boston: Harvard Business School Press.

Ireland, Universities Act (1997). (1997) Dublin: Government of Ireland. http://www.irishsta
    tutebook.ie/eli/1997/act/24/enacted/en/html
Kalfa, S., Wilkinson, A., & Gollan, P. J. (2018). Academic game: compliance and resis-
    tance in universities. *Work, Employment and Society*, *32*(2), 274–291. doi:10.1177/
    0950017017695043
Kolsaker, A. (2008). Academic professionalism in the managerialist era: a study of
    English universities. *Studies in Higher Education*, *33*(5), 513–525. doi:10.1080/
    03075070802372885
Kolsaker, A. (2014). Relocating professionalism in an English university. *Journal of Higher
    Education Policy and Management*, *36*(2), 129–142. doi:10.1080/1360080X.2013.861053
Kronman, A. (2019). *The Assault on American Excellence*. New York: Free Press.
Lynch, K., Grummel, B., & Devine, D. (2012). *New Managerialism in Education Commerciali-
    zation, Carelessness and Gender*. Basingstoke: Palgrave Macmillan.
Manosevicth, I. (2019). Deliberative pedagogy in a conflicted society: cultivating deliberative atti-
    tudes among Israeli college students. *Higher Education*, 1–16. doi:10.1007/s10734-019-00368-6
May, L. (1996). *The Socially Responsive Self: Social Theory and Professional Ethics*. Chicago:
    Chicago University Press.
Mugglestone, K., Dancy, K., & Voight, M. (2019). *Opportunity Lost: Net Price and Equity at
    Public Flagship Institutions*. Retrieved from: http://www.ihep.org/research/publications/
    opportunity-lost-net-price-and-equity-public-flagship-institutions
Norris, P., & Inglehart, R. (2019). *Cultural Backlash: Trump, Brexit, and the Rise of Author-
    itarian Populism*. New York: Cambridge University Press.
Pinheiro, R., Geschwind, L., Hansen, H. F., & Pulkkinen, K. (2019). *Reforms, Organizational
    Change and Performance in Higher Education: A Comparative Account from the Nordic Countries*.
    Cham: Palgrave Macmillan Springer (eBook). https://doi.org/10.1007/978-3-,030-11738-2
Power, M. (1999). *The Audity Society Rituals of Verification*. Oxford: Oxford University Press.
Sardoc, M. (2018). Democratic education at 30: an interview with Dr. Amy Gutmann.
    Theory and Research in Education, *16*(2), 244–252. doi:10.1177/1477878518774087
Said, E. W. (1994). *Representations of the Intellectual: The 1993 Reith Lectures*. New York:
    Pantheon Books.
Schon, D. (ed.) (1991). *The Reflective Turn: Case Studies in and on Educational Practice*. New
    York: Teachers College Press.
Spence, C. (2019). 'Judgement' versus 'metrics' in higher education management. *Higher
    Education*, 77, 761–775. doi:10.1007/s10734-018-0300-z
Spillane, J. (2006). *Distributed Leadership*. San Francisco: Jossey Bass.
Stake, B., & Mabry, L. (1998). Revelations: Documenting Classroom Teaching and Learn-
    ing through Case Study Research Methods. In C. Sugrue (ed.), *Teaching, Curriculum and
    Educational Research* (pp. 170–180). Dublin: St. Patrick's College, A College of Dublin
    City University.
Sutphen, M., Solbrekke, T. D., & Sugrue, C. (2018). Toward articulating an academic
    praxis by interrogating university strategic plans. *Studies in Higher Education*, *44*(8), 1400–
    1412. doi:10.1080/03075079.2018.1440384
Taylor, C. (1989/1992). *Sources of the Self: The Making of Modern Identity*. Cambridge: Cam-
    bridge University Press.
Tibbitts, F. L. (2019). Deliberative democratic decision making, universal values, and cultural
    pluralism: A proposed contribution to the prevention of violent extremism through
    education. *Prospects*. doi:10.1007/s11125-019-09444-2
Walker, M. (2018). Dimensions of higher education and the public good in South Africa.
    Higher Education, *76*, 555–569. doi:10.1007/s10734-017-0225-y

Woods, P., & Jeffrey, B. (1996). *Teachable Moments: The Art of Teaching in Primary Schools.* Milton Keynes: Open University Press.

Zhang, K., & Meng, T. (2018). Political elites in deliberative democracy: beliefs and behaviors of Chinese officials. *Japanese Journal of Political Science, 19,* 643–662. doi:10.1017/S1468109918000270

INDEX

Note: page references in italics indicate figures; bold indicates tables; 'n' indicates chapter notes.